THE CHURCH
FACES THE ISMS

The Members of the Faculty of the
Louisville Presbyterian Theological Seminary
Louisville, Kentucky

ARNOLD BLACK RHODES, *Editor*

Associate Editors
FRANK H. CALDWELL *and* **L. C. RUDOLPH**

ABINGDON PRESS • NEW YORK • NASHVILLE

Library of Congress Catalog Card Number: 58-5392

Scripture quotations unless otherwise designated
are from the Revised Standard Version of the
Bible and are copyright 1946 and 1952 by the
Division of Christian Education of the National
Council of the Churches of Christ in the U.S.A.

PRINTED AND BOUND BY THE PARTHENON PRESS, AT
NASHVILLE, TENNESSEE, UNITED STATES OF AMERICA

PREFACE

✠✠✠✠✠✠✠✠✠✠✠✠✠✠✠✠✠✠✠✠✠✠✠✠

THE PURPOSE OF THIS BOOK IS TO HELP CHRISTIANS, ESPECIALLY LEADERS in the Church, to prepare themselves to deal effectively and fairly with specific organized and unorganized movements which challenge main-line Protestantism in particular ways. The expression "main-line Protestantism" refers to that composite body of larger Protestant denominations which have a basic harmony in theological position and a co-operative spirit and program. Those of us who have prepared this volume are theologically neither narrow nor flat. We are evangelical and we take the Christian faith and life seriously. Obviously we are dealing with controversial issues in which both objective and subjective factors play a part. This means that it is inevitable that able men will sometimes disagree with us. We recognize that some isms are basically positive and that many emphasize truths forgotten or neglected by the Church. Without failing to recognize the positive values in a given ism and without putting ourselves in the position of enemies of those with whom we disagree, we maintain that all the isms with which we deal present certain problems from the standpoint of main-line Protestantism. Some present far more serious problems than others.

This book grew out of a course in the curriculum of Louisville Presbyterian Seminary. The selection of isms was made not only on the basis of the information and experience of professors, but also on the basis of answers to a questionnaire sent out to ministers in the pastorate. The unity of the book does not lie in the unfolding of a single thesis, but in the book's relation to the actual life experience of the Church.

A glance at the table of contents will give a clear view of the organization of the book. By way of introduction we begin with a brief statement concerning biblical interpretation and a bird's-eye view of the rise of sects and isms. We have classified the isms with which we

5

deal as "Isms Predominantly Biblical," "Isms Both Biblical and Cultural," and "Isms Predominantly Cultural." We realize that there is no sharp line of demarcation between biblical isms and isms which are both biblical and cultural, for cultural factors play a part in all isms. The word "ism" in the title of the book and in the titles of its parts is used to refer to various forms of sectarianism, as well as to other types of viewpoints and movements. Each writer has been left free to define the terms with which he deals as he sees fit in the context of his own subject.

Each unit in the book has necessarily been developed in accordance with the nature of the subject and the individuality of the author. Most of the units, however, include at least the following emphases: a brief historical sketch of the ism, a statement of its characteristic features, an evaluation of the movement, a suggested methodology for facing the ism, suggested projects for further exploration, and a carefully selected and balanced bibliography. No contributor to the volume claims to have exhausted his subject. We know our method of approach is not the only method, but we are confident that there is a need for the type of focusing we have done. All of us have sought to be constructive. Although each contributor has entered into the labors of his colleagues, he assumes responsibility for the unit or units which he has written.

We express our special appreciation to Ernest M. White, our librarian, for his untiring help in matters pertaining to bibliography and form; and to Mrs. L. C. Rudolph for her help in revising particular units and her careful typing of the manuscript.

CONTENTS

PART ONE: ORIENTATION

PART TWO: ISMS PREDOMINANTLY BIBLICAL

PART THREE: ISMS BOTH BIBLICAL AND CULTURAL

7

PART FOUR: ISMS PREDOMINANTLY CULTURAL

PART ONE

ORIENTATION

✦✦✦✦✦✦✦✦✦✦✦✦✦✦✦✦

UNIT I

THE BIBLE:
OUR POINT OF REFERENCE

POINTS OF REFERENCE ARE A NECESSITY IN ALL THE ACTIVITIES OF life. That is, authoritative guides are essential for all undertakings. The explorer carries map and compass. The builder follows the plans of the architect. The physician checks his patient's temperature, blood pressure, and other vital factors. Not only so, but the explorer must know how to use map and compass to find his way. The builder must know how to read the architect's drawings in order to avoid costly mistakes. The physician must know how to interpret the vital statistics of his patient if he is to prescribe effectively.

In main-line Protestantism the most distinctive point of reference is the Bible. By "main-line Protestantism" we mean that composite body of larger Protestant denominations which have a basic harmony in theological position and a co-operative spirit and program. In spite of the differences in biblical interpretation among main-line Protestants there is a large area of agreement and a widely accepted methodology of interpretation.

But the Bible is just as truly the chief point of reference for many sectarian groups as it is for main-line Protestants. How the Bible is interpreted, therefore, becomes crucial for Christian faith and fellowship. Herbert H. Farmer says, "It was during the era when Protestantism generally assumed the literal inerrancy of Scripture, and used it in an externally authoritarian way, that it broke up into a multitude of sects. . . ." [1]

Biblical interpretation is vitally related to the subject matter of this book. This fact is obvious when thinking of isms which are predominantly biblical. For example, Seventh-day Adventists insist that the Old Testament Sabbath is just as binding upon the modern Christian

---

[1] "The Bible: Its Significance and Authority," *The Interpreter's Bible*, ed. George Buttrick (Nashville: Abingdon Press, 1952), I, 25.

11

as upon the ancient Jew. Roman Catholicism has been placed among the isms which are both biblical and cultural. One point on which Protestants and Roman Catholics differ radically is in the interpretation of Jesus' statement to Peter in Matt. 16:17-19. Even in the consideration of the cultural isms biblical interpretation is significant, for in the evaluation of each ism the Bible is assumed as the basic point of reference. Furthermore, some people in some of the cultural isms are members of main-line Protestant churches. Some racists interpret Noah's curse on Canaan (Gen. 9:25-27) to mean that Negroes were intended by God to be slaves of the white man.

A Brief History of Interpretation

Since the interpretation of the Bible is so crucial, we take a look at the ways in which it has been interpreted. Even within the Bible itself the basic unit of revelation is the interpreted event. In the Old Testament the exodus from Egypt is interpreted as the great act of redemption by God, whereas in the New Testament the death and resurrection of Jesus are pivotal. Occasionally one part of the Old Testament is interpreted in another part. For example, Chronicles deals from a priestly point of view with the history found in the prophetic books of Samuel and Kings. Sometimes Old Testament materials are interpreted in the so-called "intertestamental" literature. The expression "son of man" found in Dan. 7:13 is referred to the Messiah in First Enoch. In the Habakkuk Commentary among the Dead Sea Scrolls the historical setting of the Book of Habakkuk is ignored, and the book is so modernized as to refer directly to the situation confronting the sectarian community at Khirbet Qumran.

The Jews were careful in transmitting the text and employed both literal and midrashic interpretation. Philo of Alexandria (ca. 20 B.C.-A.D. 54) was not a typical Jewish interpreter. Though he recognized theoretically the existence of the literal sense, he often overlooked it in favor of the allegorical.

The Old Testament was the Bible of Jesus and of the writers of the New Testament. Jesus made a distinction between the oral law and the written law (Matt. 15:1-20), a distinction between "church" tradition and Bible. Moreover, he exercised a personal authority which is superior to that of the written word. Said he, "You have heard that it was said,

12

'An eye for an eye and a tooth for a tooth.' But I say to you . . ."
(Matt. 5:38-39). In other words, Jesus was sometimes radical
in his interpretation of the Old Testament. Not everything in Scripture
is on the same level of importance (Matt. 23:23-24). When the Pharisees tested Jesus concerning the problem of divorce, he appealed to
Gen. 1:27 and 2:24 as more basic than Deut. 24:1-4 (Mark 10:2-9).
At the same time he was conservative in his approach to the Scriptures:
"Think not that I have come to abolish the law and the prophets; I
have come not to abolish them but to fulfill them" (Matt. 5:17).
He saw a basic continuity between the Old Testament and himself and
summed up the Law and the Prophets in terms of love for God (Deut.
6:5) and love for one's neighbor (Lev. 19:18).

When quoting from the Old Testament, the writers of the New
Testament ordinarily used the Septuagint rather than the Hebrew Bible.
Particular passages of the Old Testament are interpreted as being fulfilled in Jesus. Sometimes a passage which refers to a particular event
in Israel's history is interpreted in relation to Jesus. For example, Hos.
11:1 clearly refers to the exodus of Israel from Egypt; but in Matt. 2:13-
15 it is quoted with reference to the flight of Joseph and Mary with
the baby Jesus to Egypt. Parallels between the life of Israel and the
experiences of Jesus are regarded as providentially ordered, for in Jesus
Christ the Old Testament finds its deepest meaning.

The apostle Paul, along with the other New Testament writers,
lived in the light of the life, death, and resurrection of Jesus; and his
interpretation of the Old Testament is often specifically theological
or Christocentric. As an interpreter Paul has affinities to Jesus, to the
rabbis, and to those who make use of typology. The author of the
Letter to the Hebrews made great use of typology.

From the second century to the Middle Ages four schools of interpretation arose in Christendom: Marcion and his followers, who rejected the Old Testament and a large portion of the New Testament-to-
be; the school of Alexandria, noted for allegorical interpretation; the
school of Antioch, known for its historical emphasis; and the authoritarian school which sought to interpret the Bible in accordance with
the theology of the Church.

The Middle Ages witnessed a union of allegorizing and authoritarianism. Interpretation was heavily dependent upon the writings of the church fathers. Four meanings were often found in a given text: the literal, the allegorical, the moral, and the spiritual. Yet, the work of the Waldenses, Rashi, Nicholas of Lyra, and others helped to weaken the power of tradition by laying stress upon the literal and historical meaning of Scripture.

The Protestant Reformation marked a new era in biblical study. It was an era of translation and interpretation. While Martin Luther placed great stress upon the authority of the Bible and considered its message of salvation clear, he anticipated many of the conclusions of modern critical scholars. He believed each part of Scripture should be interpreted in relation to the whole and that some parts are more temporary in their relevance than others. He insisted upon the right of the individual to interpret the Bible for himself. John Calvin sometimes called the biblical writers amanuenses of the Holy Spirit, but also reached certain conclusions in line with present-day critical scholarship. For example, he questioned the Pauline authorship of Hebrews and the Petrine authorship of Second Peter.

In addition to the work of Jewish scholars and Protestant reformers, several other factors played a part in preparing the way for the critical movement which was to flower in the nineteenth century and in the early part of the twentieth—namely, geographical discoveries, the advances in natural science through the application of the inductive method, the humanists' free approach to ancient documents, and the challenge of the principle of authority.

Before Jean Astruc published his work on the sources of Genesis in 1753, literary analysis of the Bible had already begun. However, Astruc's work was the seed from which the documentary hypothesis of the Pentateuch later developed. Analytical study spread to the rest of the Old Testament as well. The chronological ordering of the Old Testament books by the critics was quite different from that of tradition. In New Testament study, search was made for the Jesus of history, Mark was declared to be the oldest Gospel, documentary hypotheses for the Gospels were worked out, and the humanity of Jesus was stressed. Ancient manuscripts bearing on the study of both Testaments were discovered, and it was claimed that the New Testament was written in everyday Greek. The value of rabbinical writings for the interpretation of the Gospels was demonstrated. The study of the Bible came to involve such disciplines as archaeology, comparative religion, eschatology, form criticism, social environment, and oral tradition.

The theological outlook of the interpreter greatly conditions his study of the Bible. On the whole the trends in biblical study are in a more conservative direction than they were fifty years ago. Though the documentary hypothesis of the Pentateuch is still held in some form by the majority of Old Testament scholars, it has often been greatly modified. The findings of archaeology have tended to undergird the historical framework of the Old Testament. At the same time, it is widely recognized that the biblical writers were not attempting to write history in the modern sense so much as they were writing confessional history. The uniqueness of the religion of Israel has been seen by comparison with the other religions of antiquity. At least in some quarters attention is being given to the meaning of the books of the Bible as whole units, for it is recognized that a book in its final form has a message. In New Testament study, attention is being given to the totality of Christ's redemptive work. The Dead Sea Scrolls have already thrown considerable light on pre-Christian Judaism and the historical background of the New Testament, and much more is yet to be learned from them. Many students of the Bible are genuinely concerned about the production of an adequate methodology for arriving at a genuine biblical theology.

Suggested Principles of Interpretation

How to get to the Bible and then from the Bible to persons, to the Church, and to the world today is the task of the interpreter. Accepting the Bible as our focal point of reference, how are we to use it?

The first suggestion is: *Interpret the Bible as a historian.* Historical interpretation is the attempt to reconstruct the original facts and meanings of a particular passage together with a study of the use made of the passage in subsequent generations.

There is ample justification of this principle. At least some of our fathers in the faith have led the way. Furthermore, it is impossible to turn back the clock of time and act as if there had never been a development of the historical method. More profoundly, the very nature of the Bible itself demands that it be interpreted historically.

The message of the Bible is a story whose framework is a series of historical events. This is one of the features which distinguish biblical religion from other early religions. Finally, historical interpretation is required by the nature of man, who is incurably inquisitive. For millennia he has kept and read records.

The process of historical interpretation seeks answers to such questions as these: How did the book or passage under consideration become part of the Bible? What is its correct text? Who is the author? When did he write? To what people and against what background did he present his message? For what purpose? What sources did he use? By means of what literary forms? Is it possible for me to enter imaginatively into the author's thought and situation and catch the emotional overtones of his message? What did the author say and mean, and how was his message received? How does his message fit into the Bible as a whole? How is the specific passage under consideration related to its immediate and larger context? In what ways has this passage been understood since it was written? Are these subsequent interpretations expressive of the author's intent? Are they helpful in arriving at the relevance of the passage?

The second suggested principle of interpretation is: *Interpret the Bible as a believer*. Christians are interested in the Bible not only as a cultural record but also as a vehicle of God's revelation. Long before the development of modern historical scholarship, men of faith interpreted the Bible and received God's message in the process. Men of faith may do a better job of biblical interpretation as judged by the message of the Bible itself than those scholars who have learning but no Christian faith. The biblical writers were men of faith, and only those with "the eyes of faith" can see the biblical message in its deepest dimension. The believer should not try to put his faith in one compartment of his personality and his historical investigation in another, for life has meaning through the integration of the whole of experience.

Some entertain the idea of approaching the Bible neutrally. It is true that in some areas of study a greater degree of objectivity can be achieved than in others. It is also true that a man of faith can be just as honest as anyone else in interpretation. But neutrality regarding the biblical message is neither possible nor desirable. Man is always more than a machine. Believer and non-believer alike come to the Bible with previous experience, study, and presuppositions. Certainly reason and tradition have a part in the process of interpretation, but faith as commitment to God through Jesus Christ goes deeper than anything else. Yet one must always re-examine the implications of his faith in the light of further study and experience.

The man of faith is interested in the theological interpretation of the Bible, and such interpretation is concerned with the unity of the Bible as history and faith are interrelated. The very existence of a canon of sixty-six books, calling to mind God's choice of and covenant with a particular people, testifies to this unity. The chief unity is seen in the activity of the one true God, who revealed himself through Israel and supremely in Jesus Christ. For the Christian, Jesus Christ stands as the fulfillment of the various forms of revelation in the Old Testament. The Old Testament is read in the light of that to which it points, the New Testament in the light of that upon which it rests.[2] This does not mean that the facts of biblical history are to be carelessly handled; rather it means that the historian who is also a believer sees not only the varied details of events in the Bible, but also the story of salvation. With this story in mind he interprets each book and passage of the Bible. The non-believer may recognize specific events as historical occurrences, but the occurrences do not have the same meaning for him as for the believer. It is through a particular elected history, elected people, and elected person that the basic meaning of all life is primarily known.

The central affirmations of biblical faith may be stated in this way: God saves, reveals himself, chooses his instruments, judges all men, creates and re-creates, reigns as king, and acts in history; he is holy, righteous, loving, purposeful, spirit, and one (triune according to the New Testament).[3] In the Bible this structure or framework of faith is in the process of being made known. Unity is seen in the basic structure, and both unity and diversity in the presentation of each affirmation. For example, the affirmation that God saves runs through most of the Bible—in this fact there is unity. But this unity is enriched for the

[2] Harold H. Rowley, "The Relevance of Biblical Interpretation," *Interpretation*, I (1947), 14.

[3] Cf. J. Coert Rylaarsdam, "Preface to Hermeneutics," *Journal of Religion*, XXX (1950), 79-89.

interpreter as he follows the theme historically. God saved Israel from Egyptian bondage, he saved both the nation and individuals from many subsequent perils, and through Jesus Christ he saves men from the bondage of sin. Along with the people of God, the believer makes these and other affirmations of faith. Thus history and faith are brought together in vital union. Those who study the Bible as historians and believers expect to hear God speak.

The principle of interpreting the Bible as a believer may be looked at in relation to the gospel. The term "gospel" views God's redemptive activity, especially in its culmination in Jesus Christ, as good news. When one reads the New Testament, he finds the gospel spoken of as "the gospel of God"—that is, having its source in him (Rom. 1:1; I Thess. 2:2); "the gospel of the kingdom," which means the good news of God's reign (Matt. 4:23); the gospel of salvation and peace— that is, dealing with the completeness of life (Eph. 1:13; 6:15); and "the gospel of Jesus Christ," for he is the one upon whom all converges (Mark 1:1; Rom. 15:19; I Cor. 9:12; Gal. 1:7). There is a sense in which there is a message of good news calling to a man from beyond himself. He may not recognize its true nature. He may examine the Gospels according to Matthew, Mark, Luke, and John, by historical procedures; yet there is more in them than a history of facts for the one who responds in faith. Paul not only spoke of "the" gospel (Rom. 10:16; 11:28; I Cor. 4:15; 9:14, 18); he also spoke of "my" gospel (Rom. 2:16; 16:25; cf. II Tim. 2:8) and "our" gospel (II Cor. 4:3; I Thess. 1:5). It is only as "the" gospel becomes "my" gospel that one can interpret as an evangelical Christian, for the central purpose of his interpretation is to help men become adequately related to God and men through Jesus Christ. At the same time "the" gospel is always calling "my" gospel into judgment, for no one can ever contain or expound the gospel in its totality. Matthew, Mark, Luke, and John, each in his own way, bear witness to the gospel. The constructive task of interpreting the Bible must go on, but no interpretation is absolute. The word of God comes to men through various forms, but the word is not to be altogether identified with the form. It is the interpreter who knows the facts and the revealer, that can best proclaim the revealer's message.

The third suggested principle of interpretation is: *Interpret the Bible as a doer.* The Bible is a book of fact and faith. It is also a book calling for action. "But be doers of the word, and not hearers only ...." (Jas. 1:22.) The Christian believer is expected to express his faith in deeds. Faith without works is not the genuine article; it is a dead faith. Interpretation, to be complete, must include action; but this does not mean that all passages of the Bible are equally a call to some specific action. The God who reveals himself through the Scriptures is a God of action. If his message is to be proclaimed by his people, they must be a people in action.

An inadequate conception of faith interferes with the practical application of biblical truth. Faith may be viewed simply as an intellectual assent to certain doctrines apart from a genuine commitment of the total person to God through Jesus Christ, or it may be viewed as an emotional feeling apart from adequate intellectual comprehension. Either of these defects will impair the exercise of this third principle of interpretation. Even when faith is genuine, wisdom and effort are essential for the interpreter.

But how does one actually learn the will of God for concrete situations? Three major factors have operated in the thinking of men in answer to this question: the Bible, the Church, and the believer. These three belong together, and it is possible to make an idol of any one of them. The Bible is best understood by those who belong to the fellowship of believers. The Church's understanding of the Bible as expressed in creeds (written or unwritten), statements, and life is to be considered seriously. At the same time we do not forget that "the Roman identification of the Church with its Lord . . . can finally lead only to the word of man being put in place of the Word of God." [4] The Bible is primary and creeds are secondary. Yet, when the Bible is regarded as the only word of God, Christ is eclipsed. The Bible is authoritative because God speaks to man through it. Within the Bible the concept of the word of God has various shades of meaning, but it centers in God's activity of salvation and revelation. Jesus Christ is the Word of God incarnate, the one to whom the Scriptures bear witness. The believer (sometimes a group) with all his powers, limitations, and relationships, is responsible for the decision he reaches.

[4] Wolfgang Schweitzer, "Biblical Theology and Ethics Today," *Biblical Authority for Today,* ed. Alan Richardson and Wolfgang Schweitzer (Philadelphia: Westminster Press, 1951), p. 140.

For any interpretation to reach its goal the Holy Spirit must be active throughout the total process. This does not mean that men are capable of perfection in interpretation or that they can control the Holy Spirit. When strong emphasis is placed upon the activity of the living God guiding in ethical action, idolatry in its basest forms may be avoided. Interpretation should be begun, executed, and completed in the spirit of reverent prayer.

The minister interprets the Bible through preaching, teaching, counseling, pastoring the flock, and attending to the business of the church. Each Christian interprets as he builds his home, educates his children, engages in community activities, and takes his recreation.

When members of a group are seeking guidance in dealing with some particular problem, let them begin with Jesus and the New Testament and then go to the Old Testament and trace the relevant teachings as those who take both history and faith seriously.

Jesus said in effect: There are two commandments—Love God with all your being and your neighbor as yourself. On these two commandments the whole *written* Word depends. Any interpretation that is out of harmony with these commandments as Jesus presented them needs to be re-examined. One reason for this book is the violence done to these two commandments by many of the sects and isms with which we deal.

Tools of Interpretation[5]

Many different types of tools are available for the student of the Bible as he applies his principles of interpretation. Carefully edited texts of the Hebrew Old Testament and the Greek New Testament, each with notes on the text, and copies of the most valuable ancient versions make textual criticism and precise exegesis possible. Lexicons give the meanings of words in relation to their derivation, usage, family relationships, and synonyms. Grammars describe how a language operates and, with the lexicons, aid in the work of translation. To some extent all translations are commentaries, and a comparison of several of them in the process of interpreting a specific passage is especially helpful for the person who does not use Hebrew and Greek.

Some commentaries concentrate on historical interpretation, while

[5] See especially B. H. Kelly and D. G. Miller, eds., *Tools for Bible Study* (Richmond: John Knox Press, 1956).

20

others emphasize theology and application. Still others give help in all phases of interpretation. Biblical introductions treat historical and literary matters almost exclusively. Concordances provide information concerning the occurrences, usage, and meaning of biblical words. They make possible the study of a theological concept through the phases of its history. Bible dictionaries and encyclopedias furnish articles on many different kinds of subjects. With the aid of archaeological publications the Israelite people and the early Christian Church can be set in their total context as never before. Archaeology shows not only the likeness of biblical religion to non-biblical religions, but also the uniqueness of biblical faith and practice. Biblical geographies and atlases enable the student to follow the biblical narrative with precision and understanding. The Apocrypha and Pseudepigrapha, the Dead Sea Scrolls, and rabbinic writings throw light on Judaism and the background of early Christianity and the New Testament. Histories of Israel, histories of Israel's religion, and histories of New Testament times, make possible an enlarged historical perspective for the student of the Scriptures. Many different kinds of material are an aid to understanding the thought world of the biblical writers. Especially significant in this respect are works on biblical psychology, which deal with the meaning of such concepts as soul, body, flesh, and spirit. It is too easy to assume that biblical concepts are necessarily the same as those in the modern world.

Theological wordbooks of the Bible trace briefly the development of the most significant words in the theological vocabulary of the Bible and provide homiletical stimulation. Biblical theologies, and works dealing with themes within the field of biblical ideology, help one in arriving at theological conclusions based upon the study of the Bible. Works on biblical preaching and on how to teach the Bible may be included among the tools of interpretation. A library of good tools is a step toward a balanced and healthy study of the written Word.

Dangers in Interpretation

The dangers facing the interpreter of the Bible are many, and those enumerated here are suggestive, not exhaustive.

The first danger is *literalism*. Not all literalism is bad. In fact, the type of literalism which is essential to historical interpretation is valid.

Such a literalism does not overlook the context of a passage or the literary types involved. It is the legalistic kind of literalism that is so dangerous for a correct understanding of the Bible. There are those who say the world is flat because the Bible mentions the four corners of the earth. Some have supported polygamy because it was sometimes practiced by leaders mentioned in the Old Testament. Some literalists are arbitrary about where they interpret literally. For example, I Tim. 2:8 ff. is sometimes interpreted to prohibit women from being officers or ministers in the Church, but the author's statement about how women are to dress is overlooked. Literalism can prevent the understanding of symbolism in such books as Daniel and Revelation.

Proof texts constitute another danger in interpretation. There is, however, a proper use of proof texts. In one sense the modern system of footnoting is an illustration of the proper use of proof texts. When texts are taken out of context to prove one's own preconceived ideas, the Bible is not being properly interpreted. The use of proof texts sometimes takes a different turn. Violence may not be done to the immediate context, but only those passages of the Bible that support one's written or unwritten creed are selected as valuable. The whole evidence is not really interpreted; selection takes the place of interpretation.

Allegorizing has plagued the Church for centuries. Allegory is to be distinguished from allegorizing. Allegory is extended metaphor, the presentation of one thing under the image of another. Examples from the Bible are the good shepherd (John 10:1-18), the vine and the branches (John 15:1-11), and the whole armor of God (Eph. 6:11-17). Allegorizing is the interpreting of a passage as allegory which the author never so intended, for example, the interpretation of the Song of Songs as teaching the love of Christ for the Church. Gal. 4:24 ff. can hardly offer any real justification to anyone for allegorizing, because Paul makes clear that he understands what he is doing in an *ad hominem* presentation. Although it cannot be commended as a method of interpretation, allegorizing kept the Church reminded that the Bible is not to be interpreted superficially.

Allegory is to be distinguished from parable. Allegory is to metaphor as parable is to simile. In the case of a metaphor one thing is said to be another; in the case of a simile one thing is said to be like another. In the case of an allegory every detail is significant for interpretation; in

22

the case of a parable there is usually one main point. It has often been said, "A parable is an earthly story with a heavenly meaning." It is an imaginary story—but not impossible—involving a comparison, with the purpose of teaching a spiritual truth.

Typology is also a danger for the biblical interpreter. Typology and allegorical interpretation are often combined when typology is taken to extremes. Typology, as the word suggests, is a study of types. Since it is a perfectly legitimate study, perhaps the word "typologizing" should be invented to indicate the finding of types which do not really exist. The word "type" occurs sixteen times in the New Testament and involves the idea of likeness. Not all of these occurrences are directly related to the study of typology. Other words are used in the Letter to the Hebrews with very much the same meaning as "type": "shadow" (10:1), "figure" (9:9 K.J.V.), and "patterns" (9:23 K.J.V.). The relationship of promise and fulfillment to the Old Testament and Christ is the basis for the existence of typology. There are types of persons, institutions, offices, events, actions, and things. For example, exodus is the great type of deliverance in the Old Testament; in the New Testament deliverance from sin comes through Christ. The two deliverances are connected for Paul when he says, "For Christ, our paschal lamb, has been sacrificed" (I Cor. 5:7). Some types are clearly designated by the writers of Scripture. Interpreters may err in finding types where no types exist and too much is left to the imagination. A type is a true picture of the person or thing it represents, it is in harmony with the story of salvation, and it prefigures something future. Paul says Adam is a type of Christ (Rom. 5:14). That is, Adam heads the human family as it stands in death; Christ heads the new humanity as it stands in life. The correspondence between Adam and Christ is providentially ordered.

Historicism is a danger sometimes encountered among interpreters. In this unit the word is defined to mean the theory or practice of confining or tending to confine the interpretation of the Bible to biblical introduction or prolegomena. In some instances there is the denial of categories beyond the historical. Objectivity tends to become an idol. There is a preoccupation with historical analysis that never gets beyond analysis. Biblical theologies are found, but no biblical theology. The danger of historicism is apt to be encountered among students whose presuppositions are basically out of harmony with those of the biblical writers. Those who are content to read the Bible only as cultural record are to be numbered here. Students of this kind are most likely to be found among adherents to one or more of the cultural isms.

Suggestions for Further Study

1. Work out a statement of your own principles of biblical interpretation.
2. On the basis of these principles examine the methods of interpretation employed by each of the groups discussed in this book, i.e., where such a procedure is relevant.
3. Visit ism groups and leaders in your community with a view to ascertaining their approach to the Bible.

Selected Bibliography

Articles in almost every issue of *Interpretation: A Journal of Bible and Theology,* 3401 Brook Road, Richmond 27, Va.

Berkhof, Louis. *Principles of Biblical Interpretation.* Grand Rapids: Baker Book House, 1950.

Dugmore, Clifford W., ed. *The Interpretation of the Bible.* London: Society for Promoting Christian Knowledge, 1944.

Farmer, Herbert H. "The Bible: Its Significance and Authority." *The Interpreter's Bible,* I, 3-31. Ed. George A. Buttrick. Nashville: Abingdon Press, 1952.

Farrar, F. W. *The History of Interpretation.* New York: E. P. Dutton & Co., 1886.

Gilbert, George H. *Interpretation of the Bible.* New York: The Macmillan Co., 1908.

Goldman, Solomon. *The Book of Books: An Introduction.* In his "The Book of Human Destiny, 1." New York: Harper & Bros., 1948.

Grant, Robert M. *The Bible in the Church.* New York: The Macmillan Co., 1948.

Grant, Robert M., McNeill, John T. and Terrien, Samuel. "History of the Interpretation of the Bible," *The Interpreter's Bible,* I, 106-41. Ed. George A. Buttrick. Nashville: Abingdon Press, 1952.

Hahn, Herbert F. *Old Testament in Modern Research.* Philadelphia: Muhlenberg Press, 1954.

Kelly, Balmer H. and Miller, Donald G., eds. *Tools for Bible Study.* Richmond: John Knox Press, 1956.

Kraeling, Emil G. *The Old Testament Since the Reformation.* New York: Harper & Bros., 1955.

Ramm, Bernard. *Protestant Biblical Interpretation.* Boston: W. A. Wilde Co., 1950.

Richardson, Alan and Schweitzer, Wolfgang, eds. *Biblical Authority for Today.* Philadelphia: The Westminster Press, 1951.

Rolston, Holmes. *Consider Paul, Apostle of Jesus Christ.* Richmond: John Knox Press, 1951.

Rowley, Harold H., ed. *The Old Testament and Modern Study.* New York: Oxford University Press, 1951.

Rylaarsdam, J. C. "Preface to Hermeneutics," *Journal of Religion*, XXX (1950), 79-89.

Swaim, Joseph C. *Right and Wrong Ways to Use the Bible*. Philadelphia: The Westminster Press, 1953.

Terry, Milton S. *Biblical Hermeneutics*. New York: Methodist Book Concern, 1911.

SECTS AND ISMS IN HISTORICAL PERSPECTIVE

Introductory Reflections

IT SEEMS LIKELY THAT LEARNING TO REFLECT BROADLY AND DISINTERestedly on the causes, the motivations, and the outcomes of sect formation as it appears in history, will better equip one to study, understand, and deal with the isms and sects of the present time. This, of course, is an immense undertaking calling for extensive knowledge of history, for delicate insight into human personality in its individual and social aspects, for great breadth of sympathy, and for the apparently opposite quality, decisiveness of judgment. What follows cannot be a substitute for such a lifelong project, but it may be a suggestive beginning of the project and perhaps a useful guide.

A brief word of definition would seem to be called for. A sect, *in religion,* has been defined as "a party dissenting from an established or parent church." [1] In distinction from a sect an ism may be regarded as a more or less coherent body of doctrine which has not been accepted as official by any established or parent church, but which has not objectified itself into a dissenting party. It is from the standpoint of the established or parent church that the dissenting opinion is called an ism and the dissenting party is called a sect. The standpoint here employed is that of main-line Protestantism. However, the implications of that term will depend to some extent upon a judgment as to which denominations do and which do not belong in the main line of Protestantism, or, in other words, which are and which are not sects.

Historically, the line of distinction between sects and established forms is neither distinct nor stable. A certain amount of "dissent," that is, of alienation from others, is an essential characteristic of a sect—but how much? To that question no definite answer can be given. Every de-

---

[1] *Webster's New Collegiate Dictionary* (2d ed.; Springfield, Mass.: G. & C. Merriam Co., 1953), p. 764.

nomination is aware of some cherished characteristic which it will faithfully maintain as against all others. When this exclusiveness becomes marked, the denomination is revealing a sectarian spirit. Nor is the line of distinction stable. It would not be difficult to point to denominations which would not now be naturally regarded as sects, but which undoubtedly were sects at one time.

Implied in the above is the fact that to call any body a sect is to pass something of a negative judgment upon it. It is not simply an objective characterization; it is to some extent a condemnation. The very assumption that we can identify main-line Protestantism implies that there are bodies which do not come under the definition of that term, and our allegiance to main-line Protestantism involves a critical rejection of such other bodies. The task that is before us, therefore, cannot be profitably performed without sitting in judgment upon others in a situation in which evaluations must often seem questionable and in which a risk of hurting people for whom one feels fraternal affection cannot be avoided. Perhaps the risks may be minimized by pointing out that others are cordially invited to exercise their own Protestant right and duty of private judgment.

A Broad Perspective

Lest too narrow an absorption in the problem of local isms and sects cause either an underestimate of their significance or an emotionally intense bias, let it be noted that sect formation has been a permanent characteristic of human societal development.

The Christian church, for example, has been involved, throughout her history, in sect formation. She herself was at first regarded as a sect by the Jewish leaders (Acts 24:14), and to her very great benefit she was regarded similarly for a long time by the Roman rulers. Indeed the book of Acts shows clearly that she was in grave danger, through the hesitations and confusions of her own leaders, of becoming exactly that. Though they were presently repudiated by the Church, the Judaizers who dogged the footsteps of the apostle Paul represented an ism of that character which, in the case of the Ebionites, actually became a sect. It has been estimated that in the first hundred years of her history the Church threw off approximately one hundred sects. Later in the period of the early Church, isms became sects in the case of the Nestorians, the

27

Montanists, the Donatists, and a host of others. The medieval synthesis, both in the long process of its formation and in the activity of its relatively finished form, created or occasioned numerous sects; and the Reformation did the same thing. So did the period of Protestant scholasticism; and so did the period when the impact of the industrial Revolution caused denominations which previously had ministered effectively to the socially underprivileged to advance socially, leaving their former constituency behind. In short, the Church has been forming isms, many of which have become sects, throughout her history. Of these sects some soon disappeared, some remain as sects, others have accepted themselves and been accepted as "respectable" members of the family of denominations.

But sect formation is not confined to Christianity. It finds expression in other religious groups also. Early in its history Islam was divided by sectarianism, and such is its condition today. Of all the greater religions Hinduism has been most successful in keeping its isms from becoming sects. Whether that represents strength or weakness may be a good question for reflection and debate. Perhaps it represents both strength and weakness. At any rate, even Hinduism has experienced sect formation. Buddhism, for example, arose as an ism within Hinduism; but in many cases it became a sect or a separate religion.

Nor is sect formation an exclusively religious process. It is every bit as richly and variously represented in the history of secular, social institutions. Most of the modern nations arose, directly or indirectly, through a process of sect formation from the largely nonnational, feudal society of the early Middle Ages. Within American political life the great political parties represent isms which have not been suffered to become sects; but the Republicans experienced a sectarian movement in the "Bull Moose" secession of Theodore Roosevelt, and the Democrats faced a similar sectarian revolt in the "Dixiecrat" movement.

The naming of a few examples is intended to make the discussion concrete. It is not intended to impose dogmatically the author's evaluation upon others, still less to confuse the discussion by arousing emotional resentments. Isms and sects, religious and secular, abound in amazing numbers throughout history and in contemporary society. If we feel that we belong in the main line of Protestantism and do not represent a sect, we should not allow that fact to cause any smug self-satisfaction.

On the one hand, the enormous number of groups which feel that we are wrong on points which seem so important to them that they are willing to live or die on the issue involved, should serve effectively to destroy smugness. On the other hand, the obvious fact that society needs sects, that sects have often stimulated correction or progress, should open our eyes to the possibility that contemporary sects may be serving precisely the same function in our own time and place.

The American Scene, Briefly Considered

Many of the religious isms and sects that have flourished or are now flourishing in America were importations from abroad. Sects have been coming to America all through our history. Indeed, the earliest settlement of America may properly be viewed as an achievement of the sects; and there is some insight into American characteristics to be garnered from viewing it in that light. Certainly, the Mayflower company were conscious and deliberate sectarians. The first settlers in Massachusetts Bay apparently desired to be Puritans, that is, to represent an ism; but they did not intend to become a sect. Circumstances, however, forced them into sectarianism also. The "Scotch-Irish" were a sect from the standpoint of the official religion of the government, and they came to America with a very pronounced feeling of sectarian resentment toward that government and its official church. Apparently they were similarly regarded by the established authorities when they sought to settle in New England. The same is eminently true of the Quakers. The colonies which they established and in which, perhaps, they were not sectarian, attracted from the start a large number of Continental sects. As early as 1653 a few Mennonites came to the Middle Atlantic colonies from south-central Europe. Their descendants, reinforced by subsequent immigration, still flourish as a sect. The Shakers came from England in 1774, established settlements in New York and as far west as Kentucky, but have recently died out. Theosophy, strongly influenced by the religion and philosophy of India, arrived here about 1873, with a host of more or less kindred but independent Indian swamis close on its heels. Various sects of that character may still be encountered here.

Since, from the standpoint of this study, Roman Catholicism is being regarded as a sect (see pp. 157-59), it should be noted that the controlling influences in the modern Roman Catholic Church came in small

29

numbers at first with the founding of Maryland. As they followed the Westward Movement, they encountered and largely absorbed the Spanish Roman Catholicism of the Southwest. More recently they have been greatly reinforced by immigration from strongly Roman Catholic areas of Europe.

Humanism came from England as one of the three or four strands which, held together by the religious genius and enthusiasm of the early religious leaders, constituted New England "orthodoxy." [2] As early as the second generation it began to separate itself as an ism, later called liberalism or modernism, which sometimes formed sects such as Unitarianism and which became increasingly prevalent until the second decade of the present century.[3] This indigenous development of the early importation was subsequently supplemented and reinforced by fresh Humanistic impulses from abroad. For example, English deism became French skepticism, and the latter strongly influenced the American Enlightenment at the time of the American Revolution. The Humanism of the German Enlightenment became a powerful influence in American educated circles in the nineteenth century.

Some of the communistic sects appeared from Europe early in the history of Pennsylvania, or communistic isms did so and became sects in this free environment. The latest, and perhaps the only dangerous member of this quite numerous brood, is Marxism, which took definite shape with the publication of the *Communist Manifesto* in Europe in 1847, and which has only recently, perhaps since the period of the First World War, become an internal threat to American security.

But, as has been noted, it must not therefore be concluded that sectarianism is a foreign product which introduces into the American blood stream something from which we would otherwise be wholly free. We must not make that mistake in considering the religious sects. The very great majority of the numerous sects now flourishing in our country originated here. Many of them—like Unity, The House of David, The Peace Mission, Psychiana, The Great I Am, and the numerous "Holy Roller" sects which, like a cloud, remain fairly constant in their totality

[2] Perry Miller, *The New England Mind; the Seventeenth Century* (New York: The Macmillan Co., 1939).

[3] Joseph Haroutunian, *Piety Versus Moralism; the Passing of the New England Theology* (New York: Henry Holt & Co., 1932).

while their individual members may be born to flourish only for a year or two—seem so far to have remained in the land of their birth, and indeed many of them are so characteristically a product of strictly American conditions that they are not likely to be accepted in any other country. But others—such as Christian Science, Mormonism, Jehovah's Witnesses, and Moral Rearmament—have become almost world wide.

Many of these sects have a history of steadfast fidelity (which a hostile critic may rather regard as "damnable stubbornness") which may appeal strongly to lovers of the Protestant principle of private judgment, to those who regard scriptural authority highly, and to all who value sturdy independence. The earlier importations consciously incurred and steadily resisted the very strongest official and social pressures in the land of their origin, they braved the hardships and dangers of early immigration and pioneering, and they were not overcome by the more subtle temptations to conformity when the environment of the new country freed them from persecution. And, though their refusal to merge in the general practices of American society may make them a source of irritation, of perplexity, or of derision to others, and may bring on the sectarians themselves the characteristic peculiarities of ingrowth, still they manifest a strength, and contribute to society a vigor and a rich variety which, if it does not awaken admiration, should at least prevent too hasty, scornful, and sweeping a condemnation.

In short, the causes and occasions, the possible values and disvalues, and any effective preventatives and remedies, are not simply racial or national problems. Not with any thought of dealing with such problems in any complete or final manner, but simply as a suggestion of the sort of thing that is involved, I shall proceed to examine them by stating a few generalizations and giving some concrete illustrations.

Explanation and Evaluation

Isms commonly arise when some forceful person becomes vividly and painfully aware of some important need or want for which no adequate provision is found in the accepted social institutions and when that person proposes a remedy which is not generally accepted. The proposed remedy, however, does not become an ism, in the usually understood meaning of that term, so long as it remains private to the originator.

However, if the "time is ripe" (whatever that expression may mean), others, though still a minority, come to sense the same need and to adopt the remedy, and then an ism is born. It will become a sect if indifference or resistance on the part of the accepted social institutions causes the ism to develop organizational expression for itself which is distinct from, and is informed with a spirit of resentment toward, the more long-standing social institutions. The sect is not simply distinct from the accepted institutions; it is usually critical of them and derives much of its inner strength and propaganda effectiveness from that criticism. When that occurs, the older institutions will characterize and condemn the new organization as a sect. The latter may feed on that charge, betraying most of the characteristics of an inferiority complex; but it may also gain sufficient self-confidence to bring the charge of sectarianism against the older institutions, in which case each side regards itself as the true way and condemns the other as a sect.

The need that has been expressed may be a genuine one, the judgment that it is being ignored or inadequately met in existing institutions may be correct, and the proposed remedy may be sound. In that case, a wholesome ism will have arisen. It may presently approve itself to and be generally accepted by society as a whole, and real progress will thus be achieved. If it is not thus accepted, it may continue to flourish as an ism within accepted institutions, hoping always for final acceptance and content meanwhile to witness to the truth. But if such a wholesome ism is steadily resisted, and if the issues involved seem important enough for the conflict to generate sufficient emotional determination, the formation of a sect would seem to be imperative and advantageous.

As examples, Protestantism and original Methodism may be mentioned. Luther certainly had no intention of dividing the Church. When the publication of his views as to the needs of the Church and the remedy had gained him a following, Lutheranism was at first an ism within Roman Catholicism. It was not until the older institution resisted with persecution that the movement became, from the standpoint of the Roman body, a sect. Even then, the Lutheran movement did not readily accept a sectarian status. Melanchthon and others labored strenuously to heal the breach. When that proved impossible, and even long before its impossibility was accepted, Protestantism claimed that it was really a return to original Christianity and that the Roman Church was guilty of sectarianism. That has been the Protestant claim throughout its history. Similarly the Wesleys detected a genuine need which was not being met. Without any intention or desire of breaking away from the established Church, they set out to meet that need in a sound and effective manner, and they gained a following. It was not until the necessities of their movement made it imperative that ordained leadership be provided and the bishops refused to co-operate in that respect, that the schismatic act of ordaining its own leadership was reluctantly performed. In each case, as in many similar ones, those who accept the standpoint of these studies would agree that, if the term "sect" must be accepted at all, it was a necessary and wholesome schism, and the resulting sect was fully justified.

But we cannot agree that all sects have thus been justified. When the formation of a sect is to be judged adversely, it may be because the alleged need was not a proper one, but arose out of the unwholesome demands of an ill-balanced personality; or the need may have been essentially real, and it may have been wholesomely provided for in existing institutions, but ill-balanced personalities may have demanded a satisfaction that would not be wholesome if it were possible.

Before examining some illustrations of each of the above types, let us pause to observe that a sect that is for any of these reasons harmful in itself may yet be historically justified in a secondary manner. Though it itself is unwholesome, it may by that very fact startle the leaders of the more settled institutions into a reaction that is wholesome, or it may occasion the formation of a new sect or ism that must be judged to be beneficial. For example, the purifying effect that Protestantism had on the Roman Catholic Church has caused some Roman Catholics to judge it in this way, and some loyal members of the Church of England similarly evaluate Methodism. Also, the highly questionable character of certain of the healing sects is probably responsible for an interest in the bearing of Christianity on physical health that at present constitutes an ism, though not yet a sect, within some of the denominations, notably the Church of England. If that judgment is correct, then the healing sects, which would probably be widely regarded as bad in themselves, have yet had an effect which many would regard as good and which must, therefore, be charged to their credit.

We acknowledged above that, under certain conditions which we specified, the formation of an ism and even of a sect may be inevitable and beneficial. In doing so we were, of course, speaking from the standpoint of the historian. From a somewhat different point of view that judgment is certainly debatable. Divisions among the followers of Christ must always be regarded as in some sense regrettable and the result of human limitation and sinfulness; but, acknowledging that human beings and human society suffer from limitation and sinfulness, it may then be admitted that the formation of an ism or a sect may be the only course available and may contribute soundly to the purification of a wrongful condition and to genuine progress. It was in that sense that we named Protestantism and early Methodism as examples of wholesome sect formation. Some further insight may be gained from considering, as a fundamentally sound ism, the strong contemporary movement known as ecumenism. It arose when sufficient Christian leaders at long last became deeply affronted by the stark contrast between the essentially catholic or universal character of Christianity, with its basic unifying quality of love, and the sadly divided, sometimes bitterly hostile, state of the modern Church; and when they proposed to correct that situation. Though some earnest Christians may not agree, it may be said that they thus became aware of a genuine need which was not until then being adequately grappled with. Thus an ism which we propose to regard as sound arose. But it may become unsound if, and insofar as, its motivations and its procedures come to involve the ignoring of other Christian values. For example, if this movement becomes so insistent on willy-nilly church unification that loyalty to doctrinal considerations is betrayed, as some critics of the movement feel has already occurred, it surely must be judged to have become unsound. Or, if a uniform, authoritarian world-wide organization should be achieved which does despite to individual freedom and the rights of individual personality, the result would be disastrous. This movement has not yet become a sect. Nor has it occasioned the formation of rival sects, but the possibility that this might occur has sometimes seemed imminent.

Turning now to examples of sects which are commonly judged to be unwholesome, it has been seen that this could occur in different ways. First, there are sects which arose out of a sense of need which depends, in part, on a subjective imbalance on the side of the founder and the followers. This sense of need may arise wholly out of a feeling of frustration caused by unrealistic demands; or more often, perhaps, there is a real, objective need, sensed with too great intensity by a frustrated person. Among such sects may be included most of the healing sects and those which have economic frustration as their basic motivation. In both cases, there is an objective lack. The legitimate demands for health and for economic justice are not adequately met in our society. Reasonably well-adjusted persons are, at least at times, quite strongly affronted by this objective lack; but others seem to be abnormally affected thereby. They seek some short-cut solution which is quite unrealistic; they find followers, but their solution is not immediately or generally accepted; and a sect is born. For example, it would probably be generally agreed that Mary Baker Eddy's concern for health was not then, and is not now, being adequately dealt with, and that, within limits at least, the concern is a legitimate one. It would also be agreed that the widespread materialism of her day prevented a recognition of the extent to which ill health is caused, and can be cured, by psychological means. But it would be agreed by all who have not become her followers that her own reaction was also motivated by her strange personality and that the need of many of her well-to-do followers arises out of their having too little significant obligation in life and could be cured if they would learn to lose themselves in some worthy cause in the service of others. Similarly, many people would agree that economic underprivilege is an objective fact in far too many cases and that by no means all of it is directly attributable to abnormal deficiencies on the part of the sufferers. Still, society does offer economic hope and many well-adjusted people, who began life in the suffering class, have found reasonably effective ways of achieving economic success. Others have learned to adjust themselves to their economic underprivilege and to live a wholesome life, either in spite of it or even because of it. But some people are abnormally sensitive to their underprivilege, or to what they, without sufficient warrant, regard as their underprivilege. They seek methods other than the normal ones for satisfying their sense of need, and thus what we have called an economic sect is born. These economic sects are of interest to us when the short-cut cures involve religious theories and lead to the formation of religious sects. But, of course, non-religious and even anti-religious nostrums may be proposed, as happened in the case of Marxian Communism.

The sects referred to above are also examples of our second type—that in which the proposed cure would not be wholesome even if it were possible. The Christian Scientist to the contrary, it is probably quite impossible to cure all illness by steadfastly affirming that matter does not exist. And, if that did prove to be possible, while it might be a wonderful cure for ill health, its results, if commonly accepted, would be disastrous in other ways. What would happen to the natural sciences, for instance, if everybody suddenly decided that whatever we should mean by matter does not exist, that only spirit is real? And if everyone could gain economic privilege simply by having some group of specialists pray for it on their behalf, the immense values in the form of character development that come from the daily struggle to earn one's bread by the sweat of one's brow would all be sacrificed. Most people sense, if they do not actually see, that the proposed remedies will not work, and they refuse the prescription; but some people do not sense it, and thus sects are born.

The third type starts out wholesomely to propose a good remedy for a real need; but somewhere, as the remedy is elaborated, wrong decisions are made, which others refuse to follow, but the founder and certain followers persist, and a sect is born. Examples to be studied in this book include perfectionism, fundamentalism, and Buchmanism or Moral Rearmament. We shall illustrate by glancing at fundamentalism.

In the heat of recent controversy, the term "fundamentalism" has been very loosely employed. It was commonly assumed and stated by the liberals of the nineteenth century type that only three basic conceptions of Christianity exist or perhaps can exist, namely, Catholicism, liberalism, and fundamentalism. Thus all of their opponents who were not Roman Catholics were classified as fundamentalists, and the worst characteristics that that term had come to connote were attributed to them. These characteristics included a reactionary attachment to past and exploded dogma, fear of new truth, ignorance that was positively willful, bitterness of spirit, and so forth. If and insofar as such fundamentalism does exist, the following may be said of it. It represents an appreciation of and a loyalty to the authority of Scripture, arising at a time when the prevailing trends of theological scholarship seemed all to be in an opposite direction, and continuing in the present when such trends seem to be strangely mixed with a return to a more positive attitude toward the Scriptures. Since a reliance on scriptural authority is basic to Protestantism, it would seem that one would have to repudiate historic Protestantism, though perhaps retaining the name for something very different, or agree that the fundamentalist's loyalty to Scripture is good. But, of course, loyalty to Scripture may have various motivations and may take different forms. If such loyalty is the fruit of ignorance asserting itself as a religious virtue (and that has happened); if it is really motivated by fear of truth which would be in effect lack of faith in the God of truth; if it leads to or springs from intellectual, moral, or spiritual arrogance; then the ism and the sects which may spring from it become unwholesome and dangerous.

Some Further Reflections

Isms, which may or may not become sects, often result from the focusing of attention by earnest people on some real value which is thus lifted out of the totality to which it belongs—a totality in which alone it is healthy and which is not healthy without it. These people feel, rightly or wrongly, that the selected value is being ignored or at least inadequately dealt with in the prevailing churches or culture. They therefore set out to give it its due. If they can do that, while still being loyal to the other values, some of which at least are being realized in the prevailing culture, a healthy ism will result. But movements of this type usually involve a certain resentment toward the alleged inadequate culture, and the resentment is commonly increased by opposition. Then the selected value is cultivated in opposition to the values of resisting society, the latter often being characterized as vices, though they may simply be ignored. It is then that the ism, and the possibly resulting sect, becomes ill balanced and unwholesome.

An illuminating example may be found in the German Pietism and in the British and American evangelicalism of the eighteenth and nineteenth centuries. Here the cold intellectualism, the dead formalism, and the consequent moral ineffectiveness of the churches and of the prevailing culture, which caused "enthusiasm" to be regarded with such superior distaste, seemed entirely to ignore the values of warm feeling in worship and of self-sacrificial activity for the moral amelioration of society and the uplifting of its victims. When the corrective movement remained an ism, working in the balancing environment of established institutions, it was thoroughly wholesome. But when and insofar as it became a sect, offering itself as a complete whole in opposition to established institutions, it tended to ignore or deny the values of sound intellectual guidance, of formal dignified expression, and of the ecumenical spirit of community. It tended to become a moralism which set up its own moral prejudices as the test of one's Christian status and to apply this test in a very arrogant spirit. But because the moral prejudices differed and the intellectual activity through which either agreement or at least toleration might have been achieved had been minimized in opposition to the intellectualism of the opposition, this movement became extremely subdivided, the various resulting sects becoming as bitter toward one another as they all were toward the culture which had originally occasioned the movement.

In closing, I turn to some examples of the same thing operating perhaps in a more subtle manner. A society or a social institution appears to be similar to a railroad train, which runs best when the pull of the engine is countered to some extent by the brakes. In other words, in order to progress wholesomely, a social institution needs both a driving force and a conservative power, the latter strong enough definitely to influence the action, but not strong enough to prevent or stop it. Something of this sort may be detected even in the psychological make-up of the well-balanced individual, in whom ideas and the superficial emotions are susceptible of rapid change and strive to create ever-changing purposes, while the deeper emotional organizations which the older psychology called sentiments make for stability, challenging the novelties to prove themselves before they are happily adopted. In society or in a social institution the progressive and conservative functions tend to become exercised through contending isms, because they locate themselves in different individuals, though, of course, there are men and movements in which the two are present in healthy balance. The true conservative is not averse to change, but he is vividly aware of the values which have proved themselves reasonably well in the past. He approaches proposed changes with hopeful caution; he is delighted if they prove to represent sound progress; but he wants them carefully tested, in somewhat the same manner and spirit as a new drug is tested by the medical profession before it is released for general use. His danger, however, especially if changes seem to be coming too fast, is to give his unchanging devotion to the *status quo* or to the past, and to confuse reaction with critical caution. The danger of the progressive, on the other hand, is that he confuse novelty with progress and the new with the true. The conservative, if he feels and fears the tug of change, is apt to become a reactionary and to form isms and sects of that character. The progressive, feeling the restraint of conservative elements, tends to confuse necessary conservatism with reaction and to form isms and sects which are designed to wipe out society's wholesome restraints.

Scientism and secularism may both be regarded as the reaction of adventurous and impatient minds, or at least of minds which regard extreme venturesomeness as a virtue, to the slowness of sound scientific progress and the strong conservatism of those who are more vividly aware of the value aspects of culture. The caution of the true scientist is well illustrated by Newton, who, when observed results differed by a small amount from his predictions, refused to accept his own theories and was willing to accept them only when a fresh measurement of the distance of the moon from the earth finally brought his predictions into correspondence with observation. But scientism is impatient of such caution. It glories in every fresh guess made in the name of science; it bitterly assails all who hesitate; it refuses to recognize the legitimacy of any search for truth other than its own mistaken conception of the scientific method. Secularism represents an impatient, unrestrained confidence in man's autonomous freedom and a resentment against the conservative pressures of religious experience.

But the same sectarian tension is abundantly illustrated in the history of Christianity. During the second century, for example, while the Church was learning, probably with some mistakes, to accommodate itself to a long-term struggle in a hostile world and substituting regularity of organization and discipline for the earlier unpredictable and often unreliable spontaneity, the Montanists refused to go along. They became a sect which was able to capture the allegiance even of the great Tertullian. The Church of Rome, having by the thirteenth century succeeded in accommodating itself to, and in accommodating to itself, the culture of Western Europe, refused to go along with the profound cultural changes which set in about that time. The result was numerous smaller sects and then the great sectarian break of the Renaissance and the Reformation.

Selected Bibliography

Broadbent, E. H. *The Pilgrim Church.* London: Pickering & Inglis, 1931.

Haroutunian, Joseph. *Piety Versus Moralism: the Passing of the New England Theology.* New York: Henry Holt & Co., 1932.

Latourette, Kenneth S. *A History of Christianity.* New York: Harper & Bros., 1953; or any standard work on church history.

Miller, Perry. *The New England Mind; the Seventeenth Century.* New York: The Macmillan Co., 1939.

Niebuhr, H. Richard. *The Social Sources of Denominationalism.* New York: Henry Holt & Co., 1929.

Troeltsch, Ernst. *The Social Teaching of the Christian Churches.* Tr. Olive Wyon. 2 vols.; New York: The Macmillan Co., 1949.

For additional materials see the Basic Bibliography.

BASIC BIBLIOGRAPHY

American Academy of Political and Social Science. *Organized Religion in the United States.* Ed. Ray H. Abrams. Philadelphia: The Academy, 1948. (Its Annals, V. 256.)

Atkins, Gaius G. *Modern Religious Cults and Movements.* Westwood, N. J.: Fleming H. Revell Co., 1923.

Bach, Marcus L. *Faith and My Friends.* Indianapolis: Bobbs-Merrill Co., 1951.

————. *Report to Protestants.* Indianapolis: Bobbs-Merrill Co., 1948.

————. *They Have Found a Faith.* Indianapolis: Bobbs-Merrill Co., 1946.

Bainton, Roland H. "The Sectarian Theory of the Church," *Christendom,* XI (1946), 382-87.

Braden, Charles S. "Sectarianism Run Wild," *Protestantism, a Symposium.* Ed. William K. Anderson. Nashville; Commission on Courses of Study, The Methodist Church, 1944.

————. *These Also Believe.* New York: The Macmillan Co.., 1949.

————. *Varieties of American Religion.* Chicago: Willett, Clark & Co., 1936.

————. "What Can We Learn from the Cults?" *Religion in Life,* XIV (1944-55), 52-64.

————. "Why Are the Cults Growing?" *The Christian Century,* LXI (1944), 45-47.

Burtt, Edwin A. *Types of Religious Philosophy.* New York: Harper & Bros., 1951.

Clark, Elmer T. *The Small Sects in America.* Rev. ed.; Nashville: Abingdon Press, 1949.

Davies, Horton. *Christian Deviations.* London: Student Christian Movement Press, 1954.

Douglass, Harlan P. "Cultural Differences and Recent Religious Divisions," *Christendom,* X (1945), 89-105.

Ebenstein, William. *Today's Isms.* Englewood Cliffs, N. J.: Prentice-Hall, Inc., 1954.

Fauset, Arthur H. *Black Gods of the Metropolis.* Philadelphia: University of Pennsylvania Press, 1944.

Ferguson, Charles W. *The Confusion of Tongues.* 5th ed.; Grand Rapids: Zondervan Publishing House, 1936.

Garrison, Winfred E. *The March of Faith.* New York: Harper & Bros., 1933.

Hedley, George P. *The Christian Heritage in America.* New York: The Macmillan Co., 1946.

Horton, Walter M., *Christian Theology: An Ecumenical Approach.* New York: Harper & Bros., 1955.

Manwell, Reginald D. *The Church Across the Street.* Boston: The Beacon Press, 1946.

Mayer, Frederick E. *The Religious Bodies of America.* St. Louis: Concordia Publishing House, 1954.

Mead, Frank S. *Handbook of Denominations in the United States.* Rev. ed.; Nashville: Abingdon Press, 1956.

Miller, Irving R. "The Prophetic Meaning of Sectarian Ecstasy," *Religion in Life,* XVII (1947-48), 104-11.

Miller, Randolph C., ed. *The Church and Organized Movements*. New York: Harper & Bros., 1946.

Muelder, Walter G. "From Sect to Church," *Christendom*, X (1945), 450-62.

Neve, Juergen L. *Churches and Sects of Christendom*. Blair, Neb.: Lutheran Publishing House, 1952.

Niebuhr, H. Richard. *The Kingdom of God in America*. Chicago: Willett, Clark & Co., 1937.

——. *The Social Sources of Denominationalism*. New York: Henry Holt & Co., 1929.

Potter, Charles F. *The Faiths Men Live By*. New York: Prentice-Hall, Inc., 1954.

Preece, Harold. *Dew on Jordan*. New York: E. P. Dutton & Co., 1946.

Rosten, Leo C., ed. *A Guide to the Religions of America*. New York: Simon & Schuster, Inc., 1955.

Roy, Ralph L. *Apostles of Discord*. Boston: The Beacon Press, 1953.

Soper, Edmund D. *Racism, a World Issue*. Nashville: Abingdon Press, 1947.

Spann, J. Richard, ed. *The Christian Faith and Secularism*. Nashville: Abingdon Press, 1948.

Stuber, Stanley J. *How We Got Our Denominations*. New York: Association Press, 1948.

Sweet, William W. "Cultural Pluralism in the American Tradition," *Christendom*, XI (1946), 316-26, 501-8.

——. *The Story of Religion in America*. New York: Harper & Bros., 1950.

Temple, William. *Nature, Man and God*. New York: The Macmillan Co., 1949.

Van Baalen, Jan K. *The Chaos of Cults*. Rev. ed.; Grand Rapids: William B. Eerdmans Publishing Co., 1956.

Williams, John P. *What Americans Believe and How They Worship*. New York: Harper & Bros., 1952.

PART TWO

ISMS PREDOMINANTLY BIBLICAL

✸✸✸✸✸✸✸✸✸✸✸✸✸✸✸✸

FUNDAMENTALISM

FUNDAMENTALISM IS AN ISM OF DEFENSE. AGAINST A VIOLATOR MOVING in upon his faith, a Christian marks a line; here he will stand and fight. Some features of the faith are under fire. To yield on these will make the faith no faith. This is no time for long thoughts on the whole of Christian truth. This is the time to stop the enemy and save the day. Fundamentalists have often been honorable if not always lovable in the story of the faith.

History of Fundamentalism

In their own way the propounders of the Apostles' Creed, the Montanists, and the Donatists were fundamentalists. Puritans quarreled with Anglicans over what was fundamental to the faith. But fundamentalism has meant something special in America. It has meant Christian defense against the infiltration of science and critical ideas. From the latter part of the nineteenth century, many Christians felt their faith was threatened. Error came masquerading as science and scholarship. Great ramparts of earnest protest were raised. Champions arose to lead the aroused ranks of believers against the invaders. And the end is not yet.

The background lies in the predominant settlement which characterized early America, settlement by Protestant groups who venerated the Bible as a holy book. Even more crucial was the Great Awakening which enlivened Christian religion in America. Allegiance was not now so much to the European national churches as to the new evangelical faith centered in the Bible. At the camp meetings and on the circuits of the frontier, conversion was expected to be witnessed from the Bible, and the Scriptures were the judge in every denominational fight. Schools prided themselves on their faithfulness to God's Word; and where some center of infidelity was formed, it was converted at least periodically by revival through the Bible.

Where the most Bible-centered of Protestants before had counted the

Scripture as inerrant in the autographs and as a rule for faith and life, in rural America it became something more. It was now a book of oracles. On the frontier the settlers did not have or understand the autographs, but they took their English King James Version as literally infallible. Here was a symbol of the true faith they had found, a faith which had just revolutionized their lives and changed the complexion of their country.

But not all the thinking world had stopped with this faith symbolized by the Bible as the rule and judge. Critics arose. Schleiermacher labored to give the faith a new base in experience valid even to the Bible's critics and the faith's despisers. Ritschl interpreted the faith in moral terms: God's love; Christ, the revealer of God's love; the Kingdom, the community of love. In America the Edwardians, Nathaniel Taylor, the Unitarians, Bushnell, and others were reformulating thought. The categories and modes of expression of the faith were changing. All these may have worked out gradually and peaceably except for three factors which brought a pressure which could not be borne: (1) evolutionary science, (2) agnostic and pragmatic philosophy, (3) radical biblical criticism. These unfortunately hit America just when urbanization and the secularization of education made her people insecure. The result was war. Modernism was storming the citadel. Let God's people stand firm.

The general pattern in each denomination was a few heresy trials in the nineteenth century, a temporary return to peace about 1900, and then a movement of protest hardening from the time of the publication of *The Fundamentals*[1] in 1912 and reaching large proportions in the 1920's. The defenders in each denomination organized and bid for control, using one or more periodicals as their organs.

Modern biblical scholars did not satisfy the defenders of the fundamentals. These scholars kept wanting to consider the textual evidence. Since this evidence was never fully in, they were disconcertingly slow in their decisions. And they lacked the ring of solid authority possessed by simple frontier reliance on the King James Version. Modern students also declared certain sections of the Bible to be poetry and the truth in these sections a poetic truth. Some even spoke of confessional truth

---

[1] *The Fundamentals: A Testimony to the Truth* (12 vols.; Chicago: Testimony Publishing Co., 1910-15).

beyond history and called it "myth." Critics were pointing out the particular historical situations of certain books of the Bible. They theorized that the Bible books were put together from several previous documents or bodies of traditional material. They concluded that not all of the Bible is on the same level of ethics or authority. The difficult passages which had long been explained through allegory could now be relegated to a lower level as primitive.

Disciples of this new biblical scholarship and of the new evolutionary science often showed the zeal of a new convert. They reveled in their new freedom and counted no reward so delightful as the shock of the uninformed. Blithe young teachers got off their college notes as solemn lectures when they had half understood their instructors and still less understood the notes. Darwin's fairly cautious and somewhat erroneous conclusions were snatched up by enthusiasts and made into an inevitable program of progression equally applicable to biology, anthropology, and biblical criticism.

Some Christian groups sounded the alarm. They rallied in scores of prophetic and Bible conferences. The Niagara Bible Conference met annually from 1876 to 1900 condemning all findings of biblical scholarship and standing firm on their understanding of classical orthodoxy. In 1895 this group issued its famous statement of five points to insist on universal Christian acceptance of: (1) the inerrancy of the Scriptures, (2) Christ's virgin birth, (3) the substitutionary atonement of Christ, (4) Christ's physical resurrection, (5) his bodily return to earth. Some later lists assert the literal acceptance of the miracles as the fifth point in place of the bodily return. Winona Bible Conferences were rallying the Midwest while Rocky Mountain Bible Conferences were rallying the Far West. The meetings were marked by vitality in their singing, prayer, and fellowship. Out of this warmth and security the new scholarship was roundly condemned.

An early mark of the conferences was their premillennial nature. But over the years the assemblies felt the increasing necessity to defend the faith, even in this world, by declaring war on the modernist invader. Let every denomination investigate the colleges and seminaries, interrogate the missionaries, indict the obstinate, and publish the story. Most of the larger colleges and seminaries were suspect, the citadel at Princeton being a truly notable exception. In every denomination the true believers were to purify their institutions. If this proved impossible, they were to set up safe Bible schools and safe mission projects, often interdenominational ones like the China Inland Mission. The defenders were to organize within each denomination and also to unite with all other defenders in pure organizations across denominational lines.

There were some who thought the main struggle was about over in the early 1900's. Then came the events that really formed and named the movement. Lyman and Milton Stewart of California got into the fray and brought their money with them. They founded the Los Angeles Bible Institute and established the Stewart Evangelistic Fund. They sent Robert Dick Wilson to the Orient to encourage missionaries out there to hold fast to the old faith. They reprinted *Jesus Is Coming* and sent a copy to every minister in the United States and Canada. They set up an editorial committee and a Testimony Publishing Company with $300,000 to publish and mail *The Fundamentals,* a total of twelve small volumes. Thomas E. Stephens, editor of *Moody Church Herald,* was business manager in charge of publishing *The Fundamentals.* The foreword to Volume I says:

This book is the first of a series which will be published and sent to every pastor, evangelist, missionary, theological professor, theological student, Sunday school superintendent, Y.M.C.A. and Y.W.C.A. secretary in the English speaking world so far as the addresses of all these can be obtained. Two intelligent, consecrated Christian laymen bear the expense, because they believe that the time has come when a new statement of the fundamentals of Christianity should be made. Their earnest desire is that you will carefully read it and pass its truth on to others.[2]

The volumes appeared over a period of five years. When the job was done, some two million copies had been distributed in the United States and another million abroad.

Articles in *The Fundamentals* were written by men known as sound in the faith. They represented England, Germany, Scotland, Ireland, Canada, and the United States. They were theological professors, evangelists, and prominent laymen. All were persuasive for the old faith and against the new trends.

These *Fundamentals,* plus the periodicals, plus the polemic preaching,

[2] *Ibid.,* p. 4.

plus the Bible conferences, plus the excesses of some liberals, plus the uneasiness and insecurity of many in the face of new society and scholarship—these precipitated a bid for control of almost every denomination by the fundamentalists. In every denomination there was a conflict. The pattern of tactics was repeated: (1) investigate the colleges and seminaries, (2) interrogate the missionaries, (3) indict the obdurate, (4) publish the story.

The Northern Baptists. Northern Baptist Augustus H. Strong was worried about what he saw on his tour of world missions. In 1917 he said, "We Baptists must reform or die." [3] *The Watchman-Examiner* registered suspicion that the seminaries were the real source of the mischief. Fundamentalist groups met for strategy caucuses ahead of the conventions in 1920 and following years to shape their defense of the faith. In 1921 the National Federation of Fundamentalists of the Northern Baptists was formed and adopted *The Watchman-Examiner* as their paper. They were against the theory of evolution and against modernism in the schools. They wanted the adoption of a creedal statement which would bind all Baptists to regularity. But they did not want to split the church and they regarded the fight as for Northern Baptists only; thus they were too tame for some defenders. That same year the Baptist Bible Union was founded with a much more violent program. They urged immediate boycott of all agencies, schools, missions, and books not orthodox and safe. They welcomed the support from any orthodox outsiders, especially Southern Baptists, and were willing to split the denomination, if necessary, for purity. Eventually this group set up its own mission program and got control of Des Moines University as their school. All professors at Des Moines affirmed that the whale had truly swallowed Jonah. William Bell Riley was a one-man army for fundamentalism. He was pastor of First Baptist Church in Minneapolis with annual receipts of over $200,000 by 1925, proprietor of a Bible and Missionary Training School, editor of three periodicals, and the moving force in a host of fundamentalist organizations, especially the World Christian Fundamentals Association. By 1923 he had already produced a forty-volume commentary, fifteen books on religious subjects, and contributions to eight other works—this in addition

[3] Stewart G. Cole, *The History of Fundamentalism* (New York: Richard R. Smith, Inc., 1931), p. 66.

to sermons, lectures, addresses, and periodicals. In 1925 he took a week's vacation to visit his children on the West Coast. While on vacation there he spoke at the Auditorium Temple, the Bible Institute, and the Church of the Open Door at Los Angeles; the First Presbyterian Church of Long Beach, and a Presbyterian church in Pasadena. And he delivered a lengthy address to a Baptist ministers' conference.[4]

Some Baptists were also disturbed about the influence of Harry Emerson Fosdick and of such men of wealth as John D. Rockefeller and Marshall Field. Fosdick and some others were receiving members without immersion. Then there was the question of the orthodoxy of the Federal Council.

To make a long story short, the fundamentalists lost out on every count among the Northern Baptists. The purge of the schools, 1918-1924, brought much noise but small results. There was no split, and the controversy died down to a continuous but not very ominous grumble.

The Southern Baptists. In the 1920's modernism was not an issue of real stature in the Southern Baptist Church. The five fundamental points were accepted on all sides. On the subject of evolution there was some difference of opinion. Nobody was really for evolution. However, three college presidents stood for complete freedom of scientific investigation and discussion. Edgar Y. Mullins, long-time president of Southern Baptist Seminary at Louisville and often president of the convention, took an ambiguous middle ground. At the conventions fairly mild condemnations of evolution and fairly mild affirmations of academic freedom were filed side by side.

This was maddening to some fire-eaters, of whom J. Frank Norris of Fort Worth was a highly successful symbol. This crusading editor, now turned flamboyant preacher, weathered formal charges ranging from arson to manslaughter and lived out his days in Fort Worth until 1952. By 1925 his church had a membership of 8,000 and a Sunday school of 7,500 plus a 600-member choir and forty instruments in the orchestra. Norris evidently feared the Catholics and hated the Jews. He championed the five points with emphasis on the Second Coming. His war on modernism and evolution kept the Baptist conventions in an uproar for the decade of the 1920's. He accused the whole lot of

[4] Norman F. Furniss, *The Fundamentalist Controversy, 1918-1931* (New Haven: Yale University Press, 1954), p. 31.

Baptist officers of warring on the truth to crush the conservatives and of catering to wealthy heretics like John D. Rockefeller and Marshall Field. In his spare time he moved in to purify the Methodists by forcing John A. Rice to resign from Southern Methodist University.

But the Southern Baptists refused to be split. At the 1925 Southern Baptist Convention at Memphis, the antievolution statement was toned down to be only fairly strong. The 1926 statement at Houston was blunt but not bitter. All institutions, boards, and missionaries were required to sign the 1926 statement rejecting every theory that man originated in or came by way of a lower animal ancestry. They signed, except for two seminaries—Southern Baptist and Southwestern Baptist. Then the argument ran out quite inconclusively. J. Frank Norris let an ethical discussion get too warm. He shot a caller three times and killed him. Norris' influence dropped, and the conventions were not so greatly stirred.

In more recent years the drive has departed from the issue of evolution in the churches. The more chastened theology of the latter twentieth century seems less likely to precipitate a major controversy among Baptists. But the adjustment of biblical literalism to critical findings must continue and that in a context of a resurgent racism and regionalism. Zeal against integration may be even greater than the earlier zeal against evolution. When biblical literalism and regionalism unite, any criticism may be explosive.

The Presbyterians in the U.S.A. The Presbyterian Church, U.S.A., had a fundamentalist controversy marked by vigor, length, and intellectual acumen. It was highly literate. *The Presbyterian Advance* and *The Continent* were usually with the liberals. *The Presbyterian, The Herald and Presbyter,* and *The Sunday School Times* were more fundamentalist, as were the even more learned publications of Princeton.

The Presbyterians were sensitive about new thought. In part, this was a heritage from their recent thirty-year split over issues of slavery, theology, and ecclesiastical control. This Old School-New School controversy had been formally concluded in 1869. The sensitivity showed when Professor Charles A. Briggs was suspended from the ministry in 1893 and Professor Henry Preserved Smith in 1894. Professor Arthur C. McGiffert withdrew from the church in 1899.

In 1910 the Presbyterian General Assembly affirmed a careful statement of the five points. In 1915 some 150 clergy, including the moderator and three ex-moderators, presented a "back to the fundamentals" statement. And in 1916 the Assembly ruled that all candidates for the ministry must subscribe to the five points in the deliverance of 1910. This was partly because New York Presbytery had recently ordained some young men from Union Seminary in New York who were quite uncertain about the Virgin Birth. Conservatives were also worried about the doctrinal implications of denominational union. The Presbyterians were discussing participation in an association of a score of denominations.

It was Harry Emerson Fosdick who sparked the explosion. The result was so devastating that a whole generation of Presbyterian preachers had to preface their quotations from Fosdick's sermons with a nebulous "someone has said . . . ." Fosdick was an ordained Baptist, since 1918 associate minister at First Presbyterian Church in New York. He took a trip to the Far East and found that conservative missionaries, backed by American fundamentalist money from the Stewart fund, were organizing to expose and discipline their more liberal brethren. This disturbed Fosdick. Back in New York on Sunday, May 21, 1922, he preached a sermon entitled "Shall the Fundamentalists Win?" He took the fundamentalists to task for their divisive ways and continued to state his own views on some controversial matters. His views did not fit well with the five points. Fosdick affirmed the uniqueness of Christ but did not find the biological miracle a helpful expression of that uniqueness for modern minds. Over against the idea of rigid infallibity he affirmed progressive revelation in the Scriptures. The coming of Christ is to be expected in the working out of his will and principles in human life and institutions, and it may be gradual. While he was about it, Fosdick sounded off against those who were pressing for antievolution laws. Then he concluded with a plea for tolerance lest the fundamentalists drive out of the churches all those who did not agree exactly with their theory of inspiration.

The result was not the toleration for which Fosdick pleaded in his conclusion. A layman named Ivy Lee was so impressed by the sermon that he had it printed and widely distributed. Ten presbyteries protested to the General Assembly. After a heated meeting, the 1923 Assembly adopted a minority committee report affirming the five points and directing New York Presbytery to see to it that preaching there conformed to the *Confession of Faith*. Now there were two distinct centers of opinion in the church. The so-called *Auburn Affirmation* was the opinion of one substantial group that the five points were acceptable but not to be used as tests of faith or fellowship. This group stood for greater freedom in interpretation of the Scriptures and the Confession and they rejected literal biblical infallibility. The conservatives, often championed by Macartney of Philadelphia, stood fast for strict interpretation and discipline of error.

In general the fundamentalists lost. Actually the extremists on both sides had yielded enough that by 1928 there might have been peace in the denomination. The issue of modernism had been deflected into a question of whether or not Fosdick could continue to be a regular minister in a Presbyterian pulpit without becoming a Presbyterian. He had resigned in 1925, and the prospect for peace looked fair.

Then Princeton blew up. Princeton had been the citadel of a new kind of apologetics—a scientific sifting and proving of the biblical facts on which and out of which an unassailable theological system could be built. There were intellectual giants there who did much to keep fundamentalism intellectually sound and widely respected. Following 1925 a serious quarrel grew up at Princeton. It involved fundamentalism, piety, administrative control, and personal issues. The men and the issues were great enough to make the controversy a spectacle for the whole church and nation. Prof. J. Gresham Machen emerged as the new champion of pure orthodoxy. He was keen, troublesome, dedicated, and in many respects admirable. If the seminaries, the missions, and the church were tainted with modernism, they must be cleansed. And if they would not be cleansed as Machen saw fit, Machen would proceed to found a seminary, a mission board, and a church of his own. In 1929 Machen, Wilson, and Allis left Princeton to found Westminster Theological Seminary. By 1933 the new mission board was established. In 1936 the fundamentalist followers of Machen formed the Presbyterian Church in America, since 1939 known as the Orthodox Presbyterian Church. From this group, in turn, sprang the Bible Presbyterian Church with its seminary at Wilmington, Delaware. Machen died in 1937 on a trip to Bismarck, North Dakota, to warn congregations there against the evils of modernism in the U.S.A. Church.

Thus the Presbyterian Church in the U.S.A. emerged from the heated years of its fundamentalism controversy with a broadened main body of the church flanked by two small and highly vigilant watchdogs of its orthodoxy. Among the noisiest critics has been Carl McIntire, suspended from the ministry of the Presbyterian Church in the U.S.A. in 1936 for violation of vows and stirring up dissension and strife. As a minister of the Bible Presbyterian Church at Collingswood, New Jersey, McIntire has edited *The Christian Beacon* while sparking the activities of the American Council of Christian Churches and the International Council of Christian Churches. To this amazing professional dissenter and self-appointed champion of "Bible-believing Christians," such stalwart conservatives as Harold J. Ockenga, Billy Graham, and Donald Barnhouse are highly suspect. McIntire's pressure has precipitated further fighting and splintering among the Bible Presbyterians in the interest of purity.

The Presbyterians in the U.S. The Presbyterian Church in the U.S. did not find fundamentalism a burning issue in the 1920's when many other denominations were torn with controversy. All major publications were conservative, and the only real concern was how vehemently to express the church's orthodoxy. When evolution agitated the Assemblies of 1924 and 1928, the insistence of antievolution forces was wisely and calmly met with reaffirmation of the Bible, the Confession, and the Catechisms—not with violent antievolution statements.

The case of H. Watson Smith, minister in Little Rock, Arkansas, stirred up the greatest contention. Smith wrote a book in 1922 and a pamphlet in 1928 affirming that evolution was not contradictory to Presbyterian belief. Following pressure in the Assembly in 1929, Smith was tried in Presbytery. By appeal his case came to his Synod and to the General Assembly with approval and vindication of Smith at each level. Charles E. Diehl, president of Southwestern at Memphis, was also accused as unorthodox; but all complaints were dismissed in 1931. There was no schism.

In 1924 the Assembly agreed that ministers, elders, and deacons should pledge to disclose any change of belief on important dogma subsequent to their ordination. That same Assembly met a demand for the investigation of missionary heresy with a fairly stringent instruction to missionaries to beware. From the early 1920's to 1931 there was dark suspicion of the Federal Council in the minds of some Presbyterians. Early protests, as in 1929, were against the Council's attempts to participate in civil or political reform through civil agencies. In 1930 there was a day-long debate at the Assembly on a proposal to dissociate from the Federal Council on grounds of modernism. The Church withdrew from the Council for a period of ten years, 1931-1941, but has remained in active participation since that time. A vocal minority has continued to protest membership in the National Council, negotiation for Presbyterian union, and modernism in the churches.

The Presbyterian Church in U.S. was not in the throes of biblical controversy concurrent with its careful stand on evolution. It faces that biblical issue in the more explosive context of racial integration and regionalism.

The Northern Methodists. Historian Norman F. Furniss says there are some important reasons why Methodists were able to escape much of the bitter strife of fundamentalism.[5] Wesley had never held to the doctrine of a completely literal, infallible Bible, and he allowed considerable room for the kinship of men to the animal world. Wesleyans were loath to consider doctrine vital to the Christian life. Heresy must reveal itself in actions rather than in ideas alone, and expulsion came not for doctrinal unsoundness but for misconduct. Fundamentalists among Methodists had no leader comparable to Bryan, Norris, or Machen, to lead their crusade. The General Conference met only quadrennially, and it was difficult for disgruntled groups to keep their followers organized and their emotions aroused so long. To Mr. Furniss' list might be added that episcopal government proved fairly effective in disciplining divisive groups and that many Methodist protestors who would not be silenced have gone off into holiness sect groups.

Even so, there was considerable stir in the Methodist Episcopal Church in the stormy 1920's. Leander W. Munhall wrote *The Highest Critics vs. the Higher Critics* and kept firing away at the liberals as editor of *The Word and Work* and *The Eastern Methodist*. Harold P. Sloan was even more persistent as president of the Methodist League for Faith and Life, organized in 1925. His paper was *The Call to Colors* and later *The Essentialist*. Methodist fundamentalists were often called "essentialists." The most common source of complaint among Methodists was the ap-

[5] *Ibid.*, pp. 148-50.

proved list of books for the ministerial course of study. Especially after the General Conference of 1908 had produced "The Social Creed," there were books on the list which disturbed good Methodists. Essentialists were always protesting to conference or sending a delegation to wait upon the bishop about this undesirable literature.

At the Kansas City General Conference of the Methodists in 1928 fundamentalist Sloan and his followers took an awful walloping. Nobody was much interested in Sloan's petition with an alleged 10,000 signatures. By convention vote he was refused time to make an address. His resolution for an investigating committee was promptly voted down ten to one. His request for a detailed creedal statement was answered by a middle-of-the-road condemnation of both liberals and fundamentalists. Sloan lost out in the vote on new bishops. He set up separate fundamentalist headquarters for the rest of the Conference, but nobody seemed to care. The essentialists were a small force indeed after 1928.

The Southern Methodists. In the Methodist Episcopal Church, South, there was less overt liberalism to fight. The hierarchy with their papers, *The Christian Advocate* and *The Methodist Review,* took a cautious but increasingly liberal stand. Bishop Denny fought all proposals for union with Northern Methodists on the grounds of liberalism up there. Bishop Candler roundly condemned modernism wherever it appeared. These statements satisfied most fundamentalists and no real champion arose among them. It was Baptist J. Frank Norris who pursued Methodist professor John A. Rice in Texas. Methodist Charles W. Rankin did found the ultraconservative Bible Union of China in 1920 to rid Asia of his heretical missionary associates. This was the organization which touched off Fosdick's famous sermon. But Rankin was cut off from the Methodist Church in 1921.

In general, Methodist official statements were cautiously fundamental and the practice increasingly liberal. This denomination probably furnished more recruits for the war on modern science than any other except the Baptist. Yet the fundamentalists never rose in effective organized revolt in the councils of the denomination.

The Disciples. It might appear the Disciples of Christ were a group with little ground for division over fundamentalism. Every congregation was theoretically free from having liberalism forced upon it. The conventions were mainly assemblies for discussion without real machinery for heresy trials. The denomination had no citadel of scholastic theology, nor was it especially doctrinally inclined. Insistently orthodox groups had broken away as the Churches of Christ by 1906. These were the most militant elements who still insist there ought to be no denominational organizations, no missionary societies, no instrumental music in the churches, and no baptism other than immersion rightly understood. They hold the five classic fundamentals plus the additional one of absolute conformance to the New Testament on the terms of their own interpretation. While some verbal allowance may be granted, this position seems, in practice, to mean denial of tolerance for any other group daring to call themselves Christian. One might hope that when this group had separated, the denomination would have a good chance for peace within.

Yet the Disciples had a long and bitter struggle. They fought over admission of convention delegates from heretical congregations and over the spending of Disciple mission money by suspect secretaries for suspect missions. Since the Bible is counted the norm for restoration, this group was most sensitive about biblical criticism. When some ministers began to dispense with immersion as an essential condition of membership, the matters of open membership and denominational cooperation became issues. Without a church structure to give official interpretations, the issues were cast squarely on the periodicals for interpretation. This they did all too stoutly, *The Christian Evangelist* for the liberals and *The Christian Standard* for the conservatives. A host of others joined in.

The schools were investigated. Along with an increasing demand for educated ministers went increasing suspicion that education was going liberal. In 1916 *The Christian Standard* charged that Transylvania College and the College of the Bible had "modernized the Scriptures and destroyed the Disciple testimony." Five Transylvania students drafted a complaint against certain instructors who had taught that "the first chapter of Genesis is poetry" and that "Jehovah was 'the tribal god of the Jews.' " [6] Eighty-seven per cent of the student body then made public their support of these instructors. *The Christian Standard* proceeded to

⁶ Cole, *op. cit.*, pp. 134, 157.

cast suspicion on the whole educational operation, and the Christian Bible College League went to the rescue. Dean H. L. Calhoun of Transylvania resigned, but the purge did not satisfy. Conservative Bible schools were founded to serve those who wanted none of the ministers trained at Chicago or Lexington.

At the same time some leaders were merging Disciple mission societies into the United Christian Missionary Society. Many conservatives feared this new union as a liberal monster. Here was the very instrument of modernism and open membership. A Christian Restoration Association was formed in protest in 1924. By 1927 the North American Christian Convention was established as a competing body with a central missionary agency pledged to orthodoxy and immersion. Each society had its schools, its missions, and its publications. In a rather remarkable exhibition of elasticity, the divided constituency of the Disciples has continued in one International Convention, all churches sending delegates no matter which mission agency they support. Differences in training of the ministry and differences in degree of interchurch cooperation are evident but not ruinous, and there appears no imminent plan of any considerable group to dislodge another as reprobate on the basis of the fundamentals.

Fundamentalists did not confine their activities to their own denominations. They found inspiration and strength in interdenominational efforts. After 1919 any right-believing church could join the World's Christian Fundamentals Association for ten dollars. At the annual conventions there was enthusiastic prayer and singing with attendance up to five thousand. William B. Riley or J. Frank Norris or William Jennings Bryan might give one of the telling addresses against the infidelity of biblical criticism or evolution. Those who could not attend the great annual conventions were not forgotten; there were local conferences on Christian fundamentals. Within a year after the founding of the World's Christian Fundamentals Association one hundred of these local conferences had already been instituted. Anywhere in the land one might hear Bryan or the dean of Moody Bible Institute or an editor of *The Fundamentals* sound the warning against modernism. Historian Cole reports that twenty-two such conventions were scheduled in Kentucky within sixty days and as many in Indiana within thirty days.[7] The members of the World's Christian Fundamentals Association were caught up in something big. They expected momentarily to receive two million dollars to found a great evangelical premillennial theological seminary. They set out optimistically for a $25,000,000 Bryan foundation for the advancement of Christian fundamentalist education. Within ten years the World's Christian Fundamentals Association had toned down to become a fairly active Bible-promoting evangelical league.

The Bible League of North America was founded in 1902. This was a scholarly interdenominational enterprise designed to combat current destructive teachings by reason, sense, and a truly scientific method. Robert Dick Wilson was one scholar for their magazine, *The Bible Student and Teacher* and later *The Bible Champion*. But the more violent fundamentalists did not count these scholars severe enough to satisfy. In 1930 *The Bible Champion* merged with *The Essentialist*, laboring to purify the Methodists. Thus one of the most admirable and promising of the fundamentalist protests was no more.

After Bryan died, George F. Washburn of Florida was one of those who felt that the mantle of Bryan the Commoner had fallen on him. In 1925 he called a special meeting at his home and offered $200,000 backing for a conservative association to combat modernism and evolution. An ambitious organization called The Bible Crusaders of America was quickly formed and promised to take leadership of the whole fundamentalist movement. The slogan of the Crusaders was "Back to Christ, the Bible, and the Constitution." They stood squarely for every tenet of orthodox Christianity. The official paper proclaimed a

threefold attack upon modernism and evolution; the boycott of unsound religious publications, missions, and educational institutions; the formation of battalions in all churches to expel liberals and elect conservatives; and the insistence upon legislative action against dangerous scientific speculation.[8]

And Washburn had in mind yet one more smashing blow—a constitutional amendment to make America Christian. There was much planning, with ample titles for all. However, the Crusaders chose to spend

[7] *Op. cit.*, p. 303.
[8] Furniss, *op. cit.*, p. 59.

most of their energy and money pressing for antievolution bills in the state legislatures. A few were passed. But the Crusaders got caught in the cooling of interest on evolution. Their nationwide plans did not materialize, and in 1927 they dropped from sight.

Not all fundamental leaders were admirable. An example of an organization which used music and fundamental symbols to prey upon thousands was The Supreme Kingdom of Edgar Young Clarke. Mr. Clarke had taken his organizational training in the Ku Klux Klan. Now on his own, he was out to smash atheism, heresy, and evolution. Incidentally, he gathered in money. The name of his paper was *Dynamite*. An aroused and enterprising newspaper in Georgia investigated Clarke and spoiled his plans after one short year. In that brief time he had castles of his Supreme Kingdom in thirty cities and was ready to use his influence in the presidential campaign of 1928.

Gerald Winrod of Kansas got his start in the midst of the fundamentalist excitement. It was against evolution and modernism that he organized his Defenders of the Christian Faith and published his *Defender Magazine* beginning in 1926. His shock troops, the "Flying Fundamentalists," held hundreds of antievolution meetings in Midwest cities and pushed antievolution bills in legislatures. "Back to the Bible" was his slogan. More lately Winrod has accused Jews and Catholics as his opponents in his "Back to the Bible" reform. The Jewish plot called the New Deal, the Negro menace, and Communism have been *Defender* targets. But there is always a mixture of fundamentalism.

The Research Science Bureau was led by Harry Rimmer who had one year of premedical work in college. He had a burning zeal to prove by science the reasonableness of fundamentalist claims. The findings of his science, social science, and archaeology fill several volumes. William B. Riley headed an Antievolution League specifically dedicated to getting the teaching of evolution out of public schools. He and his followers counted it only fair that if religious instruction was to be prohibited in the public schools antireligious instruction should also be prohibited. Add to the list the Bryan Bible League, the hosts of ultraconservative publishing houses, the Bible institutes, and the Bible conferences. This is the interdenominational atmosphere in which the conflict over fundamentalism reached its height in the 1920's.

This interdenominational atmosphere of fundamentalism, usually

without the historic issue of evolution, is still offered for all who seek
it. Education may range from a respectable Bible college or seminary,
with professors carefully trained but not "corrupted" by leading universities, to the barest memory chain of proof texts passed along firsthand or in pulp literature. Economic status may vary from the solidity
of the Christian Businessmen's Association to the poverty of some
pentecostals. Publications may vary from the carefully edited *Christianity Today* to the anti-Semitic rantings of Gerald L. K. Smith in
The Cross and the Flag. The variety is impressive and disconcerting;
one would be foolish indeed promiscuously to lump fundamentalists
past or present. But all of these constantly press for the traditional check
points of fundamentalism and claim to stand as defenders of the true
faith against the advancing enemy.

Fundamentalism lost in its historic bid for control of the denominations. Its more rational and admirable teachers served as a useful chasten-
ing force for what was naïve and extreme in liberalism. Its more violent
champions succeeded in planting suspicion of new thought in the minds
of tens of thousands of Christian people. So our major denominations
are marked by a troublesome gap between a clergy inevitably trained to
some critical judgment and a constituency heavy with members who
think of their faith in terms of that recent impassioned presentation—
defense of the fundamentals. This cleavage is kept uncomfortable by
agitators. Some of them are earnestly carrying on the struggle in terms
of the issues of thirty years ago. There is just enough unchastened
liberalism extant to warrant some perennial protest. Other agitators
are exploiting the conservative Protestant mind-set in the interest of
such causes as regionalism, racism, or private gain. Differences in understanding the Bible between Protestant ministers and their people need
to be overcome by healthy Bible study together. All who are fundamentalists by conviction need to know the whole of their faith lest
they be led astray by those who counsel pride, hate, or violent exclusion.

Evaluation of Fundamentalism

Fundamentalism in our day is not of one piece. There is pietistic
fundamentalism which is largely innocent of modern thought. The
Bible is accepted; the relation to criticism and to science are matters

not really raised. This can be a very blissful and winsome level of faith. It is not irritable or oversensitive. However, it is defenseless in the world. A year of college, a bit of reading, and it may be gone. It is not to be artificially preserved so that scientifically trained men may keep their faith set apart and in this area alone be simple.

There is rationalistic fundamentalism which has considered the facts of science, criticism, and Scripture and decided knowingly for the truth delivered, including the five points. Such a faith need not be hostile but may be quite discriminating. Truth is distinguished from error; the essential is distinguished from the nonessential. These fundamentalists feel there is demonstrable Christian doctrine from which men ought not to go away, and they will not be turned away. Doctrine is central as the right interpretation of the facts of revelation. Not all doctrine is equal and not all error is basis for refusing fellowship. But right doctrine is a conditioner of life. The truth is to be presented with persuasion and with charity. There may be real concern in social matters. Biblical criticism and science are not denied, but their claims too may be questioned. This is fundamentalism at its best.

It is fair to ask whether this rationalistic fundamentalism is fundamentalism at all. Certainly a line cannot well be drawn between "fundamentalist" and "conservative" on the basis of this description. If fundamentalism is defined necessarily in terms of a militant, legalistic, and divisive mind-set, then this rational fundamentalist is no fundamentalist. But this writer would suggest that even gracious defenders of this classical list of fundamentals, when they are nevertheless insistent on these tests for all who are truly Christian, are historically fundamentalists and ought to be less ashamed of that term than of some of the company they must keep within it. If a new name must be developed to distinguish the gracious fundamentalist from the contentious, then care must be exercised to show the relation of both to the historic fundamentalist movement in America and to the classical list of essential points.

Then there is militant fundamentalism. This is often crusading, exclusive, and violent. It pickets all ecumenical gatherings except those of its own select faction. It feels commissioned of God deliberately to disrupt every operation which does not perfectly agree with its own limitation of God's grace. In the ostensible interest of "Bible-believing" and pure dogma it yields in tactics to the vending of hatred and discord. Whether at the level of local community proselyter or of contentious national or international council, this is fundamentalism at its worst.

More profitable than fitting fundamentalists into classifications is consideration of a ministry to them and alongside them to the world. First of all, let the strength of fundamentalism be plainly seen. There are some fundamentals. Christianity is a faith rooted in fact. Every man's formulation of his experience of Christ and of God-given truth must honestly meet the Scriptures, the treasure of tradition, and Jesus Christ in history. Schleiermacher, Royce, and Tillich are subject to correction as are Hodge, Machen, and McIntire. Not all change is gain. Fundamentalists have had and do have the courage to protest; protest is often justified. In the rigidity of last century's Princeton apologetic there was a sorely needed corrective for a naïve enlightenment.

The weakness of fundamentalism is equally plain. Concentration upon a limited list of check points tends to narrowness and a misguided mind-set of suspicion. Because the old seems safe and unshakable, there may be aversion even to progress because it is change. Fundamentalism is defense, and defenders naturally seek alliance. Zealous for righteousness of the cause and impressed with the need for support, the defender seeking alliance may not be sufficiently critical. Advocates of the five fundamentals and champions of the *status quo ante* most often appear safe and trustworthy to the fundamentalist. Some are both safe and trustworthy. Others may be vicious in their exploitation of the faith. Affirmation of the five points is not of itself a valid test to distinguish the children of light from those of darkness. Nor are the five points sufficient as a basic summary of faith.

There is no comfort intended here for any who feel in condescension that their faith is so elevated that the fundamentals are beneath their concern. Considering the cogency of the points and the large place they occupy in the thought of the churches in our land, it would seem to behoove every churchman to think through his position on each and to be able to state it with candor. Conversation with a fundamentalist will hardly come by initial denial of his whole repertory.

In his stand for the Virgin Birth the fundamentalist may affirm too little rather than too much. Here is the gospel account, simple and clear.

There is a wondrous fitness about this nativity. But even this birth is at best a poor weak symbol of the majestic act of God. The birth account is no substitute for the truth and life-changing challenge of incarnation. Shall all who accept the gospel account be speaking the voice of God when they say, "Either you accept this birth precisely as I read it, or you have no part in God's saving act"? A host of Christians whose acceptance of the gospel account is earnest and studied would not so delimit God's salvation.

Just as truly, the fundamental of the substitutionary atonement is likely to be too limited rather than too large. This doctrine is scriptural. It speaks eloquently of the seriousness of sin, of man's inability apart from God's grace, of God's free gift, of the complete identification of God with man, of the great weight of guilt lifted. But this is not all. The Scriptures describe this same great salvation in terms of adoption, in terms of a debtor with his bill canceled, in terms of the power of sin and of hell broken, in terms of a union of Christ and the believer. When the point of substitutionary atonement becomes man's recital of what God *must* do to be God or to satisfy justice, it approaches blasphemy. When it is a primary expression among all the expressions of the wonder of our deliverance from the awful complexity of sin and guilt, it becomes an open door to the fullness of God's Word.

Fundamentalist defense of the physical resurrection may be no more than insistence that the Lord's body was actually gone from the tomb. Insofar as this is a deliverance from explanations of the resurrection in terms of some zephyr-inspired confidence that such a good fellow never really dies, it is a blessing. But a missing corpse is as nothing compared to the transformed body of our Lord and his appearances. And this is coupled with a promise of transformed bodies for believers, in the words of Paul. There are few areas where we know less or where the little we know is so exciting. Resurrection is surely no less than bodily resurrection. But to make our faith in the risen, living Christ and our communion with other Christians dependent upon some certain view of the essence of the body raised and the method of rising is to exceed the limits of knowledge and of grace. Here again is a fundamental which may be only an exclusive and dogged defense—or it may be the first step toward an affirmation of victory and immortality.

There are two cases where the fundamentals seem on the face of them to claim too much. One concerns the inerrancy of Scriptures. Here a claim is often made for a mechanical and technical perfection which is hardly in the spirit of the Scriptures themselves. For example, the apostle Paul was accustomed to quote the Old Testament from memory, and some of his proximate quotations appear in the New Testament without apology.[9] This kind of inexactness and some others as well do not invalidate Scriptures. The yearning for a rigid scriptural inerrancy is more likely to reflect human insecurity than defense of God's inspiration. This is not so much a high view of Scripture as a rigid and overlimited one.

The other case concerns the deity of Christ. This undeniable fundamental is often run off into heresy by loss of our Lord's human nature in the very insistence upon his "spiritual" uniqueness. So the result is not so much a high view of our Lord, as a rigid and unorthodox one. Fundamentalists are not bound to error on these points. But they are especially prone to them because of their preoccupation with a list of theological essentials among a constituency not theologically trained.

There are fundamental matters here not to be cast off. The authority of the Scripture and the nature of Christ are matters of life-shaking importance. This is all the more reason why an oversimple formulation and a summary dismissal of dissenters will not do. Sincere Christian men debated for centuries over the formula to express the nature of Christ which had been approved at the Council of Chalcedon, the official position of most churches today. It would be rash indeed to rule out modern Christians who cannot feel that a phrase like "deity of Christ" fairly embodies their belief. It is not wrong. But, as popularly understood, it may not be enough. In what it omits it may be heresy.

The fundamental concerning our Lord's bodily return calls to mind the high correlation of fundamentalism with premillennialism and adventism, though this is by no means a necessary correlation. Candid reading of the Scriptures leads many to the honorable conclusion that our Lord not only has come but also shall return in body. Equally candid reading will make it plain that there is no merit in striving to outguess the Master's plan of arrival. The command to "watch" is a direction to be attending the business to which he has set us as

[9] Holmes Rolston, *Consider Paul, Apostle of Jesus Christ* (Richmond: John Knox Press, 1951), pp. 140-44.

stewards. There is no need to stop—the arrow of the Lord can hit a moving target. Meanwhile, to exclude those who do not precisely agree on the method and timetable of his arrival is to pre-empt the seat of the Judge.

In evaluating the place of miracles, discrimination and charity are in order. Conservative Christians find a rather large area of agreement. They most often agree that miracles beyond man's prediction and beyond his ability to fit into the context of experience are not necessarily suspensions or violations of God's order and dependability. The intensity of God's presence and power is not equal at all places and times. Where that intensity is very high the miraculous may become the plain truth. Even then not all miracles are of equal importance; Elisha's floating axhead is not of the same significance as the Resurrection. But a healthy group of the conservatives part company with the fundamentalists whenever the latter put all miracles on the same level, as the buttress of a defensive system for an inerrant Bible, and deny Christian fellowship to those who cannot perfectly agree.

Every major branch of the Protestant Church has fundamentalists within it. Often they count themselves a faithful remnant more than a little disregarded and coerced by those in control. Ostensibly they are bent only on leading the denominations back to purity. Outside the main-line denominations are the host of fundamentalist sects, warm, zealous, and generally oblivious to modern scholarship. Probably half the foreign missionaries sent from the United States represent fundamentalist sects. In general neither the fundamentals nor the fundamentalists ought to be berated or opposed as evil unless the latter are rabid vendors of hate and disruption. The widespread superior attitude toward fundamentalism is probably unwarranted; in its main position fundamentalism is a continuation of classical Christianity. The insight of a university-trained minister is not always more accurate or more fruitful than the fertility of some untutored minds in the sects. Direct familiarity with the text of the English Bible is often admirable among the better-grounded fundamentalists. On the other hand, some seminary graduates are living arguments for a lay ministry. If the prophet of the fundamentals disdains the enervation of modern scholarship, little will be gained by mutual scorn. Sometimes little will be gained anyway. But the best hope lies in candid acceptance of his list of points

as an honorable view and then a movement to develop their potential
richness with him. With that may also come co-operation in constructive community service.

Suggestions for Further Study

1. By private interview, compare and contrast the position of a seminary-trained
pastor on the five fundamentals with the position of a cross section of his congregation. If any significant difference appears, prepare a plan for bridging the gap.

2. Confer with three or more ministers who classify themselves as fundamentalists
about the extent to which they are willing to co-operate in interdenominational
planning and programing with nonfundamentalist pastors and churches. Formulate
what would be the maximum interdenominational community program within the
limitations they establish.

Selected Bibliography

Cole, Stewart G. *The History of Fundamentalism*. New York: Harper & Bros., 1931.

The Fundamentals: A Testimony to the Truth. 12 vols.; Chicago: Testimony Publishing Co., 1910-15.

Furniss, Norman F. *The Fundamentalist Controversy, 1918-1931*. New Haven: Yale
University Press, 1954.

Loetscher, Lefferts A. *The Broadening Church*. Philadelphia: University of Pennsylvania Press, 1954.

Machen, John G. *Christianity and Liberalism*. Grand Rapids: William B. Eerdmans
Publishing Co., 1946.

Richards, George W. *Beyond Fundamentalism and Modernism*. New York: Charles
Scribner's Sons, 1934.

Roy, Ralph L. *Apostles of Discord*. Boston: The Beacon Press, 1953.

Shaw, J. M. *Essentials and Non-Essentials of the Christian Faith*. New York: Charles
Scribner's Sons, 1929.

Snowden, James H. *Old Faith and New Knowledge*. New York: Harper & Bros., 1928.

Younger, George. "Protestant Piety and the Right Wing," *Social Action*, XVII (May
15, 1951), 5-32.

ADVENTISM

Identification of Adventism

THE TERM "ADVENT" MEANS ARRIVAL. IN CHRISTIAN CIRCLES THE PERSON referred to by this term is Jesus Christ. Normally when we speak about his advent, we are referring to his birth in Bethlehem. But it is an orthodox Christian belief that that same person, now ascended up on high, will come again to earth in connection with the end of this age; and that anticipated event is commonly referred to as the "Second Coming" or the "Second Advent." The term "Adventism" marks groups of Christians who make this belief in the Second Advent extremely prominent, if not the primary emphasis, in their practice and advocacy of Christianity, and who commonly expect it to happen very soon. But many very earnest Christians, who would not agree to be called Adventists, give a great deal of attention to the Second Coming—for example, premillennialists. The beliefs of the Adventists are a part of a world view which they believe to be taught in the Scriptures; but such a world view is shared, in part at least, by many conservative Christians who would repudiate the name of Adventist. We shall presently define the application of the term, as it is being used in this unit, indicating and studying three groups as coming under the term; but for the present we shall employ it somewhat more widely without attempting to draw a clear line between Adventists and similar believers who would repudiate the name.

In the classification, "Adventist Bodies," the *Yearbook of American Churches* for 1957 distinguishes 5 such bodies.[1] Their statistics are for the year 1955, unless otherwise indicated. They include the Seventh-day Adventists, who claimed 2,858 churches and 277,162 members, and the Advent Christian Church, which in 1954 claimed 410 churches and 30,585 members. This group of Adventist bodies, if their claims are

[1] Benson Y. Landis, ed., *Yearbook of American Churches* (New York: National Council of the Churches of Christ in the U. S. of A., 1957), pp. 13-14.

reasonably reliable, possesses more than 3,300 churches and more than 300,000 members.

These figures are for the United States alone; and, though they indicate a type of Christian activity that is numerically imposing, they do not by any means come up to the actual situation. The Seventh-day Adventists are a world-wide people. They claim a membership of about a million, scattered over the world, and for the most part it is an amazingly loyal and active million. The figures include a per capita giving of $165.26, amounting to $44,376,669, of which $36,680,185 was for benevolences. The Seventh-day Adventists include a force of 17,774 evangelistic workers and 39,159 workers in all categories; they use 198 printed languages and 523 additional languages; they maintain 39 publishing houses with a capital investment of over twelve million dollars and a gross annual sale of more than sixteen million dollars.[2] Of the fourteen bodies referred to, this one by itself is a tremendously important religious group.

But we do not have the whole picture yet. Elmer T. Clark points out that Adventism really involves a total world view which dates from the earliest Christian times and which is at present prominent also among the Mormons, Jehovah's Witnesses, and the Foursquare Gospel.[3] The various Mormon bodies listed in the *Yearbook of American Churches* for 1957 claim a total of 3,504 churches and a membership of approximately 1,372,640;[4] but these figures do not include their churches and members abroad. Jehovah's Witnesses do not keep membership records, but officials of their governing body claim indirectly a membership of about 187,120 in the United States. In 1955 the Foursquare Gospel group seems to have had about 650 churches and more than 94,000 members.

Combining these figures, it appears that in the United States alone these Adventist bodies have more than 10,000 churches and approximately 2 million members. In addition, some of them are strongly entrenched abroad; and they are all extremely active. When it is realized that the world view characteristic of the Adventist bodies is

---

[2] James E. Bear, "The Seventh-day Adventists," *Interpretation*, X (January, 1956), 46-47.

[3] "Adventists," *The Twentieth Century Encyclopedia of Religious Knowledge* (Extension of *The New Schaff-Herzog Encyclopedia of Religious Knowledge*; Grand Rapids: Baker, 1955), p. 11.

[4] Landis, *op. cit.*, pp. 59-60.

also commonly found amoung fundamentalists and in many groups which are conservative in theology, as well as in some of the larger denominations, it becomes clear that we are confronted by an element in contemporary religious life much too important to be ignored or misunderstood. The person who shivers on a wintry street corner distributing literature for Jehovah's Witnesses does not stand alone. She is conscious of the presence with her of a body numerous, world wide, and approved of God; and she may realize that she has a powerful "fifth column" ready to be won to conscious support of her enterprise, but now abiding in the denominations. What she represents, or thinks of herself as representing, demands serious study.

Basis of Adventism

Whatever others may think about it, the Adventist bodies all appeal to the Bible as authoritative. They think of themselves as interpreting it literally and accepting it wholeheartedly. Two of the three, Jehovah's Witnesses and Seventh-day Adventists, claim that it is their sole authority. The Mormon position is slightly different, but for them too the Bible is fundamental. Thus all three Adventist groups which we propose to study in this unit take their stand squarely on the Bible.

While in no way wishing to question the sincerity of such a stand, Christians who also regard themselves as accepting the Bible as basic entertain grave doubts as to the correctness of these Adventist claims. It is maintained, in the first place, that the Adventist groups concentrate their attention upon the apocalypses, especially in the Book of Daniel and on the fourteenth chapter of the book of Revelation; that they reveal in dealing with these a strange mixture of arbitrary historical assumption, of literalism, and of symbolism; and that all of their thinking, their Scripture study, and their practice is forced into the mold so obtained. This, so it is claimed, is the way in which they arrive at their world view. A typical statement of it, which fits the Seventh-day Adventists much more closely than it does the Mormons, includes the following beliefs: The earth during the present age is regarded as the scene of warfare between divine and demonic forces. Victory for the divine forces will come catastrophically, through direct divine intervention. The beginning of this victory will be, or has been, the Second Advent of Christ. They believe in the "rapture" of the saints to meet the Lord in the "upper air"; the thousand years of peace and prosperity under the millennial reign of Christ, Satan being bound the while; the subsequent release of Satan; the great battle of Armageddon; the final defeat of Satan and his hosts. They are quite sure that this either has begun already or will begin very soon.

It will be instructive to examine some examples of the alleged arbitrariness in the Adventist interpretations which yield such a result. It is perfectly apparent that their whole interpretation of Scripture is determined by a concentration upon the apocalypses. But they understand that Scripture is to be treated as a whole and that the meaning of obscure and difficult passages is to be determined in the light of clearer utterances elsewhere in the Bible. They say that repeatedly. Well, if that is so, their selection of the apocalypses as controlling— passages which surely everyone must admit to be difficult of interpretation—must seem quite arbitrary. There are, however, sober students of the Bible who would maintain that an intense study of apocalyptic literature has now cleared up the obscurities and made the interpretation much more plain. An evaluation of that claim must be left to the reader himself. Suffice it for us to point out that the world view which these sober students derive from their study is markedly different from that of the Adventists. Since those who set the pattern for the interpretation which the Adventists offer us—such men as Joseph Smith and Pastor Russell—were not technically trained students of the apocalypses, it would seem just to claim that their interpretation does not accord with that of qualified scholarship.

Bear gives a concrete example which we cannot do better than quote. He has Adventist leader William Miller specifically in mind, but he points out that the same methods of calculation have been common to "a large host of biblical students scattered over many centuries." Bear writes:

In Daniel 9:24-27 we have the prophecy of the "seventy weeks" which are said to extend from the commandment to rebuild Jerusalem (vs. 25), till "he shall cause the sacrifice and oblation to cease" (vs. 27). Miller, along with many of his contemporaries, took these events to be the decree of Artaxerxes (Neh. 2:1) which dated in his Bible as B.C. 457 (according to the Usher chronology), and the death of Christ in A.D. 33 (also according to Usher).

71

It is seen that this rests on the theory that a "day" in Scripture represents a year, so the seventy weeks, 490 days, represent 490 years, the period from B.C. 457 to A.D. 33.

In Daniel 8:14 we read that the vision shall be "unto two thousand and three hundred days: then shall the sanctuary be cleansed." The sanctuary to be cleansed was taken to be the church on earth. The 2,300 days represent 2,300 years, and it was assumed that the 2,300 years started at the same date as the seventy weeks, so if you subtract the 490 years (minus the A.D. 1-33) you get the figure 1843.[5]

It is true that the Seventh-day Adventists insist, apparently with truth, that they have never fixed a year for the return of Christ. They repudiate this particular piece of calculation, and it will not be found among the Witnesses, whose founder fixed a date different from Miller's, or among the Mormons. But this *kind* of Scripture interpretation marks them all. Furthermore, all the Adventists, sure that the end is very near, find in the events of the contemporary world the fulfillment of Christ's prophecies of the events which are to usher in the end. They do so in spite of the fact that the same sort of thing has been going on for centuries. Critics have not been at all reticent about drawing the attention of Seventh-day Adventists to the fact that one hundred years have lapsed since they confidently proclaimed that the Kingdom "is near, even at the doors." Ever since, the same message has been proclaimed, not as an incidental part, but as a central emphasis of their preaching and propaganda; in fact, this has probably been their most effective missionary appeal. But the Kingdom is not yet. Surely it is time for the Adventists to admit that they were mistaken. Francis D. Nichol notices this criticism, and devotes a chapter to it in his *Reasons for Our Faith*. His first reply is that the critics

did not generally question the soundness of our rules of prophetic interpretation which led us to conclude that certain great time prophecies were ending and that therefore far-reaching changes impended for the world. On the contrary, our opponents a century ago were often free to admit that they likewise believed the prophecies were ending.[6]

[5] *Op. cit.*, p. 50

[6] Washington, D. C.: Review & Herald Publishing Assn., 1947, p. 130.

Since I do not know who these opponents were, I cannot know whether the claims here made with regard to them are correct or not. But that is beside the point. The point is that *the Adventists* should have changed their minds by this time but have not done so. To refer to others who, if they are correctly characterized, should also have changed their minds and may have done so, has no logical relevance whatsoever unless there is some logic in the old saying that "misery loves company." Nichol's second reply is so surprising that it must be quoted. He writes:

The mere passage of time is not in itself the measure of the validity of a prediction. We must also take into account what has happened during the period of time under discussion. Do those happenings give cumulative support to the prediction, or do they give the lie to it? [7]

He then proceeds to list eight predictions, some of which seemed at the time of their announcement as if they could not possibly happen. But all these things, so it is claimed, have happened; and somehow it seems to him that their happening gives cumulative support to—what? The assurance that, when we were told a hundred years ago that the Kingdom "is near, even at the doors," that proclamation was true? It is probably true that, in general, "the mere passage of time is not in itself the measure of the validity of a prediction." But if the very essence of the prediction is temporal, the passage of time will validate or invalidate it; and if something which was said a century ago to be "at the doors" has not entered the doors yet, only a very arbitrary mind, it would seem, will refuse to admit that something was wrong with the prediction.

Perhaps enough has been said to illustrate the claim that the Adventists do not believe the Bible from cover to cover, allowing all parts of it to speak for themselves, but arbitrarily force it all into a matrix formed by their particular interpretation of the apocalypses; that their interpretation of the apocalypses is full of questionable assumptions and arbitrary conclusions; and that their identification of contemporary events with Christ's statements about the events to indicate the nearness of his return is little, if at all, more reliable than similar identifications which have been going on for centuries.

[7] *Ibid.*, p. 133.

Another illustration of the unsatisfactoriness of their treatment of Scripture may be found in the equivocal place held by Ellen Gould White in the thinking of the Seventh-day Adventists. It is probably true that many of the personal attacks on this lady's character and claims are unjust. She apparently did not place her writings on a par with the Bible, and a careful Adventist will not do so either. But she did claim that they were "an inspired commentary," given to her through the special illumination of the Holy Spirit. Now what does that really mean, and how are the utterances of this lady actually treated in the thought and practice of her followers? Many humble Christians would claim, justly I think, to be illuminated by the Holy Spirit. Indeed, one would insist that no "knowledge unto salvation" can be derived from the Scriptures without such illumination. Presumably, therefore, many of the Adventists, perhaps all of them, have enjoyed this illumination. But Mrs. White holds a unique place in the life of the Seventh-day Adventist precisely because of the illumination which came to her. Hers must therefore have been different in kind or in degree from that which is graciously given to the rest of us. Was hers such as to make her infallible? She did not claim that, and at least some of her followers are aware of that fact and make no such claim for her. It would perhaps be too much to claim that her writings are regarded by her followers as the *Book of Mormon* is by the Mormons, that is, as an addition to the Bible. Her writings are a commentary on the Bible, not an addition to it. They are an additional corroboration and support to the Bible; and, of course, what they corroborate is the peculiar world view of the sect which she did so much to formulate.

We have given such attention to the treatment of the Bible by Adventists both because this is for them a matter of the highest importance and because it is also a matter of supreme importance for those of us who claim to belong to main-line Protestantism. Before this central topic is left, it should be pointed out further that the Adventists reject with scorn, and apparently without any careful investigation, the whole process of critical examination of the Scripture writings by modern scholars. All of that is swept aside as merely a fruit of the apostasy which they predicted and which they claim is now so much in evidence. It would probably be true to say that the overwhelming number of biblical scholars in the tradition of main-line Protestantism would reject their cavalier treatment of such scholarship. Some conservative Protestants, and probably all fundamentalists, would agree that much of recent biblical scholarship was a fruit of apostasy. Of these, some would deny that contemporary critical scholarship deserves any such characterization; and any earnest student of the Word, whatever his reaction to critical scholarship, would indignantly deny that anyone has a right to reject critical scholarship on the basis of such a superficial study as the Adventists seem to have given to the subject. They would maintain, whether they agree with the conclusions of the Adventists or not, that in the case of the Adventists they were often a result of prejudice.

The three examples of Adventism which we plan to study more closely in this unit are all products of the turbulent nineteenth century. Beginning with the outbreak of the French Revolution, Europe passed through political revolutions and through periods of political tension which might easily have become revolutions; she passed through revolutions of thought, many of them good and some extremely bad in their primary impacts (Marxism for example); she passed through the immense and accelerating revolution known generally as the Industrial Revolution. Before people could get adjusted to one major change and ready for another, repeated changes were likely to fall upon them. Those who could not keep up with the rapid changes either withdrew into social enclaves or they reacted against the changes or against their own sense of frustration in ways that seem queer to most of us today. Among the latter groups are to be included the three Adventist movements in which we are interested.

Their broader background is this rapid change that characterized the whole of Western society, but their more immediate background is to be found in American conditions. Here the Westward Movement was in full swing, offering a safety valve for Eastern society, which was slowly becoming more settled; yet it kept a volatile edge close enough to the more settled society to impart something of its turbulence to it. The settled society at first rallied to meet these conditions by joint action which had the unity of the nation in mind, giving us the period of American history known generally as the Nationalist Period. But beneath this appearance of united action, forces were building up which produced the Sectionalist Period, beginning about 1830, which presently tore the country apart in the Civil War. At the beginning of the century too a wave of religious revivalism swept the country. It soon settled down in the East; but taking quite violent forms in Kentucky, it spread through the western borders in wave after wave of orgiastic revivalism. With the close of the Civil War, the Industrial Revolution struck the country, bringing with it a period of cutthroat competition which deeply undercut the moral foundations of society but also brought wealth, a rising standard of living, labor unrest, an interest in science with its revolutionary effects and particularly religious and theological unrest. As the higher standard of living, with its efforts after culture and learning, moved westward, one of its effects was to confine the orgiastic revivalism to the economically underprivileged, though it also created among the more privileged classes an increasing number who were ripe for physical, mental, religious, and social ill health simply from having too little to do. The three movements in which we are at present interested all arose among the underprivileged—not far out on the frontiers, however, but in parts of the country where the underprivileged were in close contact with the rising standards of life.

The Seventh-day Adventists. The turbulence of the times seems to have convinced numerous earnest people that the coming of Christ was at hand. The world-wide discussion of this conviction by scholars of many denominations who based their study on Bible prophecy was the background of the Seventh-day Adventist movement.

Nichol, in championing his faith, was apparently faced by many Adventists who wished to repudiate the Millerite movement as the more immediate background of Seventh-day Adventism, for he devotes considerable space to proving their organic and necessary connection with the Millerites and to defending the latter from certain charges that, if believed, would make that connection embarrassing. According to him, the Seventh-day Adventists have never fixed a date for the Second Advent, and they recognize that Miller was led to do so by a mistake which their own movement has detected and corrected.[8] But otherwise the Millerites are defended and accepted. It is therefore on good ground that one begin with the activities led by William Miller in outlining the historical development which presently resulted in the

[8] Nichol, *op. cit.*, pp. 65-68.

Seventh-day Adventist Church. If this is agreed, then the basic steps in the formation of the Seventh-day Adventist movement may be counted as four: (1) the preaching of William Miller and its "disappointment," (2) the discovery of Miller's error and its correction in "the new line," (3) the adoption of the seventh day as the Sabbath appointed by God, and (4) developments attributed to Mrs. White.

William Miller (1782-1849), of Massachusetts, after a somewhat checkered career, was converted in 1816 and settled down to become a highly respected farmer. He began immediately a careful study of the Scriptures and came to the conclusion that "all the affairs of our present state would be wound up" between March 21, 1843, and March 21, 1844. He checked and rechecked his findings, but did not make them public until 1831. Then he won a following. Tracts, magazines, and books were published. Conferences were held. Camp meetings spread the doctrine. When the predicted year drew near, the Millerites confidently made preparations for the return of the Lord, but the reports of fanatical excesses seem either to be exaggerations or pure fabrication. The year came and went, and the Lord did not return. Miller, who had never set an exact date, confessed his disappointment but continued to expect the Advent at any time. Many of his followers, however, abandoned the cause.

Hiram Edson, who had waited out the night of October 22, 1844— a new date set by Samuel S. Snow—received a vision, the next morning, of Christ as the High Priest entering the tabernacle in heaven. He and others therefore concluded that it was that event and not the Second Advent which had been predicted. Christ had entered the tabernacle for an "investigative judgment," to examine the records of the lives of men, and his Second Advent would come when that judgment was completed. They did not set a time, but they obviously expected it soon —and they still do. That was the second of the four steps.

The third was the adoption of Saturday as the Sabbath appointed by God. Apparently it was taken through the influence of a Seventh-day Baptist group, and soon the attachment to it reached an intensity which many others would call fanatical. It became perhaps the prime "separating" feature of their doctrine. To them it is the "seal of God," and *Sunday* observance will be the "mark of the Beast." They claim that at creation God sanctified the seventh day for perpetual observance; that it has been observed since by all those loyal to God; that God has never authorized the observance of any other day, but that the change to Sunday was made by the apostate Roman Catholic Church, or by the "pagan" Emperor Constantine. Here, then, is a simple, easily applied shibboleth. Those who are prepared to obey God will observe Saturday; those who do not are disloyal to God and will drink the cup of God's anger. To the question "How do the Seventh-day Adventists know Saturday is the seventh day?" Arthur S. Maxwell makes the following reply, which to him seems obvious and final:

By the calendar. Every calendar shows Saturday as the seventh day of the week. Two unquestionable pieces of evidence confirm this: First, the fact that Orthodox Jews, from time immemorial, have observed the seventh-day Sabbath on Saturday; and, second, millions of Christians, for many centuries, have observed Sunday because Christ *rose* on the first day of the week.[9]

Thus these millions of Christians, by acknowledging that Sunday is the first day of the week, have thereby also acknowledged that Saturday is the *seventh*.

With regard to this doctrine, several things may be said at once. If the rest of the Seventh-day Adventist reasoning is correct and if the Bible is to be accepted "literally" in every detail—the Spirit-led Church being granted no liberty to introduce changes—then this would be a good test of willingness to obey God in all things. But there is at least some question about their "unquestionable pieces of evidence," and some reason to regard this feature of Seventh-day Adventist teaching as an example of arbitrary legalism.

As to their "unquestionable" evidence, there is reason to question whether the Saturday Sabbath has been observed from times immemorial. The Bible does not record the observance of the Sabbath from the time of creation. And Maxwell's straightforward appeal to the calendar ignores the fact that in times past there have been rectifications of the calendar which involved neither a correction of seven days nor any multiple of seven.

The arbitrariness of their selection of the Jewish Sabbath to be a day of perpetual observation appears when the question is raised why other

---

[9] "What Is a Seventh-day Adventist?" *A Guide to the Religions of America*, ed. Leo Rosten (New York: Simon & Schuster, Inc., 1955), pp. 134-35.

Old Testament injunctions, there appearing as divine commands, are not also regarded as of perpetual observation. They might reply, of course, that Christ himself changed some of them, such as the *lex talionis*, while he continued to observe the Jewish Sabbath; but then one might ask about Christ's promise that the Holy Spirit would lead the Church to truths for which she was not yet ready in the days of his flesh, and whether the change to the first day of the week might not be one of these Spirit-led changes, as the overwhelming majority of professing Christians claim that it is. Such a suggestion is at least plausible enough to pose a serious challenge to the inflexible insistence with which the Seventh-day Adventists employ this criterion. And the contention that it was the "pagan" Emperor Constantine who really made the change simply will not hold water. Any careful reader of the New Testament and of the literature of the early Church should know that the change was in progress in apostolic times among the Christians themselves.

The Seventh-day Adventist leaders indignantly repudiate the charge of legalism, and their reply is probably justified if and when the charge is made in too sweeping a form. They maintain that it is their faith that salvation comes through the grace of God and not through human merit. But when their tremendous insistence on the indispensable nature of Saturday observance, as indeed of other moralistic injunctions, is contrasted with Paul's counsel, "Let no man therefore judge you in meat, or in drink, or in respect of a feast day or a new moon or a sabbath day" (Col. 2:16 A.S.V.), surely the only possible conclusion must be that either Paul bore the mark of the Beast or that the Seventh-day Adventists have, in this and other respects, returned to the beggarly elements. When they insist on absolute obedience to every known command of God, they will be sustained by the consent of every true Christian; but when they make Saturday observance an inflexible test of such obedience, they are surely yielding to a temptation which dogs the footsteps of all the orthodox sectarians. The German pietist August Francke tried to make theater-going a test of one's state of grace; other sectarians give a similar role to card-playing, or to Sunday sport, or to the drinking of alcoholic beverages in any form, or to the eating of animal flesh or the flesh of some animals, or to smoking. The Seventh-day Adventists abstain from all of these things; but, for them, Saturday observance stands out uniquely.

Their third step, then, was the adoption of the Saturday Sabbath. The fourth was a number of actions taken apparently through the counsel of Mrs. White, whom they regarded as a uniquely inspired agent of the Holy Spirit. It seems to be due to her that the official name was adopted in 1860 and that the church was organized in 1863. She and her husband had moved to Battle Creek, Michigan, in 1855; and there, largely due to her visions, the publishing work was begun, as well as the health work which has since become famous in connection with the work of the Kelloggs. In 1903 her prophetic leading caused the headquarters of the church to be moved to Washington, D. C.

Concerning their belief and practice, the Seventh-day Adventists are avowedly Protestant. To the question "How do Seventh-day Adventists differ from other Protestants?" Maxwell replies: "Most noticeably in their observance of Saturday, not Sunday, as the Sabbath. But they also differ from many (but not all) Protestants in their teaching concerning the nature of man, the state of the dead, and the manner of Christ's second coming." [10] It would seem, therefore, that the Seventh-day Adventists do not differ with the other doctrines of the common Protestant creed. An examination of their formal expressions of belief on the doctrine of God, of Christ, and of the Holy Spirit seems to indicate that this is the case. But this does not mean that they characteristically accept a place as an organic part of the modern body of Protestant denominations, though some of them co-operate with other Protestants. Others may even have held the distinctive Adventist doctrines through the centuries, but now the Seventh-day Adventists officially claim to represent a new and unique fulfillment of prophecy, God's last movement in the world and his final message to all men.[11]

Jehovah's Witnesses. Marley Cole quotes the Louisville *Courier-Journal* in 1950 as describing this movement as "the fastest-growing religion in the world," and he does not believe it exaggerated. He writes that during the past quarter century "churchbook membership in the United States has increased by sixty per cent," while during the same period Jehovah's Witnesses multiplied by two thousand per cent. Through the world-wide depression, the Second World War, and the

[10] *Ibid.*, pp. 133-34.
[11] Francis D. Nichol, *Let's Live Our Beliefs* (Washington, D.C.: Review & Herald Publishing Assn., 1947), pp. 185-86.

rampage of Communism, "the Witnesses multiplied internationally by more than fifteen hundred per cent." [12] Such a rate of growth would be interesting, though it might not be very important if the numbers involved were small. But this group claims something like a half-million active members, and the rate of their activity is simply amazing. We have before us a body which cannot be ignored; and it may well be that a sympathetic study of their spirit, their teaching, and their methods—while it will undoubtedly reveal much that main-line Protestants must reject—may also serve to challenge us to emulation.

As far as the actual movement is concerned, its history began in Pittsburgh, Pennsylvania, in the seventh decade of the nineteenth century. That is to say, it is a post-Civil War development. But the Witnesses themselves would not be content with such a beginning. They would claim that their history goes back to Abel and such other faithful witnesses as are referred to in Heb. 11. Christ, the faithful and true witness, has called others to testify; and therefore Jehovah's Witnesses are the last of a long line of servants of God. Cole includes in his volume a chapter entitled "Across Nineteen Centuries," in which he links the modern movement with the persecuted minorities throughout the history of the Church, referring with special approbation to Paul, Arius, the Waldensians, Wycliffe and his Lollards, and Martin Luther.[13]

However, Cole also makes it clear that the Witnesses do not regard themselves as merely the last of a long line of servants of God. His statements are amply borne out by the emphatic rejection of all other religious bodies, and even of the claim to be a religion, by the Witnesses. They believe theirs is the only true faith; if they thought someone else had the true faith, they would preach that. Paul said there is only "one faith." Cole's estimation of their forerunners is as follows:

Martin Luther represented a movement that did more than throw off the ecclesiastical authority of Rome. Jehovah's Witnesses say that he planted the seeds of a doctrinal reformation as well, although the doctrinal reformation did not "get to first base" until the 1870's. The signing of the Augsburg Confession in April, 1530, and the Westminster Confession in 1648, by the representative Protestant faiths sealed Protestantism's cohesion to the principal

[12] *Jehovah's Witnesses* (New York: Vantage Press, 1955), p. 17.
[13] *Ibid.*, pp. 26-49.

doctrines of the Roman Catholic mother church—for example, the trinity, hell-fire, and soul immortality. Protestantism, in short, adopted the Nicene Creed.

Real doctrinal reformation, going deeper than Luther, than Wycliffe and the Lollards, than Waldo and the Waldenses, and digging back beyond Arius of the fourth century into the "first-century primitive Christian teachings set out by Jesus Christ and the apostles," was, say Jehovah's witnesses, to await the movement symbolized by a nineteenth-century Bible student named Charles Taze Russell.[14]

Like many other founders of religious movements, Charles Taze (Pastor) Russell is a highly controversial figure about whom it is extremely difficult to form an objective judgment. In this case, the reason lies partly in the bias and unreliability of the Witnesses. On the other hand, Russell seems to have invited and to have gloried in intemperate attacks throughout his life—attacks to which he responded with almost continual litigation. Such attacks apparently appealed to him, as they do to his followers, as fulfillments of prophecy and thus vindications of the man and his mission. But his adulating followers also ignore, or give a plausible exonerating explanation of, the alleged incidents which occasioned these attacks; and though they do not claim inspiration for him and will acknowledge broadly that he made mistakes, they present him in extremely flattering colors. Even where the judgments of the courts were not favorable to Russell, his defenders insinuate, if they do not openly charge, that the courts were biased.

It is suggested that this man may prove to be an interesting subject for psychological analysis; but if the outcome is not entirely in his favor, such discoveries are not likely to prove useful for propaganda purposes, at least in dealing with his modern followers. E. Royston Pike writes, "Mention Russell's name to a present-day Witness, and as likely as not you will get an uncomprehending stare." [15] Russell's books, as they fell out of print, were not reprinted; and it was Judge Rutherford, not Pastor Russell, who was accepted everywhere as the voice of Jehovah. Now very much the same fate is overtaking Rutherford. *His* books likewise are allowed to fall out of print, and his name is seldom on the lips of any save the older members of the society.

The basis for this treatment of the former "greats" may be debatable.

[14] *Ibid.*, p. 47.
[15] *Jehovah's Witnesses* (London: C. A. Watts & Co., 1954), p. 21.

Two probably justifiable reasons are given by the Witnesses. One is that theirs is a progressive movement in which, standing on the discoveries of those who have gone before, the Witnesses are searching for, and finding, new truth from their earnest study of the Scriptures and from their survey of contemporary events. They do not repudiate their forerunners, but they do emphasize further discoveries of truth. The second reason may be a desire to repudiate at least certain elements in Russell's leadership, but it is not so presented by the Witnesses. It is pointed out that, when Rutherford was chosen to lead the movement on Russell's death, he left the honored name of "Pastor" as Russell's sole possession and chose to be known as "counselor, advisor, and helper," or more commonly as "Judge." But he was confronted by the fact that until 1916 the Bible students had rallied around Russell himself. He had cautioned them against this, but forty years of listening to his sermons had caused many of them to think that "further revelation" had died out with the Pastor.

So one of the first barriers Counselor Rutherford had to demolish was the "creature worship" complex. The congregations doted on "character development."

Rutherford felt that the best antidote for "character development" would be "organization development." [16]

And so for the first time they began to perceive that the "organization" was more important than individual "personalities." This explanation seems acceptable, and it would be in line with the facts that Rutherford's writings have received the same treatment as those of the Pastor, and that the present head of the movement, Nathan H. Knorr, has kept himself so much in the background that he has refused to see people who sought to make firsthand contact with him for personal interviews. But, whatever the reason, the fact is clear: it will do the student of this movement little good to marshal the evidence about the character of leaders in the movement and to seek to employ it in dealing with the present Witnesses.

Since it is the wish and the practice of the Witnesses that the personal history of the leaders be left in the background, I refer the reader who

[16] Cole, *op. cit.*, pp. 81-82.

may wish more information on such matters to the volumes mentioned in the bibliography, while we proceed to study their organization and their doctrines. Judge Rutherford declared that the Witnesses had been on earth *as an organization* (italics mine) for more than 5,000 years.[17] The claim apparently was made orally, and it may have been misunderstood by the newspaperman who first heard it, or by others to whom it was transmitted. But it is certainly a surprising statement. That "God has never left himself without a witness" most Christians would agree, but the claim that the particular group known as Jehovah's Witnesses has existed as an organization for so long would surprise most people. In fact, it is simply not true. At present it is the phrase "as an organization" that intrigues our interest. It appears at first glance to be in flat contradiction to statements repeatedly made by other Witnesses—statements of which the following from Milton G. Henschel is typical:

"They are not an incorporated body. They use the nonprofit Watch Tower Bible and Tract Society, which was incorporated in Pennsylvania by Charles Taze Russell and associated Christians in 1884, as the governing body." [18] That the contemporary Witnesses are past masters in the *use* of organization is something that immediately strikes the imagination of students of the movement like Pike, Cole, and Harris. Though some may feel that the Witnesses have a tendency to overdo it, sacrificing other values in the process, masterly organization is probably a part of the reason for their rapid growth. And so, whatever we may think of the Judge's claim for the antiquity of such an organization, his characterization of the Witnesses as an organization would seem to be amply sustained by the facts. What, then, are we to make of the statements which seem to contradict that?

Cole gives us an explanation which seems to reconcile the apparent contradiction. It seems that they make a distinction between the Invisible Church and the Visible Church, though they would not accept such terms. Cole writes, in illustration:

Let's assume that the civil power has dissolved the legal corporation. It has banned the Watch Tower Society. This has happened in all totalitarian coun-

[17] Charles S. Braden, *These Also Believe* (New York: The Macmillan Co., 1949), p. 359.
[18] "Who Are Jehovah's Witnesses?" *A Guide to the Religions of America,* ed. Leo Rosten (New York: Simon & Schuster, Inc., 1955), p. 58.

tries. Well, then, there is no longer a legal society. But there still remains the spiritual Society. It may no longer have a central legal mouthpiece to speak through. But the real spiritual Society remains. It is held intact by a power that the civil authorities cannot touch.[19]

It was apparently this "real spiritual Society" that the Judge was referring to. But what did he mean by including in it people since the time of Abel and by calling it "an organization"? Probably their theocratic conception, reflected in their government from the top down, supplies the answer. He seems to have meant that the organization of the spiritual society is a spiritual fact, Jehovah being the direct ruler. At this point let us raise two questions. First, the reason and justification for their tight theocratic control is a matter of discussion.[20] The claim is that it was adopted on the initiative of the London Society and with the assent of other groups as the form of control most in harmony with their doctrine of direct divine control. They felt that a democratic organization was not in harmony with a theocratic control. If that statement is correct, it may still be questioned whether such a feeling is justified and whether such an organization best represents the Christianity of the New Testament and of the first century. For example, many Protestants would judge that it fails to do organizational justice to the doctrine of "the priesthood of all believers," that it therefore is out of harmony with original Christianity, that it is not in the best interest of the spiritual maturity of the members, and that their own effort to co-ordinate authority from above with a recognition of the value of the individual is vastly superior in all respects. However that may be, the question still remains whether this explanation of their theocratic control is really correct. Critics will point out that it seems to represent a grasping for power by such masterful men as the Pastor and the Judge, and that it has been resisted, if not in the lifetime of the Pastor, certainly from the beginning of the incumbency of the Judge,

[19] *Op. cit.*, p. 105.

[20] For the clearest picture of organization among the Witnesses, see Braden, *op. cit.*, pp. 363 ff. This may be usefully supplemented by Cole, *op. cit.*, p. 105. A very human picture of the way in which group organization affects the daily life of the loyal Witness is Richard Harris' article "Reporter at Large. I'd Like to Talk to You for a Minute," *The New Yorker*, XXXII (June 16, 1956), 72-105.

from within the movement itself. Braden quotes from a "former higher-up":

> Rutherford controls the organization completely. Directors' and members' meetings are a formality. The Judge sends a note stating whom he wants elected, or rejected, or what he wants done, and that is immediately done unanimously. Woe be unto that one who opposes. Anyone that opposes slightly gets a tongue lashing at the dinner table and if the opposition is serious or such one has too much independence of mind he is liquidated from the organization.[21]

Apparently this kind of autocratic control, and some resentment of it, still characterizes the organization.

In general, the membership of the movement seems not to be disturbed by this autocratic concentration of control at headquarters. They seem to accept whatever is handed down as from the Lord, though from time to time murmurings are heard, as at the convention at Cleveland, Ohio, during the summer of 1946.[22]

I should like to suggest three possible motives for it. One is that the grasping of masterful men for personal power, as a real though not openly acknowledged or even subjectively recognized factor, would not be contradicted as a motive either by the history of this movement or by the general experience of men. We often see reasons to suspect that kind of motivation even in organizations which pride themselves on their devotion to democratic theories and methods. A second suggestion is that this kind of organization seems to be characteristic of movements, sacred or secular, which regard themselves, as the Witnesses certainly do, as a warring group surrounded by powerful enemies. One can see it in the wartime powers granted to the governments of Great Britain and America. The very tight autocratic organization of the Jesuit Society is another example.

And the third suggestion is that a movement which draws its members from the underprivileged classes seems to require some such con-

---

[21] *Op. cit.*, pp. 364-5. Cf. W. J. Schnell, *Thirty Years a Watch Tower Slave* (Grand Rapids: Eerdmans, 1957).
[22] Braden, *op. cit.*, p. 365.

trol from above, or its leaders think that it does. Such an explanation fits the history of the Roman Catholic Church in the Middle Ages and is a partial explanation for its relative success in backward countries today. A similar example from the ecclesiastical world may be found in the Salvation Army, and a secular example would be Russian Communism. However, it is well to raise the question whether and to what extent it may be wise to yield to such pressures; and the history of such movements as have been mentioned would suggest that if contemporary pressures do suggest the wisdom of yielding to them to some extent, some such machinery as the British and American governments employ to reduce the centralization of authority as rapidly as circumstances permit is highly desirable.

I close this study of the Witnesses by emphasizing once more that this movement is definitely, aggressively, even bitterly, sectarian. Its street-corner and house-to-house ministry may be carried on in a spirit of patience, graciousness, and good humor; but the movement is bitter, glorying in the resistance which is stirred up by its aggressiveness.

The Mormons. Richard L. Evans, authoritative exponent of Mormon doctrine and practice, says: "Strictly speaking, there is no such thing as a 'Mormon,' and there is no 'Mormon' Church. 'Mormon' is merely a nickname for a member of the Church of Jesus Christ of Latter-day Saints." [23] Gordon B. Hinckley, another authoritative exponent, supports him in this statement and goes on to explain that "the Mormons regard themselves as saints only in the sense that they are believers in Jesus Christ and members of his Church." [24]

It should be noted that there are six bodies classified as Latter-day Saints in the 1957 *Yearbook of American Churches.*[25] Three of them are quite small, and only two of them are mentioned by Evans as being significant. In what follows, I have in mind "the doctrines and practices of the Church of Christ of Latter-day Saints, Salt Lake City, Utah, the largest 'Mormon' body in the world" with 1,246,362 members in 1953.[26]

[23] "What is a 'Mormon'?" *A Guide to the Religions of America,* ed. Leo Rosten (New York: Simon & Schuster, Inc., 1955), p. 91.
[24] *What of the Mormons?* (Salt Lake City: Church of Jesus Christ of Latter-day Saints, 1949), p. 5.
[25] Landis, *op. cit.,* pp. 57-58.
[26] Evans, *op. cit.,* p. 91.

All these bodies trace their origin to Joseph Smith, born in Sharon, Vermont, December 23, 1805. Smith was a problem to his contemporaries, awakening in some a devotion that seems fanatical, in others doubt and perplexity or violent opposition. The student would do well to consider both responses.

G. T. Harrison is an extremely bitter modern opponent.[27] According to him, Smith and his family lived in dark-age conditions. Harrison attributes to all the Smiths ignorance and gross superstition, and to Joseph almost superhuman cunning and duplicity and self-seeking. In reading his sweeping attacks, it should perhaps be noted that Harrison expresses himself as a rationalist who can reject the religious interpretation of life as a whole. The story of Joseph's finding the gold plates and translating them must surely strike anyone but a convinced Mormon as fully worthy of the treatment which Harrison devotes to it in so much searching examination.

However, Joseph found followers. A church was organized at Fayette, Seneca County, New York, with six members, the oldest of them only thirty-one years of age. This was on April 6, 1830.

The meeting was opened with "solemn prayer." . . . Joseph asked those present if they were willing to accept him and Oliver Cowdery as their spiritual leaders. All agreed. Then Joseph ordained Oliver to the office of Elder in the Priesthood, and Oliver in turn ordained Joseph. They then laid hands on the heads of the others present and confirmed them members of the Church and bestowed upon them the gift of the Holy Ghost. The Sacrament of the Lord's Supper was next administered, after which others were ordained to the office of Elder.

While the meeting was in session Joseph received a revelation in which he was designated a seer, a prophet and apostle of Jesus Christ. Since that time he has been referred to [by Mormons] as "the Prophet." [28]

But that area presently became too hot for the Mormons, and we find them next at Kirtland, Ohio, near Cleveland. The second annual conference of the church was held there in June, 1831. Already Smith's eyes were turned further west, to Missouri. Joseph claimed that it had been revealed to him that Zion would be established there. Missionaries

[27] *Mormons Are Peculiar People* (New York: Vantage Press, 1954), pp. 1-6.
[28] Hinckley, *op. cit.*, pp. 89-90.

were dispatched thither, and Mormons began at once to assemble in Jackson County. However, Kirtland was not yet abandoned, and a temple was completed there and dedicated on March 27, 1836. Persecution increased at Kirtland, and on January 12, 1838, Joseph moved to Missouri, never to return. But trouble increased in Missouri too, and in the winter of 1838-39 many of them made their way eastward to Illinois. There they sought to establish themselves, mainly at Nauvoo, near Quincy. They built this city from a swamp and established a temple there, but soon they ran into the same kind of persecution that had dogged their steps all along. Obeying a summons of Governor Thomas Ford, Joseph and several associates went to Carthage, where they were arrested and imprisoned on a charge of treason. On the evening of June 27, 1844, a mob attacked the jail and Joseph and his brother Hyrum were killed. In February, 1846, the exodus began under the leadership of Brigham Young. All agree that it is one of the most tragic but also courageous events in American history. After incredible hardship, they arrived in July, 1847, at the site of Salt Lake City, which Brigham indicated was the end of their journey; and after further hardship a city and a fertile environment to it were wrested from the inhospitable valley. The weary wanderers at last had a home; and whatever one may think about Mormonism and the Mormons, it was an achievement that must surely awaken sympathy and commendation among Americans.

Turning now to the organization of the Mormon Church, we may well begin by noticing the following statement of Mormon apologist Richard Evans:

When Joseph Smith was asked how he governed his people, he replied: ". . . teach them correct principles, and let them govern themselves."

The "Mormon" loves freedom as he loves life. He believes that there is no principle more basic to the Gospel of Jesus Christ than the God-given free agency of every man. He believes that a war in heaven was fought for freedom; that the right of choice is essential to the soul's salvation; and that anyone who seeks to enslave men in any sense is essentially in league with Satan himself.[29]

And he quotes the eleventh Article of Faith: "We claim the privilege

[29] *Op. cit.*, p. 100.

of worshiping almighty God according to the dictates of our own conscience, and allow all men the same privilege, let them worship how, where, or what they may." [30]

On the negative side, G. T. Harrison quotes the same statement by Smith. His critical comment is, "This, of course, is a deliberate falsehood and can easily be proven so." He is referring to the Mormon government and its philosophy, not to the attitude of Mormons towards others. In support of his charge he says:

As late as June, 1945, the *General Authorities' Ward Teachers' Message*, as carried by the *Deseret News* of May 26, 1945, and the *Improvement Era* of June, 1945, page 354, stated: "When our leaders speak, the thinking has been done. When they propose a plan—it is God's plan. When they point the way, there is no other that is safe. When they give direction, it should mark the end of controversy. God works in no other way." [31]

Mormons say:

The President of the Church is nominated from and by the Council of the Twelve Apostles, but he is voted upon by the membership. The same principle of common consent applies to all offices. No officer may serve without the consent of those over whom he presides. One of the established orders of business in all conferences is the "sustaining" of the officers of the organization. [32]

That would seem to confirm Joseph's statement about letting them "govern themselves"; but the possibility is suggested that this may be a mere form. If the rank and file of the membership is as ignorant, even about "Mormonism and the contents of its standard Church works and history," as Harrison claims, [33] and if their spirit toward their leaders is that of the statement quoted from the *Deseret News*, then freedom within the Mormon organization certainly is a mere form. Statements made to me from time to time, by young Mormons setting out on missionary trips and by non-Mormons who have lived in their villages, make me ready to believe that it is a mere form. On the other

---

[30] *Ibid.*

[31] *Op. cit.*, pp. viii-ix.

[32] Hinckley, *op. cit.*, p. 48; for the organizational machinery of the Mormons see Braden, *op. cit.*, pp. 432-36, and Hinckley, *op. cit.*, pp. 13-16; 47-51.

[33] Harrison, *op. cit.*, p. x.

hand, I have known Mormons whose level of education and culture make me wonder whether they could possibly possess the spirit of the *Deseret News* statement, though they might still hesitate to incur too openly the censures of the authorities of the church.

In the brief space available we can only glance, in closing, at Mormon beliefs. The two doctrines about which non-Mormons are likely to be most curious are the status of the *Book of Mormon* and the doctrine of marriage. Earlier I had something to say about the *Book of Mormon*. I noted the Mormon claim that it was translated from gold plates by Joseph Smith. Harrison maintains that this whole claim is palpable fraud and insists that Smith was merely reading from a manuscript from the pen of a deceased relative, the Rev. Ethan Smith. Braden says that:

The most commonly accepted explanation of the book's origin by non-Mormons is that it was based upon a historic novel written by a Presbyterian clergyman named Spaulding which he intended calling *The Manuscript Found in the Wilds of Mormon; or Unearthed Records of the Nephites.*[34]

Evans speaks for the Mormons:

The Book of Mormon is part of a record, both sacred and secular, of prophets and peoples who (with supplementary groups) were among the ancestors of the American "Indians." It covers principally the peoples of the period from about 600 B.C. to 421 A.D. These peoples were of Asiatic origin, of the House of Israel, and left Jerusalem during the reign of King Zedekiah, eventually to cross the sea to the Western world, where they built great cities and civilizations. Ultimately, they all but destroyed themselves in warring with one another.[35]

You are strongly advised to obtain a copy of the *Book of Mormon* to read it for yourself, and to accept it as true if you can. I cannot accept as true either its contents or the Mormon account of its origin.

As to marriage, it seems that the leader of the church in the nineteenth century had a revelation showing him that, since the patriarchs had more than one wife under divine sanction, this practice should be reinstated. Remembering what Jesus said about such matters and how

[34] *Op. cit.,* p. 424.
[35] *Op. cit.,* p. 94.

common it is for certain of the more extreme of the sects throughout history to experiment with relations between the sexes, one may well suspect the real character of this alleged "revelation." The announcement of this doctrine was a great shock to the Mormons themselves, since most of the converts to Mormonism were from Puritan New England.

Nevertheless, the leaders of the Church accepted it as a commandment from God. It was not an easy thing to do. Only those whose characters were of the highest, and who had proved themselves capable of maintaining more than one family, were permitted so to marry. Never at any time were more than *three percent* of the families of the Church polygamous. The practice was regarded strictly as a religious principle.[36]

Plural marriage was abandoned only in obedience to a decision of the United States Supreme Court. Mormons now maintain that members who have entered into such relationships subsequent to the court decision have been excommunicated.

Briefly, the Mormons claim to be Christians, but not Protestants. They believe in the Trinity, characterizing the Father and the Son in orthodox language and the Holy Spirit as a "Personage of spirit." They believe in immortality and in a literal resurrection of the body. Salvation is universal, but " 'exaltation' (with the highest eternal opportunities) must be earned by obedience to laws, ordinances, and commandments of the Kingdom." [37] They are pronounced Adventists, and Harrison claims that they all seek to control the people by instilling in them the fear of the wrath of God to come.[38] They practice baptism by immersion, but only of those who have become accountable for their actions, at the age of eight years and over.[39] Confirmation, by the laying on of hands for the gift of the Holy Ghost, follows baptism immediately. They observe the Lord's Supper with bread and water. Officially they disapprove the use of tobacco, alcoholic beverages, and hot drinks such as tea and coffee.

[36] Hinckley, *op. cit.*, p. 24.
[37] Evans, *op. cit.*, p. 95.
[38] *Op. cit.*, p. x.
[39] Evans, *op. cit.*, p. 97.

Meeting the Adventists

The parish minister must expect to attend to his ministry in the company of one or more Adventist groups. He will find much that is admirable in them: they stress the truth that Christ will reign triumphant, and they often exhibit an enviable discipline and zeal. However much he may deplore their moral legalism or their rigid exclusiveness, the minister must love and serve the Adventists according to their need, whether or not they accord him status as a pastor and preacher of the true gospel. This is least effectively done by attempting to discredit Adventism on the basis of unsavory history of the Adventist sects, even if the unsavory facts be true beyond question. Since the Adventists claim a readiness to be guided by Scripture, perhaps the best ministry is to labor in love to meet their exegesis with sound exegesis. Since they feel very strongly the appeal of an organization of the chosen people, they should be introduced to the wider communion of the elect, the Church universal.

Suggestions for Further Study

1. Compare the teaching of the Jehovah's Witnesses concerning the deity of Christ with the teaching of major Protestant groups. As part of the comparison, consider the argument of Bruce Metzger in his article listed in the bibliography following.

2. You have been called as pastor of a church in a new housing area where, by comity agreement, there is a plan for only one Protestant congregation. A team of Seventh-day Adventist missionaries has moved in with a series of audio-visual presentations in private homes preparatory to establishing a congregation. Formulate a Christian response for you and your people.

Selected Bibliography

Andreasen, Milian L. *The Sabbath, Which Day and Why?* Washington, D. C.: Review & Herald Publishing Assn., 1942.

Barclay, William. "Jehovah's Witnesses: an Ancient Heresy in Modern Dress," *Expository Times*, LXV (October, 1953), 31-32.

Bear, James E. "The Seventh-day Adventists," *Interpretation*, X (January, 1956), 45-71.

Blackstone, William E. *Jesus Is Coming.* New York: Fleming H. Revell Co., 1917.

Book of Mormon. Tr. Joseph Smith, Jr. Independence, Mo.: Herald Publishing House, 1943.

Braden, Charles S. *These Also Believe.* New York: The Macmillan Co., 1949.

Clark, Elmer T. "Adventists," *Twentieth Century Encyclopedia of Religious Knowledge.* Ed. Lefferts A. Loetscher. Grand Rapids: Baker Book House, 1955.

Cole, Marley. *Jehovah's Witnesses.* New York: Vantage Press, Inc., 1955.

Evans, Richard L. "What Is a 'Mormon'?" *A Guide to the Religions of America.* Edited by Leo Rosten. New York: Simon & Schuster, Inc., 1955.

Ferguson, Charles W. *The Confusion of Tongues.* Grand Rapids: Zondervan Publishing House, 1936. (Satirical but factual.)

Froom, LeRoy E. *The Prophetic Faith of Our Fathers.* 4 vols.; Washington, D. C.: Review & Herald Publishing Assn., 1954.

————. "Seventh-day Adventists," *Twentieth Century Encyclopedia of Religious Knowledge.* Ed. Lefferts A. Loetscher. Grand Rapids: Baker Book House, 1955.

Harris, Richard. "Reporter at Large. I'd Like to Talk to You for a Minute," *The New Yorker,* XXXII (June 16, 1956), 72-105.

Harrison, G. T. *Mormons Are Peculiar People.* New York: Vantage Press, 1954. (Bitterly opposed.)

Henschel, Milton G. "Who Are Jehovah's Witnesses?" *A Guide to the Religions of America.* Edited by Leo Rosten. New York: Simon & Schuster, Inc., 1955.

Hinckley, Gordon B. *What of the Mormons?* 3d ed.; Salt Lake City: Deseret Book Company, 1950.

Knorr, Nathan H. "Jehovah's Witnesses," *Religion in the Twentieth Century.* Edited by Vergilius Ferm. New York: Philosophical Library, Inc., 1948.

Landis, B. Y. *Yearbook of American Churches.* New York: National Council of Churches of Christ in the U. S. A., 1957.

Maxwell, Arthur S. "What Is a Seventh-day Adventist?" *A Guide to the Religions of America.* Edited by Leo Rosten. New York: Simon & Schuster, Inc., 1955.

Mayer, F. E. *The Religious Bodies of America.* St. Louis: Concordia Publishing House, 1954.

Metzger, Bruce M. "Jehovah's Witnesses and Jesus Christ," *Theology Today,* X (April, 1953), 65-85.

Nichol, Francis D. *Let's Live Our Beliefs.* Washington, D. C.: Review & Herald Publishing Assn., 1947.

————. *Reasons for Our Faith.* Washington, D. C.: Review & Herald Publishing Assn., 1947.

Pike, E. Royston. *Jehovah's Witnesses.* London: C. A. Watts & Co., 1954.

Smith, Joseph F. *Church History and Modern Revelation.* 2 vols.; Salt Lake City: Council of the Twelve Apostles, 1953.

Stuermann, Walter E. "Jehovah's Witnesses," *Interpretation,* X (July, 1956), 323-46.

DISPENSATIONALISM

Origin and Definition

A DEFINITION OF THIS TERM DOES NOT APPEAR IN BIBLE DICTIONARIES and encyclopedias until the twentieth century, for the simple reason that no one conceived of this system of thought before. It started with John Nelson Darby (1800-1882) of Britain. In 1825 he began the practice of law, but left the bar to take "orders" in the Anglican Church. Almost at once he questioned the scriptural foundation for "church establishments," leaving the church entirely in about two years. We are concerned, not with his condemnation of a paid clergy, but with his theological ideas and their development by his followers. In attempting to establish a "consistent eschatology," he was willing to dispense with the historic doctrine of salvation, the nature of the Christian church, and other related teachings.

The most familiar current source of dispensational teaching is found in the Notes of the Scofield Reference Bible. These Notes must be distinguished from the Scofield Bible itself, which is simply an edition of the King James Version. An additional important statement of dispensational beliefs occurs in *Bibliotheca Sacra* (see bibliography).

In brief, the teachings of dispensationalism are as follows:

1. The Jews are to be saved by repentance; they are to be left here on earth as God's earthly people.

2. The Gentiles are to be saved by faith; they will be taken to heaven after the Rapture.

3. The Church is a parenthesis in God's plan and will end in apostasy.

4. The kingdom of heaven and the kingdom of God are sharply differentiated, the first being the Davidic kingdom and the latter being God's universal world-wide kingdom.

5. God deals with men according to seven dispensations.

Its Distinguishing Feature

Its distinguishing feature is its seven[1] "dispensations," or "periods of time, during which God tests men by certain requirements." These dispensations are: Innocency (Gen. 1:28–3:13); Conscience (Gen. 3: 22–7:23); Human Government (Gen. 8:20–11:9); Promise, from the call of Abraham to the giving of the Law (Gen. 12:1–Exod. 19:8); the Law (Exod. 19:8–Matt. 27:35); Grace (John 1:17; Heb. 9:3-8; 10:19, 20); the Fullness of the Times (Eph. 1:10). It is claimed that the seventh dispensation is identical with the kingdom covenanted with David (II Sam. 7:8-17) and that it is yet to come.[2] When men failed these successive tests, falling under judgment, God inaugurated a new dispensation, a new period of testing with new requirements. Along with these seven testing periods, there are eight covenants.[3] Why they should not correspond in number, Scofield does not make clear. Whenever it makes the final test of man his failure or success in keeping God's requirements, dispensationalism is dangerously close to a new form of righteousness by works.

This system of seven dispensations differs radically from the teaching of the rest of Christendom—Eastern Orthodox, Roman Catholic, and Protestant—as it does also from the plain meaning of the Bible itself. Having been made aware of many criticisms leveled against their doctrines, the dispensationalists now find it useful to defend their name by saying that all Christians are dispensationalists: "Any person is a dispensationalist who trusts the blood of Christ rather than bringing an animal sacrifice. . . . Any person is a dispensationalist who observes the first day of the week rather than the seventh." [4] Again Chafer says: "The term *anno Domini* is intensely dispensational in itself and, like Augustine's (354-430) familiar dictum, 'Distinguish the ages and the Scriptures harmonize,' can hardly be considered modern." [5]

To be sure, Christians do believe in the distinction between the Old and New Testaments; in that sense, they may be said to believe in two

---

[1] Today dispensationalists are divided concerning the exact number of dispensations.

[2] For an outline of these dispensations see the Scofield Bible, p. 5, n. 5. Each dispensation is discussed as Scofield identifies its place in the Bible.

[3] See the Scofield Bible, pp. 5 and 6, n. 6.

[4] Lewis S. Chafer, "Dispensationalism," *Bibliotheca Sacra*, XCIII (October-December, 1936), 391.

[5] *Ibid.*, p. 393.

dispensations, but that does not put them in the category of those who identify seven or more dispensations. Since the word "dispensationalism" is in bad repute, it hardly clears the reputation to say, "You too are one, if you are a Christian."

The Church has not taught seven dispensations because they are not in the Bible. As the main body of Protestants observe two sacraments rather than seven, with no concern about being incomplete Roman Catholics, just so they accept two dispensations rather than seven without concern about being incomplete dispensationalists. In both cases the line is drawn on the basis of careful Bible study. Chafer implies that Christians who accept only two dispensations are "partial" dispensationalists, who can be completed only by coming over into the dispensational camp and observing the full quota of seven dispensations.

The "Virtues" of Dispensationalism

The strong points of dispensationalists are two: (1) their intention to be completely loyal to the Scriptures of the Old and New Testaments and (2) their zeal in propagating their "faith." Let us look at the latter first. In commending their zeal, we must remember that Paul encountered much zeal among the Judaizers. The book of Acts lists more than twenty attacks made by the Judaizers upon him and his co-workers; almost every Pauline letter reflects the Judaizers' opposition to real Christianity. The zeal of the Judaizers was to defend the letter of the law; they considered Christianity, as Paul taught it, a heresy. Paul replied that the letter kills but the Spirit gives life (II Cor. 3:6). He urged the Romans to serve with newness of spirit and not in oldness of letter (Rom. 7:6). Paul acknowledged the zeal of his persecutors, but said it was a zeal without knowledge, "For they being ignorant of God's righteousness, and going about to establish their own righteousness, have not submitted themselves unto the righteousness of God" (Rom. 10:3 K.J.V.). The very zeal of dispensationalism is a part of its danger because it is misdirected; it is bent to preserve a special status for the Jews for which the New Testament offers no hope. Nothing can justify the freezing of the religious status of any people short of the full provision of God's grace, or the overruling of the New Testament with the thought of Ezekiel or Daniel.

Let us now look at their first virtue mentioned above: their avowed intention to be loyal to the teaching of the Bible. Their method of biblical interpretation has been called "irrational," "illogical," "fantastic." They are often mechanically literalistic, and can resort to allegorizing with equal ease. One of the best examples of their allegorizing occurs on page 1331, note three of the Scofield Bible. The messages to the seven churches (Rev. 1–3) are said to be descriptive of the Church in its seven successive ages. Each is identified as a period of declension in purity. Ephesus is supposed to represent the ideal Church of the first century. But one cannot read the Acts or First Corinthians and suppose the first-century Church was ideal. The other unfortunate feature of their interpretation of Revelation is that the portion (chs. 4–22) which is obviously highly figurative is taken literally. When the historical is allegorized and the figurative apocalyptic is taken literally, one is as far away from the meaning of Revelation as it is possible to get.

The proof-text method is worked harder in this system of teaching than in any other I know. There is a legitimate use of the proof text, but in order that it be legitimate the interpreter must observe carefully the context to determine what the text was intended to mean. The dispensationalist ignores context completely. The Scofield method is to build up a doctrine from the Bible as a mosaic is made. Florence, Italy, is famous for its hard-stone mosaics. Nothing can be more beautifully done than that which the workman produces as he polishes many fragments of stone of many colors, making a delicate piece of jewelry from them. I have a pin, about the size of a quarter, which contains a bunch of white lilies, with green stems and yellow stamens, on a black background. Twenty-seven pieces of stone were used in making it. It is truly a work of art, but if one should conclude that this mosaic supplies the key to the understanding of the geological formation of the environs of Florence, he would be sadly wrong. So it is with "Dispensational Truth"; it is a mosaic made up of verses taken at random from the Bible. Since it is biblical material there is good in it, but it is not a key to what the Bible means.

It is impossible to discuss all the Scofield notes, for that would take a very large book. There is yet another limitation under which I labor: the copyright agreement under which the Scofield Bible is published forbids anyone to quote any considerable part of these notes. This means that in paraphrasing or giving the gist of these notes, one may be accused of unfairness.

Errors of Dispensationalism

It is the claim of dispensationalists that they have discovered the differing purposes of different parts of the New Testament: the Synoptic Gospels are for the Jews; the Acts, the Pauline Epistles, and the Gospel of John are for the Gentiles. They assert that the Jews will be saved by repentance: "Repent, for the kingdom of heaven is at hand" (Matt. 3:2; 4:17); the Gentiles will be saved by faith, by believing.[6] However, careful examination of the Synoptic Gospels reveals that faith is called for by Jesus more often than repentance. In the Gospel of Mark (1:15), the first words from Jesus' lips represent him as saying: Repent ye, and believe the good news that the kingdom of God is at hand. Matthew, the most Jewish of the Synoptics, maintains that Christianity is the fulfillment of Judaism. This same idea is beautifully illustrated by the Epistle to the Hebrews, which shows that everything in Christianity is better than its prototype in Judaism.

It is true that the Pauline epistles speak much more frequently of faith than of repentance, for they were written to Christians. The Acts demands both faith and repentance from both Jewish and gentile followers of Christ: "Testifying both to Jews and to Greeks of repentance to God and of faith in our Lord Jesus Christ" (Acts 20:21). The dispensational theory is contradicted by the New Testament evidence itself.

The dispensationalists say the kingdom of heaven must be distinguished from the kingdom of God. This is contradicted by the examination of any good harmony of the Gospels: Mark and Luke use "kingdom of God," while Matthew uses "kingdom of heaven"; but these uses are interchangeable. Matthew wrote for Jewish Christians who were accustomed to the Jewish hesitancy to use the name of God where a proper substitute could be found. Mark and Luke, who wrote for gentile readers, had no compulsion to refrain from the use of the word God. The dispensationalists say the kingdom of heaven is the Davidic kingdom of the Messiah to be set up here on earth and that the kingdom of God is God's universal reign. The redeemed Jews will live here on

[6] *Ibid.*, p. 436, n. 10.

earth for a thousand years, as God's "earthly people." The redeemed Gentiles will be taken to heaven at the Rapture. The Jew will be saved by his "physical birth" as a Jew; the Christian will be saved by his "spiritual birth": "Ye must be born again" (John 3:7 K.J.V.).[7] But we must remember that according to their theory John was written for Gentiles. This requirement for entering the kingdom of God was not addressed to a Gentile, but to Nicodemus, a member of the Sanhedrin (John 7:46-47), a ruler of the Jews (John 3:1). Paul was also emphatic in his denial that it was enough to be born a Jew (Rom. 2:28, 29). Every man of whatever race must be born again. Or, in Paul's words, "If any man be in Christ, he is a new creature" (II Cor. 5:17 K.J.V.). Both Jew and Gentile must pass through a transforming spiritual experience.

The dispensationalists' doctrine of the apostate church is the most serious of all their errors, because it fosters a spirit of contention, suspicion, and slanderous criticism of professing Christians. Yet nothing is more urgently yearned for by Paul than a spirit of brotherly love. This is a central idea in Philippians, in First Corinthians (chs. 12–14), and in other letters. Christians form the Body of Christ. If one member suffers, the whole body suffers. The thirteenth chapter of First Corinthians is a remedy for contentiousness, jealousy, and slander. Christians, if really Christians, are still babes in Christ, devoid of spiritual insight, as long as they are marked by these things: "And I, brethren, could not speak unto you as unto spiritual, but as unto carnal, even as unto babes in Christ. I have fed you with milk, and not with meat: for hitherto ye were not able to bear it, neither yet now are ye able" (I Cor. 3:1, 2 K.J.V.). If a man is contentious, he at best can only be called a childish Christian. Christians are warned to avoid contention (I Cor. 1:11; Tit. 3:9).

Scofield states that the most important passage in the Bible to support dispensational teaching is Acts 15:13-17. To get this before us for examination, it is well to copy it from the version endorsed by Scofield adherents, the King James Version. There are four important words or phrases which they misunderstand; it is from these that they draw the heart of their system. These I am italicizing:

[7] *Ibid.*, p. 431.

And after they had held their peace, James answered, saying, Men and brethren, hearken unto me: Simeon hath declared how God at the *first* did visit the Gentiles, to take out of them a people for his name. And to this agree the words of the prophets; as it is written, *after this I will return,* and will build again the tabernacle of David, which is fallen down; and I will build again the ruins thereof, and I will set it up: *that the residue of men* might seek after the Lord, and all the Gentiles, upon whom my name is called, saith the Lord, who doeth all these things (Acts 15:13-17).

1. Scofield takes the word "first" to be a statement of the order in which God will save the Jew and the Gentile: The Gentile will be saved in this "the church age," and then the Jew will be saved after the Second Advent of Christ. If Scofield had read the fifteenth chapter of Acts carefully, he would have seen that "first" refers to the fact that God used Peter to take the gospel to the Gentiles, Cornelius' family and friends (Acts 10–11), before he used the other apostles to take the gospel to the Gentiles. If Scofield had read Acts 15:7 carefully, he would have seen that James, in vs. 14, referred to Peter's account of this event, unless he had failed to recognize that Simeon and Peter were the same man. No doubt he was familiar with "Simon Peter" as a name for the Apostle, but Simeon is the unusual Palestinian spelling of the same name (cf. II Peter 1:1). It is obvious that this word "first" has no reference to any order in which God plans to save the two peoples. On the contrary, in the New Testament the gospel was presented to the Jew first and also to the Greek. Each Christian assembly contained both Jews and Gentiles; this was especially true of the church in Rome. It does no good to try to give this passage a dispensational turn by adding a number of irrelevant passages, none of which has any bearing on this doctrine. The mosaic of passages may be impressive, but it adds nothing to the evidence.

2. We must consider next the phrase "after this." In the Greek, it is "after these things," *meta tauta.* Scofield was aware that most of this passage (Acts 15:13-17) is a quotation from Amos 9:11-12, but did not know that the first line is not from Amos at all, but rather from Jeremiah 12:15. If he had read more carefully, he would have noted that James quoted "the prophets," not the prophet. Again by ignoring the context, he completely missed what James meant. He understood him to say that after God had gathered together the Gentiles into the

"parenthesis Church," and the "times of the Gentiles" had come to an end, then the parousia of Christ would occur, and the Jews would be saved in the Davidic millennial kingdom. In Jeremiah 12:15, this phrase refers to God's plucking Israel and Judah out of their captivity, when every man would be brought to his heritage, "and every man to his land." It has no reference whatever to gathering in the Gentiles. The prophecies in both Jeremiah 12:15 and Amos 9:11-12 refer to the restoration of the Israelites from the captivity for a new start, when God will build again the tabernacle of David. It is not a prophecy of something to take place after the church age, but something that did take place in the days of Zerubbabel and Nehemiah, when God began to restore the fallen fortunes of his people. The children of Israel lost the promise because they rejected their Messiah, and again they were by God rejected for a time (Matt. 8:11-12; 21:43).

3. "I will return" is said to be a promise of the Second Advent of the Lord after the parenthetical church age ends in apostasy, as God has planned that it should. The Greek word translated "I will return," *anastrepso,* is never used anywhere of the Second Advent. It means "to turn upside down," as Jesus upset the tables of the money changers (John 2:15); it also means "to turn back and forth"; so it often describes one's manner of life (I Cor. 1:12; Eph. 2:3). Here it is used of God's turning back to redeem his people after sending them into captivity. It is then that the fallen tabernacle of David will be restored. David's greater Son came to restore the kingdom of David, which He always called the kingdom of God or heaven. The Christian church is the New Israel (Gal. 6:15-16), the heir to the promise to Abraham (Rom. 4:9-13). This is the point of the Gospel of Matthew, which, as I said earlier, is the most Jewish of all the Gospels. The Church is composed of both Jews and Greeks; the two have become one new man in Christ (Eph. 2:11-22).

If Scofield had used a correct Greek text, such as Westcott and Hort's, he would have discovered that the Church is composed of both Jew and Greek. The King James Version has an error in the text of John 10:16, for this passage is translated, "There shall be one fold and one shepherd." The correct reading is "there shall be one flock and one shepherd." The difference is this: one fold may have several flocks. At daybreak when the shepherds come to take out their flocks, each "calleth his own sheep by name, and leadeth them out" (John 10:3 K.J.V.). Where the sheep all belong to one flock, one shepherd calls them all out. There are no dual flocks in the Church.

We need badly to recover the biblical doctrine of the Church. Dispensationalist error makes this imperative, unless we are to be carried away into an apostasy resulting from false teaching.

4. "The residue of men" Scofield identifies with the Israelites. In Amos, it refers to the Edomites who shall be called by God's name. Now the Edomites were never identified with the Israelites. This passage in Amos is a prophecy of first restoring the fortunes of Israel and then winning converts to worship the God of Israel. Amos saw no farther than the conversion of the Edomites. It is difficult to explain to the person who knows no Hebrew, so that he will understand, how *Edom* in Hebrew became "man" (Adam) when Amos was translated into the Greek Septuagint. It is plain to one who knows Hebrew, the consonantal letters of the two words being exactly the same. What does this mean to Christians? Amos had a vision of God's redeeming Israel's enemies, the Edomites; the Alexandrian Jews who translated the Old Testament into Greek had a wider vision of the redemption of mankind, so they put in the vowel points reading *man*. The vowel points to make the word read *Edom* were not put into the Hebrew manuscripts until about eight hundred years after Christ. James takes the Septuagint reading to support his point that Gentiles are welcome in the Church. The Scofield interpretation is exactly opposite to the meaning of this passage in either Hebrew or Greek.

It is manifestly clear that Scofield misunderstood every crucial word in this whole quotation. This is fatal for dispensational teaching, for it is here that Scofield stakes his claim to prove his case. There is no dispensationalism in this passage.

Other Incorrect Definitions

Not only is Scofield's sovereign indifference to the context of a passage fatal for his correct interpretation of the Bible, but also his arbitrary definitions of words are ruinous to his understanding of biblical teaching. Let us look at a few additional examples.

The most important of these is the word *oikonomia*, which Scofield chooses to translate "dispensation," "a period of time," in which God tests men by laying demands upon them which they fail to observe, then judges them for their failure. After this, God gives them a new dispensation. A careful study of the word *oikonomia* reveals the fact that no Greek lexicon gives it this meaning, and nowhere in Greek literature is the word used in this sense.

But our concern is with the meaning of the word in the New Testament. It occurs nine times, in the sense of a plan, the managing of a household, a stewardship. The English word "economy" is taken directly from this Greek word. It is used three times in Luke 16:2-5 of the "unjust steward," who was required to give an account of his stewardship (*oikonomia*), his handling of his responsibility. It is used in I Cor. 9:17 of Paul's responsibility to preach the gospel; it is used in Col. 1:25 of Paul's responsibility as a servant (*diakonos*) of the Church. It is used in I Tim. 1:4 of the service rendered to God through faith, being translated in the King James Version as "godly edifying" of the Christian worshiper. In the Revised Standard Version it is more correctly translated "divine training." None of these passages shows the word in Scofield's sense.

Two other examples should be mentioned. In Eph. 3:9, *oikonomia* is used of the management of the mystery of God which had existed from the ages, but was revealed in Christ. In this verse is found the expression "fellowship of the mystery" (K.J.V.), because a mistake in the text substituted *koinonia* for *oikonomia* in the Textus Receptus. Westcott and Hort's text shows this correction of the error in the Greek text that lies behind the King James Version. But Scofield claims that their work showed that the King James Version text is correct. This is another Scofield claim contradicted by the facts.

The one and only passage where *oikonomia* might possibly refer to a period of time is Eph. 1:10. Scofield places that in the millennial age; the New Testament dates it at the coming of Christ and his ministry. The fulfilling of the time is referred to three times in the New Testament. In Mark 1:15 Jesus said, "The time [*kairos*] is fulfilled, and the kingdom of God is at hand" (K.J.V.). This was the point in history when Jesus began his ministry. Paul said that "when the fulness of the time [*chronos*] was come, God sent forth his Son, made of a woman, made under the law" (Gal. 4:4 K.J.V.). This referred to the incarnation, to Christ's redemptive work for those under the law. Why should "the fulness of times" in Eph. 1:10 refer to an age yet future after the Second Advent? Obviously it does not. It plainly refers to the redemptive work going on at the time this letter was written, and to the continuing of the making of both Jew and Greek "one new man" in Christ, the "third race." Before leaving this discussion, it should be said that no other one of Scofield's seven dispensations is called a dispensation. The word occurs in connection with none of the other six so-called dispensations. This one example in Eph. 1:10 Scofield misunderstood. There is no ground in this word for Scofield's doctrine of dispensations.

Another arbitrary definition which has no justification in the New Testament is that of the word *genea* in Matt. 24:34; Mark 13:30; and Luke 21:32. Scofield says that the primary definition is "race, kind, family, stock, breed (so all lexicons)." This meaning can be found in classical Greek authors, but it is not correct for the New Testament. The New Testament word for "race, tribe," etc., is *genos*. It occurs more than twenty times in this general sense. The real reason for translating it "race" in Matt. 24:34 is that the dispensationalist interprets this passage as referring to the Second Advent. Since Jesus did not return in the lifetime of that generation to set up the kingdom of David, to protect Jesus against seemingly having made a mistake in his prophecy, the dispensationalists say it must mean "race," that the Hebrew race is still with us. But it must be noted that Mark 9:1 refers to those standing before Jesus who shall see the kingdom coming with power. The disputed word is not used in this verse, so there is no way to postpone this statement by a false definition. In the Septuagint *genea* translates *dor*, the people living at a given time. "All these things" in Matt. 24:34 does not refer to the Second Advent, but to the destruction of Jerusalem and the gathering of the elect. Jerusalem did fall within the lifetime of Jesus' contemporaries, and the gathering of the elect was begun, and still continues today. It was a more extensive job than Jesus' followers realized at that time. This false definition is just one more effort to make the Bible support a theory which grows out of misunderstanding the words of the Bible.

Textual Criticism

Scofield began his theological "education" at the age of thirty-six and did it "privately." He professed interest in scholarship, but frequently did not digest the fragments of information that he gathered. For example, in referring to textual criticism, he speaks of such scholars as Griesbach, Lachmann, Tischendorf, Tregelles, Westcott and Hort who "cleared the textus receptus of its minor inaccuracies," giving us the amazingly accurate text (?) which lies behind our Authorized Version. This is just the opposite of what these scholars did. For several centuries scholars knew of the corruptions that had entered the text through repeated copying. The textual critics by their work cleared out these errors, as we noted for example in John 10:16, and gave us the purified text which lies behind the English Revised Version, the American Revised Version, the Revised Standard Version, and nearly all of the twentieth-century translations. Scofield could not be more confused on the significance of textual criticism.

False Chronology

Scofield accepts all of the Ussher chronology appearing in the margin of some editions of the King James Version. Many of his disciples think these dates are an authentic part of the Bible, in spite of the fact that they were not inserted as notes into the Bible until about the eighteenth century, even though Ussher worked these out earlier (1581-1656). This chronology forms a barrier to the understanding of the Bible. The most famous date is 4004 B.C. for creation. There are disciples of Scofield who call men "communists" who question this date. Archaeological discoveries reveal that the Ussher chronology is completely untenable.

The Doctrine of the Apostate Church

Dispensationalism appears in its most vicious form in this doctrine. Napoleon Noel's *History of the Brethren* (see bibliography) reveals the dispensationalists as a group continually quarreling with one another. They still exhibit this same characteristic. This is quite natural, for they are taught to expect apostasy in every professing Christian. They form a sort of spiritual gestapo, looking for grounds of accusing the man in the pew to their right or to their left, to the front or to the rear, including the man in the pulpit, if he is not a militant dispensationalist. Their practice is consistent with their principles. One young minister I know, pastor of a large church, has been driven almost frantic by constant persecution day in and day out. He is an able, orthodox preacher with a distinctly prophetic note in his preaching. Because he does not preach dispensationalism, his congregation will acknowledge no good in him. He has repeatedly been driven to the point of resigning and taking another church, but feels it his duty to save this church for the Christian faith.

Another example is in a small county seat. One industry dominates the town, employing many of the leading men. A new executive came in to head this enterprise. He called a meeting of all the influential men under him. The men went because they supposed it was a business meeting. He used the occasion to attack the churches of the town, in what seemed to be a religious address. He announced a weekly meeting which the men were expected to attend. At these he kept up his attack on all the churches. The men talked to the pastors; the pastors had a meeting to decide what to do, for the men felt that their standing with the company depended on their attendance. The pastors managed to hold the line, but they could not answer the attack too well for lack of knowledge. They had not been trained in their seminaries as to the falsity of this teaching. What is the scriptural evidence for the complete and final apostasy of the Church? The Scripture nowhere speaks of an apostate church. Failure, sin, moral declension among God's people, occurs frequently in both the Old and the New Testaments, but there is no word from God to the effect that he expects his Church to apostatize. The word "apostasy," *apostasia*, occurs in the New Testament twice. In Acts 21:21 we are told that the Jews accused Paul of teaching the Jews of the Dispersion to apostatize, forsake Moses, telling them not to circumcise their children or to observe the Jewish customs. This conflict is reflected in every Pauline letter. To the Jews, in the main, the teaching of Paul was apostasy, but to the Christian church it was the continuation of Jesus' teaching. The New Testament writers said the Church was the New Israel, made up of both the circumcised and the uncircumcised (Gal. 6:15; Eph. 2:11-22; John 10:16). The charge of apostasy against Paul has its roots in the same soil as the dispensationalist charges against the Church today. We must recognize that we are confronted with a Judaizing, legalistic movement. In II Thess. 2:3, the word "apostasy" is used once more. If one will take the trouble to read the first twelve verses of this chapter, it will become manifest that Paul was talking about something that would happen in the life of his converts in Thessalonica. It is not something yet in the future. The outbreak of evil was, no doubt, conected with Nero's diabolic reign. Also an examination of the verb *aphistanai* reveals no expectation of apostasy in the Church.

The passage most frequently cited as proof of apostasy occurs in the words of Jesus, Luke 18:8: "Nevertheless when the Son of man cometh, shall he find faith on the earth?" (K.J.V.). This is understood to be an authoritative word from the Lord himself that apostasy is the sure end of the Church. Two things should be noticed:

(1) There is nothing in the Greek to indicate a negative answer to this question. The introductory word for such a question would have been *mē*. The word used is *ara*, which does not suggest either a "yes" or "no," but is a sort of challenge. We might interpret it, "What are you going to do to keep faith alive?"

(2) The other important point is that Jesus did not say "Will he find faith on the earth?" but rather "Will he find *the* faith on the earth?" There is a rule in Greek grammar called the "anaphoric use of the article." This question means: Will the Son of Man find faith such as this widow displayed in Luke 18:1-7? In no sense is it a prediction of apostasy, but it is a challenge to loyalty.

Another claim for apostasy rests upon II Tim. 3:1-8, "in the last days perilous times shall come" (p. 1280). The Christian must remember that the "last days" does not refer to some time yet in the future. John told his readers that they were already living in the last time (I John 2:18). They are not to look for antichrist, for many antichrists have already come (I John 2:18). It was the "last days" when Jesus was here on earth teaching (Heb. 1:2). All this kind of use of Scripture by the dispensationalist is more building of a mosaic. It is constructing a system of teaching that is unbiblical. A passage (II Tim. 3:1-8) which was intended to guide Christians in Ephesus in the first century is being offered as proof of what the Church will be like when the Lord comes again.

A still further evidence for apostasy Scofield finds in I John 4:1-3 and Phil. 3:18. He says this apostasy is the denial of the deity of Christ and the rejection of his atoning and redeeming sacrifice. Again he has missed the point of the passages. The heresy with which First John dealt was the denial of the incarnation, that is, that Jesus came in the flesh (I John 4:1-3). Philippians 3:18 is not something that Paul prophesied for the age of apostasy in the Church; it had already taken place. The enemies of the Cross are as old as Golgotha.

Meeting the Dispensationalists

One dislikes to criticize the work of a man who attempted to do a service for the Lord Jesus, but every Christian is called upon to defend the truth of the gospel. There are some good notes in the Scofield Reference Bible, but many that are false, even pernicious. They have become a menace to the faith of the Church. It is our duty to lead Christians who have gone astray theologically back to what the Bible teaches. The dispensationalists have infiltrated almost every branch of Protestantism, but their ideas are often not recognized for what they are. At least one major denomination, Presbyterian U.S., at the General Assembly of 1944, declared dispensational teaching out of harmony with the doctrines of that Church. However, this action did not greatly lessen dispensational teaching in the local churches.

In order to cope with dispensationalism, church leaders must know the theology of their church and the content and teaching of the Bible thoroughly. They must know how to recognize dispensationalists and prevent their taking over the places of leadership in a given church. The church leader must study carefully the notes in the Scofield Bible and compare them with his own careful exegesis of the passages involved. Let him remember that many people are led into the dispensationalist camp because the leadership of the Church has failed in the task of Christian education.

Suggestions for Further Study

1. After studying the Scofield Notes, visit Bible classes taught by dispensationalists and interview the teacher of the class.

2. Examine the literature which is published for dispensationalist teachers.

3. Interview pastors whose churches have been split by dispensationalists.

Selected Bibliography

Allis, Oswald T. Prophecy and the Church. Philadelphia: Presbyterian and Reformed Publishing Co., 1945.

Bear, James E. "Dispensationalism and the Covenant of Grace," Union Seminary Review, XLIX (July, 1938), 285-307.

Bowman, John W. "Dispensationalism," Interpretation, X (April, 1956), 170-87.

Chafer, L. S. "Dispensationalism," *Bibliotheca Sacra*, XCIII (October-December, 1936), 385-449.

Chamberlain, William D. "Dispensationalism," *Twentieth Century Encyclopedia of Religious Knowledge*. Ed. Lefferts A. Loetscher. Grand Rapids: Baker Book House, 1955.

Larkin, Clarence. *Dispensational Truth or God's Plan and Purpose in the Ages*. Philadelphia, 22-2 N. Park Avenue: Rev. Clarence Larkin, Est., 1918.

Noel, Napoleon. *The History of the Brethren*. 2 vols.; Denver: W. F. Knapp, 1936.

Pieters, Albertus. *A Candid Examination of the Scofield Bible*. Swengel, Pa.: Bible Truth Depot, 1938.

————. *The Seed of Abraham: A Biblical Study of Israel, the Church, and the Jew*. Grand Rapids: William B. Eerdmans Publishing Co., 1951.

Scofield, Cyrus I., ed. *The Scofield Reference Bible*. New York: Oxford University Press, 1909 ff.

Whitfield, E. E. "Plymouth Brethren," *The New Schaff-Herzog Encyclopedia of Religious Knowledge*. Edited by Samuel M. Jackson. Vol. IX, 1911.

PERFECTIONISM

FEW STATEMENTS OF THE CHRISTIAN FAITH HAVE PROVED SO APPEAL-
ing to certain types of people as the various expressions of perfectionism.
Yet few have been fraught with such treacherous pitfalls for the soul,
as the highest-minded leaders of perfectionist teachings have themselves
been keen to note and quick to warn. The wide range covered by doctrines of holiness makes it difficult to point to any one formulation and
say, "This is it." Even standard reference works differ in their emphasis
when describing the somewhat complicated points of view represented
under the blanket title of this unit.

The Meaning of Perfectionism

Many treatments of perfectionist doctrines lay the stress on an act
of attainment in this life. There is the dictionary definition, "The doctrine that a state of freedom from sin is attainable, or has been attained,
in the earthly life." [1] Sin is here thought of largely as deed, or perhaps
even particular deeds. When such a view is taken, the grosser sins are
naturally magnified. The hunted soul that has found itself tempted
beyond resistance by the beastly appetites and that has often suffered
in shame because of the inability to overcome passions that are obviously
wrong, finds surcease from strife and the joy of victory in the perfectionist faith. God has freed the soul once for all from the sins of the
flesh and even from unholy desires.

But the meaning of perfectionism is not always so completely centered on this life. Another standard authority defines the term as "The
completeness and blessedness of Christian experience which has attracted the wistful desire of orthodox and sectarian alike." [2] Such a
point of view evidently has back of it the thought of sin as a state of

---

[1] *Webster's New International Dictionary of the English Language* (2d ed.; Springfield,
Mass.: G. & C. Merriam Co., 1952), p. 1818.

[2] Frederic Platt, "Perfection," *Encyclopedia of Religion and Ethics*, ed. James Hastings (New
York: Charles Scribner's Sons, 1908-27), IX, 728.

the soul. It is not so much concerned with the outward and the gross as with the inward and the spiritual. Can pride and jealousy, self-centeredness and anxiety, be overcome? Can life be saved from its contradictions? Can split personality be mended? And the answer of perfectionism, so conceived, is the pointing to a new kind of life, an experience where the "completeness and blessedness" that one looks for in his relation to Christ has become a reality. Perfectionism so defined would certainly hold up the possibility that such an experience may be attained in the present life and would point to the utter joy of some Christians in their devotion to their Lord. But the stress would not here be on the attainment of a state; it would rather be on what the Lord can bring about within the soul that trusts him absolutely.

The Appeal of Perfectionism

That such a possibility should move the Christian heart is surely understandable. Every child of God believes that he has been made in the image of his Creator. He has been taught to worship God as supremely and perfectly holy. Such a psalm as the ninety-ninth sings of the holiness of God with wondering adoration. The Old Covenant bade the children of Israel to be holy because their God was holy. While the ambition to be like God may be terribly presumptuous if it arises in an unconsecrated mind, in the heart of men whose lives have been devoted to their Maker it is inevitable. "Like father, like child."

Moreover, whenever a Christian knowingly does wrong, there follows a sense of guilt. And that guilt arises primarily from the consciousness of doing, not something socially unacceptable or morally unjustified, but something which goes against the very nature of God. The scriptures of both Old and New Testaments are filled with examples of men who have striven in agony because they have marred the image of God within their soul. Classic among such examples is the prophet Isaiah (Isa. 6:1-8). Here in autobiographical lines that spring from a heart completely bared before its God, Isaiah reveals his awful consciousness of the difference between the holiness of God and his own uncleanness. And his only solace is in the fact that God's seraph has flown to him with the burning coal that purifies his soul and makes him ready for God's commission. Classic also is Paul's sense of the vast void between God's purity and his own sin, a consciousness which led him not only to seek the purity of God, but also to writhe in anguish because he was not able to maintain that purity within his own soul, but suffered a frequent sense of contradiction and defeat (Rom. 7:13-25). Yet it was just at this juncture, when his evil conscience had led him to exclaim wildly, "Wretched man that I am! Who will deliver me from this body of death?" that he could cry aloud for joy, "Thanks be to God through Jesus Christ our Lord!" If the conscience of the man who has given his life to Christ remains keenly alive, it ought to be shocked by every failure to live up to such a far-reaching profession. The guilt of a broken dedication leads more readily to despair than the earlier sense of being at enmity with God. What more glorious than faith in a keeping power that destroys the possibility of failure! Such power might readily become a "second blessing."

Indeed, to the soul that is fixed on God all relativisms seem disappointing and unreal, and the many ways of accounting for them but excuses of confused and wayward minds. And how inventive those excuses can become! "My intention was good, but I slipped when I wasn't on guard." "No one knows how hard I struggled against my besetting sin, but the temptation was just too great." "Jesus taught the moral ideal, but we cannot hope to attain it." "Jesus anticipated the end of the world in his generation, but we cannot hope to keep up day after day going the second mile, turning the other cheek, loving our enemies." "It may be that the ideals of Jesus are good for any age, but the fact that we don't keep them only drives us back again and again upon the mercy of God and keeps us humble as we realize our weakness."

Many of these ready answers to the Master's words, "You, therefore, must be perfect" (Matt. 5:48), have become the backbone of successive theologies of ethics in the twentieth century. Others are the common replies of the man of the street. But all of them sound weak to the soul of genuine sincerity. The hunger for the absolute in life is deep, and the appeal of perfectionism to our human nature, out of keeping as it may seem at times, is certainly to be expected in the face of claims as sweeping as those of the gospel of Christ. Indeed, we may safely say that the core of our faith would be corrupt if we could look with tolerance upon repeated sin or if we failed to respond in some positive way to the challenge of the complete. After all, the Psalmist had rested his sin-wearied soul on the assurance, "Purge me with hyssop, and I shall be clean; wash me, and I shall be whiter than snow" (Ps. 51:7). The prophet of the last chapters of the book of Zechariah could look forward to a time when holiness would be so universal in Israel that it would even be "inscribed on the bells of the horses" (Zech. 14:20). And that perfectly simple and yet deep epistle of the New Testament that has always been associated with the apostle of love insists in no uncertain terms that sin and the Christian life are irreconcilable and that there is no sin in the one who abides in God (I John 2:9-10; 3:4-10). The saint who yearns to be perfect is by no means to be laughed out of the fellowship as an idle dreamer; he has much within his own soul and within the word of God that invites him to some such hope.

Historical Sources of Perfectionism

Within the Church, both Romanist and Protestant, perfectionist tendencies have often been expressed. In the ideals of purity, poverty, and obedience that form the framework of more than one of the Roman Catholic orders, the tendency has frequently been to expect perfection in these virtues. Often some group within the church has been allowed to adapt a still stricter and more detailed code of living in the hope of producing qualities of deportment that are exact. Romanism has proceeded in such cases in accord with its general policy; it has permitted and even praised these attempts, while keeping close control over them and pointing out to the faithful the wrongs of which they are composed.[3] More often still, however, one finds perfectionist leanings within Romanism in the lives of individuals of mystical temperament. Here holiness often lives in souls that are quite robust, though it is also to be found in those vaguely pantheistic spirits who feel themselves near to being merged in God.

Within modern Protestant circles perfectionist emphases have generally sprung from Arminian rather than Calvinistic groups. Whether this is due to basic differences in theology between Arminius and Augustine appears difficult to determine. But in the modern scene, and especially on the American frontier, the lines come rather clear. Calvinistic groups were of course in the ascendancy in the early days of American life. As civilization forged its way westward, well-trained

---

[3] See, for example, Theodore Maynard, "Noble Fallacy," *Catholic World*, CLXXVII (August, 1953), 352-357.

Calvinistic preachers of stern and uncompromising morality followed in its wake. They soon became scandalized by what they saw in the wilderness. Men broke away from the old moorings and, in the wild and free life of the woods and streams, often without the gentler influence of the companionship of women, sank into the depths of gross degradation. Drunkenness, personal revenge, and more unspeakable sins were of almost regular recurrence. For such ways of living the Calvinistic preacher had strong and justifiable denunciation. He brought the word of the Lord to bear in no uncertain terms on the immoralities of the hour. But the frontiersman could see no hope. He felt himself caught in a vise where his life was out of control and his elementary appetites ruled his will. He might agree in theory with the preacher's denunciation of his wrongdoing; he might accept as his due the curses of the law; he might tremble at times before the vivid presentation of the future torments of hell. But he longed for some present deliverance. Into such an environment came many preachers of repentance. They were of various faiths. Calvinists as well as others proclaimed the love of God and the forgiving mercy of a heavenly Father. The "Great Awakening" had Calvinistic, as well as other, roots. Lesser revivals of religion took place from time to time. But much of the preaching was directed toward deliverance in a life beyond the grave or a spasmodic urging of men to turn to God. There were few settled pastors, and after the revivalist had left, the woodsmen, like the Israelites in the days of the judges, would return to their old sinful ways.

The preachers of perfection, on the other hand, while they came with as strong a hatred of sin, declared with more eager persuasion a belief that God could deliver here and now. If they went to extremes in their hopes and promises, this is to be understood in the light of the extreme immorality they so readily observed. It is small wonder that their preaching of hope for a complete and often instantaneous experience of holiness led to frantic searchings of heart, to terrific orgies of wrestling with sin, and to wild paroxysms of joy when victory seemed to be real. It was because men had seen sin in the raw that they could pull up saplings by the roots in their frenzy to overcome it and could lie prone all night before God in an ecstasy of glory when the burden of guilt was lifted. Perfectionist tendencies in American revivalism persisted and found perhaps their loftiest expression in the work of

Charles G. Finney and others of the "Oberlin School." I can testify to the moral thrill which the reading of Finney's autobiography gave me in my middle teens.

These Western-world developments of the idea of perfection stemmed, as is well known, from the Old World and particularly from the Wesleyan movement. John Wesley himself had been strongly influenced by other thinkers and writers, from men like Thomas a Kempis and Jeremy Taylor to William Law. In Law's *A Serious Call to a Devout and Holy Life* one finds, under the allegory of two sisters, extreme contrasts between a life of pride and arrogance within the Church and a completely humble and self-abnegating piety. To anyone who reads it with open mind this "serious call" must appeal as no theoretical treatise but as a sincere coming to grips with the problems of living. John Wesley came upon the scene of the English church in days when it had fallen into the twin pitfalls of formalism and hypocrisy. His Aldersgate experience of the warming of the heart must impress the reader of any theological or temperamental background as genuine. In it one can feel the musty cobwebs of the Church's staid and ingrown life swept away as if by magic. It is the personal purity of men like Law and Wesley that argues most strongly for their convictions.

John Wesley's doctrine of perfection has been the subject of all sorts of comment. Behind such works as those of Green, Flew, Linstrom, Sangster, and Peters (see bibliography), the present-day Christian who has come in contact with groups that stress holiness ought to read for himself here and there in Wesley's *Journal* and in those portions of his works where the subject is specifically treated. Wesley was critical and cautious in his approach to his own profound conviction. When he wrote of the possibility of perfection in this life, he did so with care to guard against seeming to suggest that men can become absolute as God is absolute. Infallibility, Wesley knew, belongs to God alone, and any doctrine of perfection that oversteps these bounds is *ipso facto* false. Moreover, Wesley shrank from accepting evidence of sudden and complete attainments of holiness. He gradually came to the position of allowing for them, but he always warned against the too ready claim. Especially did the founder of Methodism urge his followers to beware of "open testimony," by which he referred to the public announcement of holiness by one who thought he had attained it. Later leaders of the movement welcomed this public claim; Wesley never did. He recognized full well the temptations it involved to display and pride. In harmony with this it is to be noted that Wesley never laid claim to perfection for himself. Nor did he feel that the majority of Christians could attain it. Again and again he stresses the fact that the moral ideal lies ahead even for the most saintly. Even those who have holiness may lose it again, though they can recover it under God. In fact, Wesley was not slow in moving toward the climax of his belief, namely that Christian perfection is not a matter of particular morals, but is perfection *in love*. While his use of language at times seems to deny this, he reiterated frequently his teaching and insisted that perfect love is possible only to the most genuine faith. He admits that a Christian's judgment is still affected by insufficient knowledge, and thus he allows room for growth even within his doctrine of complete sanctification in love. If only some of his followers had been as modest and reserved!

Perfectionism as Found Today

The associations of perfectionism today are of a different order. In most parts of America one finds little stress on the teaching in current Methodism. But a strong revival of interest in extreme doctrines of holiness has arisen in various of the sects. Though they differ somewhat in their emphasis, there is a general underlying agreement. A state of freedom from sin has been attained, or may be attained, in this life. The "first blessing" given by God is justification of the sinner as an act of His grace; and this is followed by the "second blessing," sanctification, which is also thought of as an act. The farther one moves toward the type of sect that is aloof from the main body of Christendom, the more likely he is to find the stress on this sanctification as instantaneous. In some of our mountain districts a preacher may even be stopped by public objection from the "saints" in the audience if he refers to growth or progress in the Christian life. To many believers life is so strongly either/or that one must be altogether Christian in all of his reactions or not Christian at all. There is no room for conversion in different areas of his being at different times. He must be regenerated throughout his soul all at once or regeneration is not real. Some of these sects do indeed allow that sanctification, instantaneously affected, may be lost if the soul gets out of touch with God and may be gained back by a return to him. Some of them will even admit that instantaneous sanctification is the gift of only a minority of Christians, and that others who are real believers in Christ may attain complete sanctification at death. In this last belief they of course find Calvinists and other groups in essential agreement. But generally the perfectionist sects that condemn others the most fiercely are those that insist on the drawing of sharp lines, that stress holiness as a blessing already completely bestowed on those within the circle, that preserve the revivalistic tendencies to proclaim their faith noisily, and that (logically enough) proselyte from churches of a quieter and more orthodox belief. Many a small town is split badly between the members of the "regular" churches and those who have "found sanctification" through some of the sects, and many a soul in these regular churches is sorely troubled. He instinctively distrusts the extreme claims and questionable methods of those who seek to convert him or his children, but he is at a loss to give an answer for the faith that is in him.

Among these modern sects with perfectionist teachings the Nazarenes have been quite prolific. In many smaller communities especially they have been the ones to stress sanctification as an instantaneous act of God and to decry the most loudly any need for spiritual growth. They have laid great stress on the doctrine of the Holy Spirit, but they have magnified his more spectacular gifts, especially what they believe to be his direct action on believers to make them perfect. In larger communities the Nazarenes are tending today to soften some of their more extreme dogmas and to co-operate with the more orthodox churches. They retain their inclination to frequent revival meetings but are not so denunciatory of those who do not share their views as they once were. The Pilgrim Holiness group is a smaller body, quite similar to the Nazarenes but a little less conservative. The Christian and Missionary Alliance is also a holiness body, but their stress is often more on the verbal inspiration of the Scriptures. Their relation to the Nazarenes comes at the point of their strong emphasis on the baptism of the Spirit. In larger communities they are sometimes related to the Peniel Missions. There are many groups which call themselves "The Church of God," some of which practice the use of the "gift of tongues." In some circles this seems to be thought of as an ability to speak in a dialect that none may understand unless the one who has received the power from God is able to interpret it. Thus the experience is thought of as the repetition of the Day of Pentecost in the early Church as recorded in the second chapter of Acts and as literally interpreted. In other groups, however, speaking in tongues seems to have a broader and freer interpretation as a spiritual ecstasy before God, ecstasy growing out of the joy of freedom from sin. The Church of God, which has its headquarters at Anderson, Indiana, does not practice speaking in tongues and prefers to think of itself as a movement within the Church universal rather than as a separate denomination.

In more recent years the strongest perfectionist emphasis, especially in urban centers, has come from those first known as Buchmanites or Oxford Groupists, now generally referred to as Moral Rearmament or simply MRA. They have been known for their large gatherings and testimony dinners in spacious city hotels. They have often sought as deliberately to reach those of higher income brackets as the Nazarenes, for example, have frequently specialized among the poorer classes. They have delighted in bringing back to the church leaders of professional and business life who have for years been only technical members of some ecclesiastical body, particularly of some church that has been cold and formal. The stress of the Moral Rearmament group is on the absolutes—absolute purity, absolute honesty, and so on—and on confession of sin, not only to God but also to one another. In the vein of perfectionism they take a Christian ideal and teach it as completely realizable in this life, and from this there generally follows the corollary that unless it is completely realized it is not the true article at all. One is not honest, for example, unless his honesty covers scrupulously the most minute detail. Again they take a Christian practice, that of confession of sin, and lift it out of context. For while all Christians will recognize that any wrong done against any man should be confessed to that man as well as to God, the Moral Rearmament group generally expects that sin to be publicly as well as privately acknowledged, and that repeatedly.

Dangers of Perfectionism

Even from such a brief sketch as the preceding, some of the chief dangers of perfectionism are not hard to discern. Morally the deepest of these dangers is just what Wesley foresaw, the tendency to pride.

No one can continually emphasize the need of being perfect and the possibility of attaining perfection without tending to develop the assurance, "This blessing is mine; I have it." And no one, threatened by the pitfalls that beset our human nature, can long rejoice in an attainment without tending to sit in judgment on those who have not attained and without feeling himself lifted up above his fellows. Perhaps it was this sequence of tendencies, more than anything else, that made John Wesley shrink from ever claiming the perfect state for himself, even when that state was defined as perfection in love. Pride is certainly among the deadliest of sins. Jesus spoke more of humility than of any other virtue. It would be idle indeed if one could be freed completely from the power of all the grosser instincts only to find himself enmeshed in the net of haughtiness.

Anyone who has come to know those who think themselves to have attained, will appreciate the boredom they can produce in the religious life of a small, cohesive neighborhood. One of our pioneers in co-operative enterprises between various denominations, a man of inimitable personality, used to tell the story of his most grievous trial at the hands of a perfectionist. While conducting a meeting in an overgrown town, his efforts were constantly stymied by a woman who was sure she had not committed a sin in twenty years. At each service she managed to proclaim her perfect sanctification, and she always left the impression that there was no salvation for anyone who had not shared her experience. One night when the preacher felt he had stood all he could from her, she started down the aisle in the midst of the sermon, shouting to high heaven of her triumphant state. "I've been made so perfect," she cried as she waved her hands aloft, "that if I just had one more feather in my wings I could fly away to heaven." Only one who knew the dynamic little minister well and understood his rare combination of wit and reverence could appreciate his response. He stopped his sermon, folded his hands over his breast, closed his eyes and prayed, "O Lord, send her that feather, and let her go!"

Recording such an incident by itself would, of course, be to caricature the doctrine of perfectionism. Nevertheless there are many braggarts, not so loud or so unruly, whom the average community, fed up with their ambitious claims, would be glad to "let go." They can be found, to be sure, not alone in the company of perfectionist sects, but in many an orthodox church. They may give lip service to the doctrine that they are sinners, but if anyone points to some particular wrong, they deny it vehemently. Often their pride manifests itself in their passion for ruling others, either in their own families or their own neighborhood or their own church. Anyone who combines pride with selfishness can easily give a religious tone to any of his own whims. He is not insisting on having his own way, for he and he alone knows God's way. The father who is sure of the occupation his son ought to follow, the mother who is certain that all her children as they marry should settle down in the community where she lives, the church officer who can quote Scripture to prevent anything being done differently from the way he likes—these all may actually be thinking of themselves as perfect in knowledge rather than in love.

Again, perfectionism leads often to moralism as the sum and substance of the good life. Now it is quite true that religion which is a matter of form and ceremony chiefly and which is devoid of the ethical emphasis of the prophets and Jesus, is no kin to the Christian faith. But to substitute a satisfaction in "being good" for the worship of God, as many have done, is also a gross misrepresentation of our faith. Inevitably it leads to legalism. If you follow this prescription, that set of rules, you will attain to godliness. Often the devotee of holiness will lay down the law that a convert must pray so many times a day or at such hours. Or, with more mystical tendencies, a member of MRA may urge that if you take paper and pencil and sit down before the Lord in meditation for half an hour and then write down the first thing that comes to mind, this will be what God means for you to do. Now all such prescriptions hold the element of truth that there is in the legalistic approach. It is indeed well to have hours of prayer, and meditation before God is one of the finest of the forms of prayer. But the tendency, in seeking a ready absolute, is to lay down the requirements so that the result may be assured. Quite as inevitably too the temptation grows to be satisfied with negatives in morality. If one never takes a drink or has never been arrested, that it is which makes him essentially better than his fellows. The perfectionist, in his careful prescription of detailed rules for living, often becomes so anxious that he really tries to take matters out of the control of the Holy Spirit. In effect he does not trust the Spirit to do his work in the souls of men. The natural wellspring of truth and virtue, of which Jesus spoke to the woman at Sychar's well (John 4), gets clogged in such an emphasis, and the positive goodness of great souls receives but scanty attention.

Perfectionism leads also to the oversimplifying of life's problems. If the family will just follow a budget, if the overworked individual will only adhere absolutely to a schedule, everything will work out all right. This particular temptation can always be met satisfactorily if one will follow certain prescribed rules; that particular sin will be easily overcome if attacked in a certain way. Problems of corporate living too come in for abuse at the hands of those who have the perfect answer. In the tremendous issue of war and peace that confronts the world today, both pacifism and militarism often loom as perfectionist programs. It is easy to feel that if every Christian would only refuse to fight that would be the end of conflict. On the other hand, one often hears in these days of superheated armament races some smug statement to the effect, "If we just maintain an air force superior to that of any other nation, or if we develop a bomb so powerful that no one will have the temerity to attack us, all will be well." Though there are capable Christians who believe in the pacifist procedure, just as there are those who believe in militarism as a necessity, either of these schemes can become a perfectionist snare when taken as the one simple remedy for all our ills.

There are subtle theological fallacies with which perfectionism easily allies itself. Certain doctrines, such as the verbal inspiration of the Bible or the virgin birth of Jesus or the laying on of hands, may be stressed out of all proportion. Perfectionism is a ready partner to fundamentalism. Or the perfectionist gets absorbed in the question of the Lord's return and how soon the judgment and the reward of the faithful will take place, and his hope becomes grounded in some form of millenarianism. He may become fascinated by the spiritual gifts and graces, especially such a showy one as "speaking in tongues," and he tends to honor the gift for its own sake without considering what good it will do. He gets so engrossed in his feeling that the Church has missed some important doctrine that he becomes schismatic. He feels that light and darkness are trying to dwell together in the Church. He is constantly calling on his friends to come out from the corruption, to be separate from the error that he feels has engulfed the body of Christendom. He seeks to redeem those who are outside the pale of any religious influence, not so much by the slow and careful means of cultivation which the church has generally employed, but by a quick revivalism which becomes a ready substitute for genuine evangelism. He has forgotten that fellowship among believers is one of the subjects of Christ's most elaborate recorded prayer (John 17). He would be willing to break an existing fellowship to set up a distinctive group of those who underscore the one little belief that he finds most important. Men often live by small pet hobbies. Sects germinate in the soil that is over-fertilized for some one crop. Even in this day of great union efforts, the Church universal suffers at the hands of the church particular. The revival of the sects parallels the ecumenical movement.

Now in all fairness to the perfectionist it must be pointed out that these are only tendencies. He does not *necessarily* align himself with any of the cults and isms that have been suggested. But it may also be noted that there is a very strong pull in that direction. It is extremely difficult to relate perfectionism to the entire body of Christian faith and practice. It is much easier to support it at the point of some one or two specialties. And so the perfectionist *tends* to latch on to some rule or essential belief or cure-all.

The history of perfectionism in dealing with the grosser sins of the flesh has been most interesting. Some perfectionists have become so scrupulously upright in all their dealings that they have avoided, wherever possible, even the commonest contacts of life lest they be defiled. Others have pitched headlong into the flotsam of the social order, believing that nothing could cause them to lose their salvation. This latter variety has produced some of the most objectionable of the sects.[4]

Meeting the Perfectionists

The Church may either make or break itself by its attitude toward relatively small schismatic groups or toward the presence of some extreme form of teaching in its own membership. If that attitude is one of indifference or disdain, the evil that is in the schism tends to grow

[4] See, for example, the findings of an examination into a morally loose perfectionist group as told by S. H. Holbrook in the article entitled "When Sex Flourished in Oneida," *American Mercury*, LXX (February, 1950), 202-8.

in despite. If the attitude is one of benevolent tolerance, the evil often spreads underground for a long time and then suddenly erupts at some crisis in the Church's life. If harsh, unyielding discipline is employed, the sectarian spirit sometimes cowers like a whipped dog for a while, only to turn in revengeful anger when its opportunity finally comes.

In dealing with perfectionism, in the form of either some sect or some tendency within the body of the regular Church, sympathy and understanding ought to be foremost. There is almost certainly a need that has brought the new emphasis into the picture, out of focus though it may be—a need of which someone has become aware while the leaders of the church were asleep. In the case of perfectionism, especially of the variety that stresses the showier spiritual gifts, this need may be for more of an emotional outlet. Through the centuries the Church tends to return ever and anon to a formalism by which the more ardent expressions of feeling are squelched. To find some good way to let emotion manifest itself wholesomely may be to make use of the truth that there is in the error which is being perpetrated. There ought to be too in all dealing with perfectionist movements an appreciation of the high ideals and moral challenge that are in the best of them. And while, in meeting these challenges, as in giving freer rein to emotion, the Church may well seek to educate its membership against extremes, it needs to admit, not grudgingly but willingly, the worthwhileness that led to the extreme.

Further than this. While modern perfectionist groups have tended to get away from John Wesley's emphasis on perfection in love and have oftener stressed perfection in moral character, even here the Church ought to be readier than it is to allow for the rich possibilities in Christian living. It is simply true that we have often been content with the lower levels of Christian experience. The overcoming of sin goes on at a slower pace than is needed. Indeed believers are often encouraged to be satisfied with slight progress, for the urgency of kingdom-living deserts the Church for long periods. "Professor," interrupted the seminary student whose conscience had been stung by the lecture on the Christian life, "sanctification is a slow growth, isn't it?"

"Yes," shot back the aroused professor who knew his student well, "but it doesn't need to be as all-fired slow as you are making it!"

The process of the Christian life is not necessarily even. It has its climactic moments, and in one such the soul that is united with Christ may really experience some mountaintop of transfiguration where he can meet and have done with a particular sin once for all. Some fairly good people toy with a bad habit for years, though they have had resources of grace at their command to settle it in short order. Many a man who does not actually yield to a besetting temptation fights it over and over again along the very edge of some moral precipice when he could have struck away from the dizzy spot altogether. A revival of religion may actually include complete deliverance of some person or some community from a specific evil way of life. The perfectionist has often done the Church a real favor by calling it back to face this possibility. To recognize such service from whatever source it comes and to show gratitude for it is the part of humility.

The error of the perfectionist does not lie in his arousal of the souls of men to greater faith and effort. The Church is always in need of the injunction, "Take time to be holy." The error of the perfectionist lies rather in his too easy transfer of a sense of triumph and joy in one moral victory to the entire experience with sin. He grossly over-simplifies that transfer. He is inclined to forget the fearful odds there are in our world against righteousness. He is apt to lack at the same point where so much of the theology of our day is lacking: in realizing that the cross of Christ must always be supplemented by the believer's cross if victory is to be won at any point. There is abroad in our world a revived tendency to worship Calvary. There is a fine new recognition that the cross of Christ does for men what they cannot do for themselves. But the Church dare not forget that it was Jesus himself who reminded his disciples at the very time he spoke of his approaching passion, "If any man would come after me, let him deny himself and take up his cross daily and follow me" (Luke 9:23). In this great saying it is evident that the taking of the cross is no mere burden-bearing; it is the denial of the self. Nor does this mean the denying oneself of something, such as drinking or smoking or going to the movies or buying a television set; it is the very renouncing of one's own independent running of his own life. It is as truly the death of self-centeredness as the cross of Christ was a death. And apparently Jesus did not anticipate this death of the believer occurring all at once. He said that his followers must take up their cross "daily." What this suggests is that the death to sin is not completed in one experience; the giving up of oneself to the Lord is done by degrees and done every day.

It may indeed be ideal that conversion should change the whole nature at once—all its appetites and powers. And conversion does bring real repentance and commitment. But what happens, in most lives at least, is that we are changed in this part of our nature today and in that tomorrow. One experience of Christ leads us to take the cross of Christian living in our home. It is apt to be some time after that before we see the relevance of the cross to our business or profession, to our politics, to our relations with our social set; and then we are apt to see it only partially. The gradual transformations of our lives in their varied relationships are all the outgrowth of our first commitment of ourselves to Christ as Lord. But to claim that these transformations are readily attained is not only to run the moral dangers we have discussed; it is to minimize how deep the doctrine of the cross must go in life. The worldliness around us fights against the Christian at every turn. Friends, family, social groups, government, even the Church may make it nearly impossible for one to give himself up in a particular area of life. Even the soul that is consecrated must needs go again and again through some Gethsemane of torture before he is willing to pay the price, especially in his social relations. The perfectionist is often a crass individualist. It is his private sin he believes Christ has removed. The Church in meeting him must emphasize the family nature of the religious experience and the social application of all virtue and vice. One may shout for joy over deliverance from some peccadillo; one can find glory in the highest possibilities of life on this earth only by "counting the cost" in a godless society. To think of sanctification as a growth in grace is not to deny its reality, but to affirm the fury of its battle "where cross the crowded ways of life." It is to trace patiently the gradual work of the Holy Spirit in committed lives, an ever-broadening work that leads at last, by the mercy of God, to perfect peace.

That word "perfect" has bothered many people. Does not Jesus himself command his disciples to attain perfection (Matt. 5:48)? It should be pointed out that the Greek word for "perfect"—*teleios*—does not generally refer to moral sinlessness. In the Septuagint, the Greek version of the Old Testament, this word often translates Hebrew words that denote "end" or "purpose." (See, for example, Luke 1:45.) Such a significance is frequent in the New Testament use of the term. Jesus must "finish his course"—complete or perfect it (Luke 13:32). He must accomplish his Father's work (John 4:34; 5:36; 17:4; 19:28). This meaning of "complete" or "rounded out" for the word translated "perfect" is especially seen in the Epistle to the Hebrews where it is used of Jesus completing his task (2:10; 5:9), of the law being brought to its completion in the gospel (7:11), and of Christians finding the completion of their purpose in life (11:40; 12:23). Paul sometimes uses the word thus, especially in his thought of love (Rom. 12:2; I Cor. 13:10; Col. 3:14). So also does John (I John 2:5; 4:12). More often Paul employs it to denote the freedom from childishness that Christians ought to attain—their "maturity" in Christ, as the Revised Standard Version generally translates it (I Cor. 2:6; 14:20; Eph. 4:13; Phil. 3:15; Col. 1:28; 4:12). This is the sense too in other New Testament passages (Heb. 5:14; 6:1; Jas. 1:4, 25; 2:22; 3:2). But Paul denies that he has attained full perfection of God's purpose in him (Phil. 3:12), and both he and the author of Hebrews speak of the old order's failure to bring the purpose of life to completion and of perfection or maturity being wrought only by Christ (II Cor. 12:9; Heb. 7:11; 9:9; 10:1, 14; 12:2). It is noteworthy that in Matthew 5:48 Jesus' injunction, "You therefore, must be perfect, as your heavenly Father is perfect," has this same note of becoming mature in the purpose of God. Noteworthy also is the fact that Luke, in the parallel passage (6:36), substitutes an entirely different phrase, "Be merciful, even as your Father is merciful." Hence, to pin the word of Jesus down to a meaning of moral sinlessness would certainly be to base a strict dogma on a very free saying.

It is quite generally recognized that John deals in absolutes, especially that he paints absolute contrasts. It is in this light that his positive statement in I John 3:9 must be understood: "No one born of God commits sin; for God's nature abides in him, and he cannot sin because he is born of God" (cf. v. 6). It is not that such a statement pictures an ideal which John knows cannot be realized. Rather, it pictures absolute states. It holds them up to the clear light that men may actually see them. As absolute states they are real. Righteousness and sin are opposites. The essence of the Christian life, God's "nature" abiding in the heart, as John puts it, is a different sort of nature altogether from that of worldliness. But this nature is only what the King James Version called God's "seed"; it is not a completed plant. Growth is still anticipated in John's picture, absolute though his contrasts are. That John actually anticipates in this growth some remaining experience with sin is evident from his injunction to pray for the "brother" who is committing sin that is not "mortal" (I John 5:16). In this growth John also sees the attaining of the complete purpose for the Christian's life. This is the *telos*, the end or the goal, toward which the Spirit of God leads his followers. He most often leads them toward it, not by quick jumps or long strides, but by the painful and yet triumphant road of the cross. It is only by an ever-steadier yielding to that leading that we may come at last to the full experience of that "holiness without which no man shall see the Lord."

Suggestions for Further Study

1. Try each day for several weeks setting aside some prayer time simply for meditation and quiet waiting before God. Note whether new drives to action or greater experience of freedom develop.

2. Attend one or more meetings of some holiness sect; make a careful estimate of the good and bad elements in the procedure. Try also to get acquainted with the persons most prominent in leadership and with the most faithful followers. See if you can estimate the amount of reality and of make-believe in their lives.

Selected Bibliography

Boobyer, G. H. "New Testament Perfectionism and Christian Citizenship," *Hibbert Journal*, LI (1952-53), 143-48.

Brown, J. S. "Social Class, Intermarriage, and Church Membership in a Kentucky Community," *American Journal of Sociology*, LVII (1951-52), 232-42.

Flew, Robert N. *The Idea of Perfection in Christian Theology*. London: Oxford University Press, 1934.

Foss, Martin. *The Idea of Perfection in the Western World*. Princeton: Princeton University Press, 1946.

Green, John B. *John Wesley and William Law*. London: The Epworth Press, 1945.

Holbrook, S. H. "When Sex Flourished in Oneida," *American Mercury*, LXX (1950), 202-8.

Johnson, George A. "From Seeker to Finder," *Church History*, XVII (1948), 299-315.

Law, William. *A Serious Call to a Devout and Holy Life*. Philadelphia: Westminster Press, 1948.

Lindström, Harold G. A. *Wesley and Sanctification*. Stockholm: Nya Bokförlags Aktiebolaget, 1946.

Maynard, Theodore. "The Noble Fallacy." *Catholic World*, CLXXVII (1953), 352-57.

Pauly, Herta. "The Bond of Perfectness." *Review of Religion*, XI (1946-47), 261-72.

Peters, John L. *Christian Perfection and American Methodism*. Nashville: Abingdon Press, 1956.

Sangster, W. E. "The Church's One Privation," *Religion in Life*, XVIII (1948-49), 493-502.

————. *The Path of Perfection*. New York and Nashville: Abingdon-Cokesbury Press, 1943.

————. *The Pure in Heart*. Nashville: Abingdon Press, 1954.

Warfield, Benjamin B. *Perfectionism*. New York: Oxford University Press, 1932.

Wesley, John. *Journal*. Abridged by Nehemiah Curnock. New York: Philosophical Library, Inc., 1951.

————. "A Plain Account of Perfection," in his *Works*, VI, 483-531. New York: B. Waugh and T. Mason, 1835.

Williamson, Geoffrey. *Inside Buchmanism*. London: C. A. Watts & Co., 1954.

PART THREE

ISMS BOTH BIBLICAL AND CULTURAL

JUDAISM

JUDAISM HAS BEEN DEFINED IN A VARIETY OF WAYS: (1) AS THE RE-
ligious beliefs and practices of the Jews; (2) as the composite of the
thoughts, sentiments, and efforts of the Jewish people; and (3) as a
civilization or way of life. The word "Jew" is ultimately derived from
the word "Judah." To define the word "Jew" in present-day society is
rather difficult. Some people think of a Jew as one who belongs to a
particular racial group. However, this is not strictly accurate. Biology has
no doubt played a part in the creation of the Jewish people. Yet, throughout the centuries there have been converts to Judaism and intermarriage
between Jews and Gentiles. Some say a Jew is a member of a particular
nation or nationality. The word "nationality" is sometimes used to refer
to a nation in a *cultural* rather than in a political sense. Still others say a
Jew is one who holds particular religious beliefs and practices. There
is truth in all of these definitions. In this unit we shall be thinking
of Judaism primarily in religious terms.

It may seem strange to some to find Judaism included in such a
volume as this. Judaism is a world religion and is often included in
courses on comparative religions. Furthermore, Christianity began as
a movement within Judaism. It is included here for two reasons. First,
the Church does face the Synagogue in many American communities.
Jews and Christians go to school together, work together, play together,
and occasionally worship together. We desperately need to understand
each other and to carry on a conversation about the deep meanings of
our faith and life. Second, the Christian church is called upon to acknowledge its share in the responsibility for anti-Semitism and to bring
forth fruits that will help to abolish it.

Literary Sources of Historic Judaism[1]

Although very few scholars ever really master the chief literary
sources of Judaism, anyone who studies Judaism at all should know

[1] Some of these sources in full and others in part are available in English translation.

what they are and something of their significance. The Hebrew Scriptures, which are known to the Christian as the Old Testament, are the basic point of reference for studying the later developments of Judaism. This is especially true of the Torah or Pentateuch. Though the Old Testament was in part produced by members of other tribes, it was in large measure the product of Jewish leaders. Furthermore, under God the literature which composes our present Old Testament was first canonized by the Jews in the process of history. Jews have through the centuries played a significant role in translating and interpreting the Old Testament. For example, the Septuagint, the chief translation of the Hebrew Scriptures into Greek, throws light on Alexandrian Jewish scholarship and theology from the third to the first century B.C. The Targums are a kind of combination translation and interpretation of the Hebrew Scriptures in Aramaic. In pre-Christian centuries many Jews began to speak Aramaic, and Aramaic Targums came to be made orally in the synagogue services in conjunction with the reading of the Hebrew Scriptures. Only gradually did Targums become fixed and put into writing. Targum-making continued for centuries into the Christian Era.

The Apocrypha are also a Jewish product and are valuable for studying the so-called "intertestamental period." The books which we refer to as apocryphal were included in the Septuagint and are included in the canons of the Greek Orthodox Church and the Roman Catholic Church.[2] Traditional Jews and Protestants have not accepted these books and parts of books as canonical.

The Pseudepigrapha are for the most part pre-Christian Jewish religious works which form no part of the Jewish or Christian canons. These books are useful in studying Judaism and the background of Christianity. Some of them and some of the Apocrypha are being brought into prominence today in relation to the Dead Sea Scrolls.

The Dead Sea Scrolls themselves are excellent sources for studying Judaism and the background of Christianity in and about the New Testament period. In the judgment of many able men the inhabitants of Khirbet Qumran, who placed the scrolls in the caves, were the Jewish sect known as Essenes.

[2] The status of the Apocrypha in the Greek Church is ambiguous.

The writings of Flavius Josephus (ca. A.D. 37—ca. A.D. 100) may be considered sources for studying the history of Judaism and the Jewish people. These writings include his *Jewish War, Antiquities, Vita,* and *Contra Apionem.*

The Mishnah is one of the greatest sources of Judaism. The Mishnah par excellence is the collection of Jewish *Halakoth* (rules) made by Judah Hanasi in the third century A.D., the culmination of an oral interpretation of the law which had developed into a written tradition. The Mishnah is authoritative in traditional Judaism.

The Tosephta is a supplement to the Mishnah. It is composed of the teachings and traditions of the Jewish scholars known as the Tannaim.

Just as the Jews had felt a need to have the biblical law interpreted, as found in the Mishnah, so the time came when it was felt the Mishnah itself should be interpreted. This is the basis of the origin of the two Talmuds, the Palestinian and the Babylonian. The Palestinian was brought to an end about A.D. 400 and the Babylonian was completed A.D. 500. In each case the Talmud is composed of the text of the Mishnah plus a commentary on the Mishnah known as the Gemara. The Palestinian is the shorter of the two Talmuds and is incomplete. It contains 750,000 words and is written in Hebrew and Western Aramaic. The Babylonian contains 2,500,000 words and is written in Eastern Aramaic and Hebrew. To Orthodox Jews the Talmud has divine authority.

Whereas the composers of the Mishnah and the Talmud approached the law to give legal and authoritative teachings, the formers of the Midrashim (searchings) sought to penetrate deeply into the *spirit* of the Scriptures. The purpose of Midrash Halakah is to treat more fully a biblical law; the purpose of Midrash Haggada is to warn and edify. The Midrashim are more frequently of the latter type. Midrashic exegesis is homiletical or devotional interpretation. The most creative period of Midrashic activity was the third and fourth centuries A.D. in Palestine, but Midrashic activity continued to the eleventh century.

In Judaism as well as in other religions there have been many types of movements with varied emphases. The cabalistic movement laid emphasis upon mysticism. The Zohar (splendor) is the chief collection of Jewish mysticism. Its authorship is ascribed to Simeon ben Yohai (second century A.D.), who was famous for his mystical inclinations. It is probable that it is a collection of writings by many mystics, and it was issued in Spain in the thirteenth century.

Maimonides or Moses ben Maimon is considered the greatest Jewish philosopher and codifier of the Middle Ages. He was also a famous physician. He was born in Spain (1135) but did most of his work in Egypt. He both suffered at the hands of Moslems and was favored by them. Maimonides was author of several important works. His *Mishneh Torah* (copy of the law) is a codification of Talmudic knowledge together with "dogmatics, physics, metaphysics, ethics, and dietetics," and it is divided into fourteen books. Another of his most influential works is the *Guide of the Perplexed,* a philosophical defense of Judaism. Maimonides was influenced by Greek thought and sought to rationalize Judaism. His *Guide* was used by Arabic and Christian scholars. However, some of his teaching was opposed by his own people.

The *Shulhan Aruk* (prepared table) is the authoritative code of Orthodox Judaism. It was based on the *Turim* (rows) of Jacob ben Asher (1280-1340). Joseph Karo (1488-1575) was the author-compiler of the *Shulhan Aruk,* though it was later modified to conform to the practices of Ashkenazic as well as Sephardic Jews. This code covers the details of traditional Jewish life.

There are other books which may be classified as literary sources of Judaism, but the ones mentioned above are sufficient to indicate the types of materials which are usually placed in this category. It will be observed that the sources which are authoritative in traditional Judaism emphasize Torah (Law).

A Brief Outline of Jewish History

It is assumed that the reader is already well acquainted with the main facts in Jewish history. In the event he has not read an account of Jewish history written by a Jewish scholar, it is recommended that he do so as soon as possible. Many churchmen who have carefully studied church history as written by other churchmen, have never taken the time to read much of the same story written from a Jewish point of view. To say the least, it is a humbling procedure. The most that can be done here is to give a very brief synopsis of the Jewish story.

Jewish history is rooted in the history of Israel; Israel's history is rooted in Hebrew history; Hebrew history is rooted in Semitic history;

and Semitic history is rooted in the history of man. Jewish history may be divided into four periods. The first period is that of formative Judaism, extending from the Babylonian captivity (586 B.C.) to the end of the Patriarchate (A.D. 425). This was the period of the return from exile, the rebuilding of the temple and Jerusalem, the rise of the high priest and the scribe to places of great importance, the beginning of the reign of Law, the origin and growth of the synagogue, the struggle of the Maccabees against Syrian persecution, the turmoil of the Hasmonaean state, the rule of Rome, the events connected with Jesus, the formation of the New Testament, the rise of the Christian church, the rebellion of Bar Kochba, and the production of the Mishnah and Talmud.

The second period is that of the Diaspora, extending from the end of the Patriarchate (A.D. 425) to Columbus (A.D. 1492). This is the period of the Middle Ages. Among the notable events of the period were: the scattering of the Jews, the triumph of Christianity, the rise of Islam, the many literary and academic achievements of the Jews (including such things as the responsa, the work of the Masoretes, translations of and commentaries on the Hebrew Scriptures, the literary works of Ibn Ezra and Maimonides, the Zohar, and Kimchi's Hebrew grammar), the Crusades and the horrible persecution of the Jews on almost every hand, and the discovery of the New World. In spite of the intellectual, moral, and spiritual darkness in much of Europe and the persecutions suffered by the Jews during the Middle Ages, learning reached great heights among Jewish scholars, notably in Spain.

The period from Columbus (1492) to Napoleon (1815) was a transition period in Jewish history. Jews played a significant role in the Renaissance and Reformation by teaching Christian scholars, through scientific pursuits and through literary productions. The Jewish population as a whole in Poland was raised to a high intellectual level. Persecution of the Jews continued. Though the ghetto arose in the preceding period, its horrors continued in this period. As in former generations Judaism was torn by sectarianism within. The new world offered hope to some Jews. The first synagogue in the United States was established about 1654 in New York. The formulation of the American Constitution gave promise of a better day for the Jewish people.

The fourth period of history is the modern era, extending from Napoleon (1815) to the present. This period was ushered in by two revolutions, the one in the United States and the other in France; and world revolution in many forms is still going on. Among the many events and movements of significance for the Jews in the modern era, three stand out: the Reform movement, the Nazi persecutions, and Zionism. The Reform movement began in Germany. Moses Mendelssohn (eighteenth century) began to break down the mental ghetto of his fellow Jews by teaching them the German language, translating the Torah into German, publishing a magazine of general culture in Hebrew, and establishing a school where both traditional and nontraditional subjects were taught. Israel Jacobson of Westphalia (1768-1828) introduced changes in the synagogue ritual. When he moved to Berlin, he carried his reform with him. In Hamburg, Germany, the name "synagogue" was changed to "temple." Thus reform spread far and wide. Samuel Holdheim (1806-1860), rabbi of the Reform congregation in Berlin, was one of the most radical reformers. He placed emphasis upon man's intelligence rather than upon tradition. Of course there was strong reaction by the orthodox to the reform movement. At the other extremes from Holdheim was Samuel R. Hirsch (1808-1888), who emphasized the Torah revealed at Sinai. Through Hirsch many Jews were won back to orthodoxy. Between the extremes of the ultra-orthodox and the reform were such moderates as Zechariah Frankel.

Reform spread to England and the United States. As early as 1820 there were persons in this country who advocated reform. The most lasting impression on the Reform movement in America was made by Isaac M. Wise, who came to America in 1846. He was the founder of the organization which became the Union of American Hebrew Congregations and was also the founder and first president of Hebrew Union College in Cincinnati, Ohio. Conservative and Orthodox Jews also established their institutions. Today there are numerous kinds of Jewish institutions and organizations.

The Nazi persecution of the Jews could not have taken place if there had not been so much foundation laid for it in anti-Semitism and previous persecutions, for expressions of anti-Jewishness in the modern period are by no means confined to the Nazis.

Zionism did not originate in the twentieth century. Throughout the

138

centuries traditional Jews regarded Israel as being in exile (*Galuth*) and expressed the desire to return to the homeland. This hope was often expressed in relation to the Messiah, whose coming was expected to bring justice and peace to the world. Modern Zionism has been stimulated in large measure by the pressure of terror under which Jews have lived and died. Theodor Herzl may be regarded as the father of the modern movement, though he had predecessors. The trial in France of Captain Alfred Dreyfus was the immediate occasion for Herzl to seek a solution to the problem of Jewish persecution in Europe. In a pamphlet, *Der Judenstaat,* he proposed the re-establishment of a Jewish nation in Palestine, a proposal which met with both support and opposition. Herzl worked hard for the accomplishment of his goal, but died a disappointed man. The opposition to Zionism among the Jews themselves took a variety of forms.[3] Opposition was particularly strong among Reform Jews, Isaac M. Wise, for example. However, it should be remembered that there have been and are Zionists within the various branches of Judaism. Many Jews in the United States give aid to Israel, whether they classify themselves as political Zionists or not. New stimulus was given to the Zionist movement by the Balfour Declaration, a letter written by Arthur James Balfour, England's secretary of foreign affairs, on November 2, 1917.

At the conclusion of the First World War Britain was given the mandate over Palestine. The cornerstone of the Hebrew University was laid in Jerusalem on July 24, 1918, and the University was opened in 1925. It is estimated that Hitler and his anti-Semites were responsible for the death of six million Jews. Furthermore, before, during, and after the Second World War Jewish refugees were seeking a home. Russia and the Western nations received some of them, and Palestine was permitted to receive others. Yet many lost their lives because they had no refuge opened to them. In 1947 Britain placed the Palestine problem in the hands of the United Nations. Late in this same year the United Nations made a recommendation to divide Palestine into Jewish and Arab states, but made no provision for enforcing the recommendation. Britain was unwilling to enforce any plan which was not acceptable to both Jews and Arabs and announced that she would

[3] See Solomon Grayzel, *A History of the Jews* (Philadelphia: Jewish Publication Society of America, 1947), pp. 679-84.

give up the Mandate on May 15, 1948. The Arabs refused the partition. On May 14, 1948, Israel was proclaimed a republic. War between the Arab and Israel forces followed. On January 29, 1949, Great Britain granted *de facto* recognition to Israel, and *de jure* recognition by the United States was announced by President Truman on January 31, 1949. Israel was granted membership in the United Nations on May 11, 1949. To the best of my knowledge, many more Jews are supporting political Zionism today than formerly; yet it is still a hotly debated issue among both Jews and others. The Israel-Arab controversy is still at white heat, and both sides continue to suffer. It is not possible to give a critical evaluation of this controversy here. However, it should be recognized that this is a problem which ought to be heavily upon the consciences of the nations of the world which have through sins of both omission and commission contributed so largely to creating it.

Israel is faced with many internal problems: economic, social, educational, and religious. Zionists, while working together, are divided within Israel into several political parties with varying emphases and objectives. Most refugees have entered Israel with little or no means, and the Israelis receive heavy financial support from Jews in the United States. Jews from many varied cultural and social backgrounds have been precipitated into one small melting pot. This inevitably means a certain degree of conflict. The conflict between orthodoxy and secularism is vigorous. Can orthodoxy, which was wrought out at least in part in the ghettos of Europe, adapt itself in such a way as to be acceptable to the modern Israelis?

It is estimated that there are approximately twelve million Jews in the world at the present time. They are scattered throughout many nations, but the largest groups are found in the United States (5,200,-000), Russia (2,000,000), and Israel (1,550,958).

Jewish Religion Today

Judaism has been called a way of life. Certainly Jewish religion has been designed to deal with the whole of life. This way of life is rooted in the Talmud and the Old Testament (especially the Law of Moses). Since there are variations in certain particulars among Jewish groups, the description here is a generalization based on traditional practice which continues among the majority of observant Jews today.

The Jewish calendar is a key to understanding much in Judaism. The Sabbath is of paramount significance. It is rooted in God's activity as creator and deliverer. The Sabbath is considered a day of rest, joy, instruction, and worship in the home and the synagogue. The three major festivals are *Pesach* (Passover), *Shabuoth* (Pentecost or Feast of Weeks), and *Sukkoth* (Tabernacles). Passover first marked the early harvest, but this meaning is secondary to its historical significance in commemorating the exodus events. Pentecost was early celebrated as the festival of the first fruits, fifty days after the first omer of barley was brought. Later it was given the meaning of the season of the giving of the Law. Tabernacles is designated as the feast of ingathering and came to commemorate the journey through the desert. The two holy days of the Jewish calendar are *Rosh Hashana* (New Year) and *Yom Kippur* (Day of Atonement). These two days are closely related and the whole season marked by them is a time of repentance. New Year is Tishri 1 and the Day of Atonement is Tishri 10. Work is forbidden on any of the above mentioned festivals or holy days. The minor festivals are *Hanukkah* and *Purim*. The former is celebrated for eight days beginning with Kislev 25, which commemorates the victory of the Maccabees over the Syrians in 165 B.C. *Purim* (Adar 14) celebrates the deliverance of the Jews as set forth in the Book of Esther. There are other significant days in the Jewish calendar.

The most important institutions in Jewish religious life are the home, the synagogue, and the school. The home is of primary importance. Here prayers and benedictions are said, ceremonies enacted, and the dietary laws observed. Special features of the synagogue are the ark which contains copies of the Torah; the perpetual light, symbolizing the golden candlestick (Exod. 27:21); the *bema* or platform; and the galleries for women in some synagogues. Both daily and special services are held in the synagogue. The order of service includes benedictions, prayers of gratitude, selections from the Scripture, psalms and hymns, the *Shema* (Deut. 6:4-9; 11:13-21; Num. 15:37-41), the *Amidah*, supplications for Israel in exile and expression of hope for future redemption, the Messianic hymn *Alenu*, a special psalm for the day, and optional elements. Judaism has always emphasized education as well as worship. Jewish children are enrolled in many different kinds of schools. In addition to theological schools for the training of rabbis, there are four other institutions of higher learning in the United States. The four symbols of Judaism are also educational. These are the *tallith* (a garment with fringes which are reminders of the Law), the *Tefillin* (phylacteries worn on the left arm and forehead during prayer), the *mezuzah* (a parchment scroll containing Deut. 6:4-9 and Deut. 11:13-21 enclosed in a small box and attached to the doorpost), and the Covenant of Abraham (circumcision).

The rabbis are the chief religious leaders of the Jewish people. The word "rabbi" literally means "my master" but in ordinary usage "teacher." However, the rabbi does not usually lead the worship service. He is responsible for religious education; worship in the synagogue; the ceremonials connected with birth, confirmation, marriage, and death; and for pastoral counseling.

Observing Jews have emphasized *deed* rather than formal *creed*. Nevertheless, they have believed and do believe certain things about God, man, and salvation. To them God is one and the Father of all men. He is eternal, incorporeal, omnipresent, omnipotent, wise, just, long-suffering, merciful, transcendent, and immanent.

While no one outside of the Jewish faith is bound by the rules of Jewish ceremonial discipline, Judaism draws a distinction between the adherents of monotheistic faiths—including Christianity and Islam, which are recognized as each making a distinctive contribution to the realization of the Kingdom of God on earth—and nonmonotheistic faiths.[4]

Man is made in the image of God and is therefore a child and creature of God. The fatherhood of God involves the brotherhood of man. God's character is the point of reference for the development of man's character. Human conduct should be motivated by love for God. Ethics are to be applied to all the details of life. Ordinarily a Jew is expected to give between one-tenth and one-fifth of his income to philanthropic causes. Judaism recognizes the fact of sin but does not believe in original sin. The Day of Atonement recognizes the social as well as the personal nature of sin. God's love makes it possible for

---

[4] Louis Finkelstein, "The Jewish Religion: Its Beliefs and Practices," *The Jews: Their History, Culture, and Religion,* ed. Louis Finkelstein (New York: Harper & Bros., 1949), II, 1329. Used by permission.

men to escape some of the consequences of sin. Repentance is possible for men in most circumstances, but wicked rulers who have led nations into evil cannot repent.

If a man [not a wicked ruler] injures his neighbor, he will not be able to repent completely or win peace of mind until he has won the forgiveness of his neighbor. . . . Thus, for example, if a person has been guilty of theft, repentance requires not merely restitution of the stolen article and a determination never to steal again, but also a study of the motives that led to the theft, and an endeavor to prevent them from being effective in the future.[5]

The Code of Maimonides includes among its tenets the belief in the resurrection and human immortality. The doctrine of the future life helps to solve the problem of human suffering. Some Jews believe in a period of purification for some persons in the next life before they are admitted to all the joys of the blessed. At one time Jews believed in heaven and hell in a rather literal manner, but this is not generally true today. Many believe that the wicked person does not survive death; his disintegration is complete.

There are three major religious groupings among the Jews in America today: the Orthodox, the Conservatives, and the Reform. In addition to these major groups there is a movement known as Reconstructionism, which cuts across religious group lines and seeks to interpret and develop Judaism as an evolving religious civilization. The Orthodox are the strictest traditionalists in Judaism. They accept the Old Testament and the Talmudic traditions as authoritative. They are meticulous in the keeping of significant days of the calendar and in keeping the dietary laws. They use more Hebrew in their services than the other groups. They look forward to the return of the Jews to Palestine, to the rebuilding of the temple, to the reinstitution of sacrifice, and to the coming of the Davidic Messiah.

Reform Judaism[6] is the most liberal branch of the Jewish religion. It lays stress on the progressive nature of revelation and the use of human reason and science. It departs from orthodoxy in form at a

---

[5] *Ibid.*, pp. 1340, 1341.
[6] The Columbus Platform adopted at a meeting of the Central Conference of American Rabbis in 1937 may be found in Finkelstein, *op. cit.*, pp. 1344-47.

number of points. Reform Jews believe in a Messianic Age rather than a personal Messiah.

Basically, Conservative Judaism is traditional, but it has caught something of the spirit and practice of the Reform movement. It stands between the two extremes.

Both Orthodox and Conservative Judaism are much stronger numerically in the United States than Reform Judaism. The estimates on the exact number of observing Jews in this country vary all the way from two million to five million. In my judgment the three branches of Judaism have been drawn closer together in our time through the sufferings of European Jews under Nazism.

Besides the organized movements in Jewish religious life, there are independent Jewish thinkers who are pursuing their own lines of theological interest. Many Jews are concerned with Jesus as Jesus of Nazareth.

Contributions of Judaism to Christianity

The contributions of Jews to civilization are too numerous to catalogue here. The major contributions of Judaism to Christianity will serve as a token of the larger indebtedness. The first gift is the Old Testament. Actually Protestants get their canon of the Old Testament from Palestinian Judaism, and the Greek Orthodox and Roman Catholics get theirs from the Septuagint, the work of Alexandrian Jews. Origen, Jerome, and later Christian scholars learned Hebrew from Jewish teachers. The traditional Jewish scholars known as Masoretes standardized the Hebrew text and inserted vowel points about A.D. 700, making the learning of Hebrew easier for Christians as well as for Jews. A study of Jewish influence on the King James Version leads to the following conclusions: (1) that Jewish help was essential to the production of the King James and other versions of the Bible; (2) that the Jews of the Middle Ages kept Hebrew scholarship alive, so that there was something to be taught and someone to teach it at the time of the Renaissance and Reformation; (3) that such significant names of Christian scholars as Nicholas of Lyra, Reuchlin, and Münster are associated with the names of the great Jewish scholars, Rashi, Kimchi, and Elijah Levita; (4) that the works of Kimchi and Rashi have played an outstanding role in the production of the English Bible.

Jesus is the supreme contribution of Judaism to Christianity. Christians recognize that from the standpoint of Christianity this is only a part of the truth. We cannot account for Jesus simply on the basis of his Jewish heritage. At the same time we cannot account for him wholly apart from that heritage. According to the flesh, he was the son of David. In the context of his Jewish heritage he fulfilled his ministry. As far as the records go, he was never outside Palestine but twice. Though he was a member of no Jewish party, he had much in common with the Pharisees and the Essenes. Along with the religious leaders of his day he emphasized the Ten Commandments and the two great commandments. He spoke Aramaic, the language of the people of his time and place. His parables were built from the raw material of his own world.

Jesus' apostles and other early disciples were Jews. In fact, the earliest Christianity operated within the framework of Judaism. As far as we know, every book of the New Testament was written by a Jewish Christian, except the Gospel of Luke and The Acts.

Jews and Christians share certain basic theological affirmations and a strong concern for ethical behavior. A part of Jesus' uniqueness as a teacher lies in the fact that he lifted that which is central out of the mass of Jewish teaching and stamped it with a new integration. The kingdom of God and the fatherhood of God are cases in point. When a Christian reads what was said earlier in this unit about Jewish faith, he immediately recognizes a similarity to his own faith at points.

Judaism passed on to Christianity the linear view of history. The peoples about ancient Israel thought largely in terms of the cyclic view of life. In the Old Testament and in subsequent Judaism God marches on toward his purpose of consummating the kingdom.

The Christian church entered into the Jewish pattern of worship. Jesus and Paul, to say nothing of others, participated in the worship of both temple and synagogue. The following aspects of public worship were already employed in Judaism before Christianity began its distinctive career: prayers, benedictions, the amen, singing, Scripture reading, preaching, teaching, bowing, processing, baptizing, and eating a sacred meal.

Christianity inherited the family nature of religious life from Judaism. The covenant as interpreted in a large part of Christendom emphasizes both the personal and the corporate nature of Christianity. In fact, Christianity owes something of its concern for religious education to Judaism. Moses stands as the first educator in the Hebrew-Christian tradition, as well as the human deliverer of God's people. Through him God gave the Torah, which is basically "instruction." Thus he taught the people of the covenant how they should live in distinction from the people around them. Through prophet, priest, sage, scribe, and rabbi, the process of education was perpetuated. Jesus was known by his contemporaries as prophet, rabbi, and teacher. The New Testament contains both *kerygma* (preaching) and *didache* (teaching).

Differences Between Judaism and Christianity

Just as we have looked at some of the contributions of Judaism to Christianity with an attempt to state the case honestly, so now we attempt in the same spirit to examine some of the differences between the two faiths. In speaking of Christianity we are thinking primarily of main-line Protestant Christianity.

First of all, Judaism centers in a people; Christianity in a person. There is no attempt here to set God-centeredness over against Christ-centeredness. Nor is there any intention of supporting a unitarianism of the second person of the Trinity. Judaism sees the Jewish people as the elect community of the covenant. Even though a person born of Jewish parents does not share their religious beliefs and does not participate in the religious life of the home and synagogue, he may still be considered a Jew. However, having said this, we must recognize the fact that Judaism, as Christianity, lays great stress on the dignity and worth of the individual. Christianity takes its name from Jesus Christ. To Christians, Jesus is the Christ or Messiah (anointed one) for whom God's people looked. Therefore, they are called Christians and their religion Christianity. It is the religion of the Messiah. If one may coin a word, Christianity is "Messianity." In Protestant Christianity the person who never makes a profession of faith, is not usually thought of as a Christian. The words "Gentile" and "Christian" are not synonymous. The Christian church sees itself as the New Israel (Gal. 6:16; I Pet. 2:9), the people of the new covenant. In other words, there is a strong emphasis in Christianity upon the community, especially in the doctrine of the Church as the body of Christ. But Christ is the head of the body and our point of uniqueness. Christians see both continuity and discontinuity between Old Israel and New Israel. Many Jews still look forward to the coming of a personal Messiah but others look forward only to a Messianic Age. Though Christians differ among themselves in their interpretation of the second coming of Christ, there are certain parallels between that doctrine and Jewish messianism.

Judaism rejects the incarnation, vicarious atonement, and resurrection of Jesus Christ; the doctrine of the Trinity; and the New Testament as canonical. These are basic elements in historic Christianity. The Jewish concept of monotheism at the present time leaves no room for real incarnation and Trinity. Concerning the concept of mediation Morris N. Kertzer says:

Nor can Judaism accept the principle of vicarious atonement—the idea of salvation *through* Christ. It is our belief that every man is responsible for his own salvation. We believe that no one can serve as an intermediary between man and God, even in a symbolic sense. We approach God—each man after his own fashion—without a mediator.[7]

Jewish scholars study the New Testament and many Jewish people read the New Testament, but they do not accept it as a part of their Bible. Judaism does not claim that its postbiblical literature records the fulfillment of Old Testament promise; Christianity claims that the New Testament records such a fulfillment. While expressing his respect for the values in Judaism and without desiring to appear argumentative, H. H. Rowley has this to say on the subject:

While post-Biblical Judaism is completely unintelligible without the Old Testament, however, it is not the case that the Old Testament is unintelligible without post-Biblical Judaism, whereas it is claimed that the Old Testament is not fully intelligible without the New Testament. For if the New Testament looks back to the Old which preceded it, the Old looks forward to something which should follow it, and *that something is not post-Biblical Judaism*.

It [Judaism] has no Messiah to offer, no Suffering Servant that can gather to Himself the things predicated of the Servant in the fifty-third chapter of Isaiah, no new revelation of God to authorize the dispensing with sacrifice,

---

[7] "What Is a Jew?" *A Guide to the Religions of America*, ed. Leo Rosten (New York: Simon & Schuster, Inc., 1955), p. 67.

no vital sense of a mission to win the world for its God, no overmastering passion to communicate the Law of God to all men.[8]

In other words, the historical perspective of Judaism may be diagrammed as a triangle pointing to an expected Messiah or Messianic Age yet to come, whereas the historical perspective of Christianity may be diagrammed as an hourglass with Christ at the center. He has come to fulfill the promise; he will come to consummate it.

Judaism tends to be nationalistic; Christianity is missionary and universal. In the ancient world Israel existed as a united nation and later as two separate nations. Today a part of the Jewish people live as the republic of Israel in Palestine. Some Jews outside Palestine think in terms of nation or nationality when thinking of all Jewry. This concept, however, does not mean that these Jews are not loyal citizens of the countries in which they reside. Judaism has not always been nonmissionary. In fact, Isa. 40-66 and Jonah contain strong missionary emphases. Persecution is at least a part of the reason for the present-day position of Judaism on this matter. Jews still understand Judaism as having a mission in the world. Of course, genuine converts to Judaism have been and are welcomed by the Jewish community. Christianity is in no sense a nation or nationality. A denomination in a given country may be a national church, but not so in the United States. Main-line Protestantism has a strong sense of the ecumenical Church. Denominations are parts of one world-wide Church. The Christianity of the New Testament is missionary to the core, and historic Christianity has been missionary through the centuries.

Judaism emphasizes law; Christianity emphasizes faith. Law refers basically to the law of Moses. It sometimes refers to the way of Jewish life as based on the authoritative decisions of Jewish scholars. This does not mean that faith plays no part in Judaism; actually faith is the presupposition of Torah. Main-line Protestant Christianity emphasizes faith as commitment of oneself to Jesus Christ as Savior and Lord. Faith is used in a secondary sense to refer to creed or dogma. It is often said that Judaism emphasizes deed, not creed. The fact that Christianity emphasizes creed does not mean that deed is unimportant. The deed is thought to be bound up in genuine faith. We are created in Christ

[8] *The Unity of the Bible* (London: Carey Kingsgate Press, 1953), pp. 94, 118. Used by permission.

Jesus for good works (Eph. 2:10), but we are not justified by them. "For by grace you have been saved through faith; and this is not your own doing, it is the gift of God—not because of works, lest any man should boast" (Eph. 2:8-9). Furthermore, Christianity is not antinomian. Notwithstanding, Christianity needs to pay more attention to sociology, and Judaism to theology.[9]

Approaches to the Jew

An approach of many Christians as well as others to the Jew has been lamentably that of persecution. Such persecution did not originate, however, after the arrival of Christianity on the scene of history. The Old Testament and extrabiblical literature bear witness to the fact. The Book of Esther speaks clearly to the point. Early in the history of Christianity Christians were sometimes persecuted by Jews, but such persecution was extremely short-lived in comparison with the long centuries through which Jews have suffered at the hands of Christians. In no case would two wrongs make a right.

After the Council of Nicea (A.D. 325) the persecution of the Jews at the hands of Christians increased. In Spain at one time the Jews were ordered to become Roman Catholics or leave the country.[10] "The climax was reached around the year 700 when it was decreed that anyone found practicing a Jewish ceremony should be sold into slavery, and the children of the people under suspicion of being Jews should be taken from them to be brought up by the Christian clergy." [11]

The Crusades from Europe to the Holy Land were the occasion for persecution and murder of Jews. Inasmuch as the purpose of the Crusaders was to free the Holy Land from the Moslems, some got the idea that there was no point in going so far away from home to fight God's battles when the Jews were in their midst. Hence the cry, "Kill a Jew and save your soul!" When the army of the first Crusade captured Jerusalem, they drove the Jews there into the synagogue and then set fire to the building.[12] Such behavior, however, did not go altogether unchallenged. For example, at the time of the second Crusade Bernard

[9] Cf. James Parkes, *Judaism and Christianity* (Chicago: University of Chicago Press, 1948), p. 198.
[10] Grayzel, *op. cit.*, p. 303.
[11] *Ibid.*
[12] *Ibid.*, p. 342.

of Clairvaux denounced the monks and priests who urged the murder of the Jews. At the time of the third Crusade the Jews of York in England took refuge in the royal castle. After holding out against the mob for a while, they committed suicide as a group to prevent being butchered at the hands of their enemies. Sometimes during the period of darkness in Europe Jewish babies were baptized against the will of their parents, taken away from their parents, and brought up as Christians. Even the Talmud was put on trial, and much Jewish literature was burned. Upon occasion Jews were *forced* to listen to Christian sermons. False accusations were brought against the Jews. One was that Jews murdered Christian children to obtain blood for ritual purposes. Another was that Jews poisoned wells in Europe. Martin Luther was at first friendly toward the Jews but later turned against them. Whereas religious differences played a large role in the persecution of the Jews in the Middle Ages, economics and politics have played a larger role in modern times. Modern anti-Semitism reached its peak in Germany under Hitler. In addition to the many other forms of Nazi persecution, many Jews were exterminated in huge gas chambers and crematoriums. Though many Christians also suffered under Hitler and though many came to the aid of their Jewish neighbors at risk to themselves and their families, it would have been impossible for Hitler to have used the Jews as a scapegoat if the Christian church had really faced the problem of anti-Semitism effectively in previous years. At the present moment anti-Semitism is still a reality even in the United States.[13] The forged *Protocols of the Elders of Zion* still circulate.

Some of the sources of anti-Semitism and persecution of the Jews are: religious intolerance and the desire for uniformity, ignorance, jealousy, insecurity, the desire for a scapegoat, and the dislike of the unlike.

Jews have been called "Christ-killers" and have been accused of deicide. Passages from the New Testament have been used in such a way as to promote hatred for the Jews. In the Middle Ages there was a strong desire for religious and political uniformity. Nonconforming Christians sometimes suffered for the same reasons their Jewish neighbors suffered. As Christians we have an overwhelming responsibility to

[13] See Ralph L. Roy, *Apostles of Discord* (Boston: The Beacon Press, 1953), pp. 26-58.

interpret the crucifixion of Jesus and passages throughout the New Testament in accord with God's eternal love for all men. We must help our people to understand that only some Jews participated in bringing Jesus to trial and that the earliest Christians were Jews. But more profoundly we must see that from the standpoint of our own theology all men as sinners put Jesus to death. It is the nature of sin to put to death the best that God himself can do. It was not Paul's desire to stir up trouble for his Jewish brethren; he loved them more than life (Rom. 9:1-3). To seek to force anyone to accept the Christian faith is as foreign to the New Testament as anything can possibly be.

Prejudice thrives on ignorance. Unfortunately many Christians do not know their Jewish neighbors. It has been my privilege to number among my warm personal friends Jewish neighbors, businessmen, professors, and rabbis. My contacts with these friends have greatly enriched my appreciation for the Jewish people. Christian leaders have the opportunity of helping their people to know their Jewish neighbors and the contributions of Judaism to Christianity.

Often people dislike the unlike. This is closely related to the desire for uniformity. No doubt the elements in Jewish separatism have had a part in stimulating anti-Jewishness.

Yet none of these sources of anti-Semitism and persecution really gets at the heart of the matter. Hostility to the Jew arises out of the deep cleavage in the human will. The root of hostility toward the Jew is also the root of hostility toward the Christian, for such hostility is a hatred of or alienation from God which expresses itself especially in tense situations. Men are not necessarily conscious of hating God, just as they may not be conscious of hating themselves at the same time. One cannot love God and hate his neighbor (cf. Matt. 22:34-40; I John 4:20). The gospel of reconciliation is the ultimate answer to the problem.

A second approach of Christians to Jews is that of co-operation. Through the centuries Christian and Jewish biblical scholars have worked together. Today such co-operation has reached an all-time high. Too, there have been numerous occasions of co-operation along other lines between Christians and Jews, but a more forceful accent is being made at this point in our own time. Both Christians and Jews are becoming aware of their need to know each other better. The devastating consequences of anti-Semitism have shaken the Christian conscience of the world and show the need for overcoming such barbarism. All deeply religious groups sense the threat of secularist materialism to our very existence.

The movement for co-operation has not been undertaken without misgivings on the part of both Christians and Jews. Some Jews are afraid of the evangelistic intent of the Christians, while some Christians are afraid of compromising their evangelical convictions. Nevertheless, as a general policy it is understood that there is to be required no compromise of the distinctiveness of any group which participates in the program.

Organized co-operation on a big scale began in 1923 when the Federal Council of the Churches of Christ in America set up a Committee on Good Will between Christians and Jews. On the basis of the work done by this Committee the National Conference of Christians and Jews was launched in 1928. Chief Justice Charles Evans Hughes drafted the Constitution and bylaws and gave the Conference its name. He, Newton D. Baker, S. Parkes Cadman, Carlton J. H. Hayes, and Roger Williams Straus founded the Conference. This is a movement of co-operation among Protestants, Catholics, and Jews. Its purpose is "To promote justice, amity, understanding and co-operation among Protestants, Catholics, and Jews, to analyze, moderate and finally to eliminate intergroup prejudices." Its program is basically educational. Most people are acquainted with the annual Brotherhood Week sponsored by the Conference. Somewhat similar movements have been launched in Great Britain, Canada, Australia, Switzerland, France, Italy, Hawaii, and perhaps elsewhere. Furthermore, International Conferences have been held. World Brotherhood has its address at the Centre International, Geneva, Switzerland.

Co-operation between Christians and Jews is by no means confined to the activities sponsored by such organizations. Individual religious leaders and particular groups often undertake programs of their own.

A third approach of Christians to Jews is that of missions or evangelism. The approach of co-operation and the missionary approach are not mutually exclusive. In thinking about the missionary approach, the place to begin is with the New Testament. Jesus was a Jew and his earliest followers were Jews. He called men to be his disciples and sent them forth to do his bidding. He had a mission to his own people (John

1:11) as well as to the world (John 1:29; 3:16). The world mission of his disciples is emphasized in the Gospels. We read in Acts 1:8, "But you shall receive power when the Holy Spirit has come upon you; and you shall be my witnesses in Jerusalem and in all *Judea* and Samaria and to the end of the earth." [14] In Peter's sermon at Pentecost among the forms of address used are: "Men of Judea and all who dwell in Jerusalem" (Acts 2:14) and "Men of Israel" (Acts 2:22). Paul was a Jew who became a Christian, and as a Christian he often preached the gospel to his Jewish brethren. Peter had a special mission to the Jews. According to Paul the gospel is for Jew and Gentile alike: "There is neither Jew nor Greek, there is neither slave nor free, there is neither male nor female; for you are all one in Christ Jesus" (Gal. 3:28). According to the Letter to the Romans, Gentile and Jew alike are sinners standing in the need of God's salvation through Jesus Christ. Like his Master, Paul loved his Jewish brethren deeply, and he grieved that so many of them had not accepted Jesus Christ: "For I could wish that I myself were accursed and cut off from Christ for the sake of my brethren, my kinsmen by race" (Rom. 9:3; cf. Luke 19:41-44). God has not rejected his people as Paul makes clear in the doctrine of the remnant (Rom. 11:1-6). Though the Jews as a whole have not accepted Christ, the time will come in God's purpose when Old Israel and New Israel will be *one* Israel (Rom. 11:25-26). As long as they stand apart, the full purpose of God for neither of them is complete.

Though many Christians through the years have dragged the name Christian in the dust by unchristian methods of evangelism, Christianity is a missionary religion to the core. To exclude the Jew from the Christian witness would be a type of discrimination that would ultimately undermine the whole witness of the Church. Some Jewish leaders recognize the fundamental missionary nature of Christianity. Here is the statement of one Jewish rabbi:

Since Christianity is a missionary religion, you have not only a right, but also a duty to include the Jews in your evangelistic program. The only test of the ethics of this type of endeavor is sincerity. The Talmudic rabbi said, "God desires the heart."

As a Jew I can only admire your missionary zeal, which is a direct in-

[14] Italics mine.

heritance from the Pharisees whose moral teachings I try to perpetuate. I regret that historic reasons have prompted my people to give up our missionary efforts.

It goes without saying that all missionary work should be conducted on a high level. In that case, it should not lead to friction between Jews and Christians.

Missionary work among Jews is likely to serve as a challenge to us and it may drive us not only to intensify our efforts to save the Jew for Judaism, but also to carry our faith to the gentile world. A number of my colleagues share this view.[15]

It should be recognized also that there have been and are converts to Judaism. Though Judaism is not missionary in the usual sense of the term, it is because Judaism gives a witness that there are converts to Judaism.

Where genuine friendship reigns between Christian and Jewish neighbors, a conversation at the deepest religious and theological level can be carried on in freedom. This I know from personal experience.

One of the reports received by the World Council of Churches in 1948 undergirds the missionary approach to the Jews.[16] In fact *The Church and the Jewish People*[17] is the volume which was produced in response to a recommendation of this report. The missionary approach to the Jew is included in the program of the International Missionary Council, the National Council of Churches of Christ in America, and particular denominations. These organizations are opposed to all approaches to the Jew which are unworthy of the name Christian. Some of the methods being used in evangelization of the Jews may be found in Hoffman's *What Now for the Jews*, and *The Christian Church and the Jewish People* (see bibliography).

David N. Freedman, professor of Hebrew and Old Testament literature in Western Theological Seminary in Pittsburgh, has written a most

[15] As quoted in Conrad Hoffman, Jr., *What Now for the Jews?* (New York: Friendship Press, 1948), p. 59. Cf. W. W. Simpson, "Co-operation Between Christians and Jews," *The Church and the Jewish People*, ed. Göte Hendequist (London: Edinburgh House Press, 1954), p. 124. Used by permission of Friendship Press, Inc.

[16] "The Christian Approach to the Jews," *The First Assembly of the World Council of Churches*, ed. W. A. Visser 't Hooft ("Man's Disorder and God's Design"; New York: Harper & Bros., 1949), pp. 160-64.

[17] Göte Hedenquist, *op. cit.*

helpful article entitled "Jew and Christian: Is Reconciliation Possible?" [18] After pointing out what Christianity and Judaism have in common, Freedman prophesies, "When the Church exhibits in its life the Messiahship of Jesus and his Lordship over its life, then the whole world and the Jews especially, will take notice." [19] Certainly the Church through the centuries and today by its failure at this very point has incurred the judgment of God. Christians are called to repent of their sins against the Jews and other minority groups. Too often we have preached the gospel of salvation without the gospel of Christ's lordship. At least in part for this failure the whole world is groaning and travailing in pain until now.

Suggestions for Further Study

1. Attend Orthodox, Conservative, and Reform Jewish services, and compare and contrast the three services.

2. Interview at least three rabbis, one from each major branch of Judaism, and ask them questions to which you desire answers from a Jewish point of view.

3. Discuss the Israel-Arab controversy with informed persons.

4. Write to the proper person in your denomination for information and literature concerning your church's program as it relates to the Jews.

5. Ascertain the status of Jewish-Christian relations in your community and work out a plan undergirded by prayer and your own theological convictions that will meet the needs of the people involved.

Selected Bibliography

Abrahams, Israel, Bevan, Edwyn R., and Singer, Charles J., eds. *The Legacy of Israel.* New York: Oxford University Press, 1948.

Allport, Gordon W. *The Nature of Prejudice.* Cambridge: Addison-Wesley Publishing Co., 1954.

Burrows, Millar. *The Dead Sea Scrolls.* New York: The Viking Press, 1955.

Eckardt, Arthur R. *Christianity and the Children of Israel.* New York: King's Crown Press, 1948.

Finkelstein, Louis, ed. *The Jews: Their History, Culture, and Religion.* 2 vols.; New York: Harper & Bros., 1949.

Ganzfried, Solomon. *Code of Jewish Law.* Tr. Hyman E. Goldin. New York: Hebrew Publishing, 1927.

Gaster, Theodor H. *The Dead Sea Scrolls in English Translation.* Garden City, New York: Doubleday & Co., 1950.

[18] *Presbyterian Life* (March 3, 1956), pp. 10-11; 26-27.
[19] *Ibid.,* p. 27. See Matt. 11:2-5; Luke 7:19-22.

Gittelsohn, Roland B. *Modern Jewish Problems.* Cincinnati: Union of American Hebrew Congregations, 1943.

Grayzel, Solomon. *A History of the Jews.* Philadelphia: Jewish Publication Society of America, 1947.

Hedenquist, Göte, ed. *The Church and the Jewish People.* London: Edinburgh House Press, 1954.

Hoffman, Conrad, Jr. *What Now for the Jews?* New York: Friendship Press, 1948.

Johnsen, Julia E., comp. *Palestine: Jewish Homeland?* New York: H. W. Wilson Co., 1946.

Kertzer, Morris N. "What Is a Jew?" *A Guide to the Religions of America.* Ed. Leo Rosten. New York: Simon & Schuster, Inc., 1955.

Landman, Isaac (ed.) *The Universal Jewish Encyclopedia.* 10 vols.; New York: Universal Jewish Encyclopedia, Inc., 1939-1943.

"Modern Palestine: Chronology and Commentary," *Social Progress* (February, 1957).

Moore, George F. *Judaism.* 3 vols.; Cambridge: Harvard University Press, 1932-1940.

Parkes, James W. *Judaism and Christianity.* Chicago: University of Chicago Press, 1948.

Rall, Harris F. and Cohon, Samuel S. *Christianity and Judaism Compare Notes.* New York: The Macmillan Co., 1927.

Simon, Maurice. *Jewish Religious Conflicts.* London: Hutchinson House, 1950.

Singer, Isidore, et al., eds. *The Jewish Encyclopedia.* 12 vols.; New York: Funk and Wagnalls Co., 1901-1906.

Stern, M., ed. *Daily Prayers,* New York: Hebrew Publishing Co., 1928.

The Christian Church and the Jewish People. Addresses delivered at a Conference in New York City October 7, 1947. Published by the Committee on the Christian Approach to the Jews, Home Missions Council of North America, 297 Fourth Avenue, New York 10, N. Y.

Torrance, T. F. "The Israel of God," *Interpretation,* X (July, 1956), 305-20.

Waxman, Meyer. *A History of Jewish Literature.* 2nd ed.; 4 vols.; New York: Bloch Publishing Co., 1938-1945.

ROMAN CATHOLICISM

Claims and Counterclaims

THE ROMAN CATHOLIC CHURCH CLAIMS TO BE THE "ONE TRUE church established by Jesus Christ." [1] If all Christians found this claim to be true, all Christians would of course be members of this church. Non-Catholics vary widely in their attitude to the Roman Catholic Church. Some non-Catholics are nonreligious and ignore or oppose the Roman Church just as they do all churches and all faiths. Other so-called non-Catholics are non-Roman rather than non-Catholic—as for example the Greek Orthodox or the Anglo-Catholic communions—setting great store by the Catholic tradition as they understand it, but repudiating the claim of Rome and in turn being repudiated by the Roman Catholic Church. Some of these non-Roman Catholics are very friendly to the Roman Church and doctrinally are scarcely to be distinguished from it, though they do not acknowledge the supreme authority of the Pope.

On the other hand, there are individuals and groups which claim to be Christian and are generally accounted as such, who take a strongly negative or hostile attitude to the Roman Catholic Church. *The Westminster Confession of Faith,* an influential seventeenth-century Protestant statement, used to identify the Pope with antichrist.[2] A fundamentalist weekly, *The Christian Beacon,*[3] made the accusation that "Romanism is a pagan, false religion that enslaves and damns the souls of men."

The viewpoint taken here is different from any of these. We shall consider Roman Catholicism as *a sect of Christianity.* The reader will be better able to see the grounds for this point of view after considering this unit. Some preliminary remarks may be in order, however, for the sake of clarification.

---

[1] *Baltimore Catechism, A Catechism of Christian Doctrine* (Paterson, N. J.: St. Anthony Guild Press, 1941).
[2] Chapter XXV: 6, 19th century editions.
[3] November 8, 1945.

Roman Catholicism is surely Christian. One cannot possibly call it pagan; it is not to be classified with any other religion. It is one of the forms of the Christian religion. The name "Christian" cannot in fairness be denied to a church in which the members pray to the Father, Son, and Holy Spirit; regard as God's Word the same Bible as other Christians read (even though with additions);[4] honor the same Christ; and draw similar distinctions between right and wrong.

Nevertheless, Roman Catholicism can fairly be classed as a sect or even an ism. Its great size (15,914 churches in the United States with 32,575,702 members) has nothing to do with it. As Elmer T. Clark says, sectarianism is not a matter of size but of spirit.[5]

For one thing, the Roman Church is no longer universal. Since the Eastern Church swung away in the eleventh century—or as the Eastern Church would say, since the Roman Church seceded!—the claim of the Roman Church to be the true and sole representative of Christendom, is obviously exaggerated. Most Christian denominations are in fact, in some sense, offshoots from the Roman Church. If all the churches which are not now within the domain of Rome had lost the true Christian faith and spirit, then the Roman Church might have some reason to think herself the only true church; but since many or most of these denominations do show marks, scarcely to be questioned, of being parts of Christ's body, then the claim of the Roman Church is seen to be doubtful. Its claim, as we see it, is the claim of a part to be the whole; to use a Niebuhrian phrase, such a claim "absolutizes the relative," and comes close, as we shall see, to self-idolatry.

The Roman Catholic Church exhibits some of the most characteristic features of a sect. It is narrowly dogmatic and exclusive. That is, just as Communism has a "party line" from which the least deviation is regarded as major offense, so there is an ecclesiastical, dogmatic line in the Roman Church; that is to say, dogmas once settled on are not open to question nor subject to review. Furthermore, what has been defined as *de fide*, "of the faith," must be "believed" (whether understood or not), doubt on such points being regarded as mortal sin. All this is

[4] See Henrici Denzinger and C. Rahner (eds.), *Enchiridion Symbolorum* (1951), p. 2009. See systematic index under "Revelationis fontes" for references to numerous deliverances regarding the Bible.
[5] *The Small Sects in America* (Rev. ed.; Nashville: Abingdon Press, 1949), p. 20.

familiar to students of sectarianism. Further, while claiming to be ecumenical, this church shows a very weak sense of ecumenicity, to say the least. Here we must recognize a difference between attitudes of individual Catholics, who are often truly ecumenical in spirit, such as Father Tavard (see bibliography), and the official attitude of the church. Its abstention from the World Council of Churches, even to the extent of refusing to permit observers from the clergy, goes beyond the simple hands-off attitude of many Protestant sects.

Another compound reason for regarding this church as a Christian sect will be developed in more detail presently. In general, it can be said that the Roman Catholic Church not only permits but also stresses doctrines and practices not in line with Scripture. This again is a feature common to Christian sects everywhere—surrounding a hub of true Christian life and teaching by a skewed wheel of ideas and practices varying from the eccentric to the harmful.

To defend this church as exclusively the true one or to condemn it as wholly false would be alike unjustified. But the position that it is a sect can be better evaluated after some consideration of the facts.

What We Owe the Roman Catholic Church

The history of the Christian church for one thousand years is the history of the Roman Catholic Church, as far as western Europe is concerned. The first debt of gratitude we owe the Roman Church, then, is for preserving the Church itself. If it had gone out of business with the coming of the Dark Ages, it is most doubtful whether what we call the Reformation would have come at all.

Another debt of gratitude we must pause to pay is for the Roman Church's preservation of the Bible. That church claims credit for the production of the Bible in the first place, but this is generally denied by Protestants. To affirm that the apostles Paul and John, not to name other New Testament writers, were Roman Catholics, is like saying they were Presbyterians or Baptists. All Christians owe these pioneer prophets a great deal, but pinning our labels on them will not do. However, there is no doubt that by the sixth century what eventually became the Roman Catholic Church was a going concern. And one of its great concerns was the preservation and teaching of the Word. It did much to preserve the Bible in Western Europe.

The Roman Church for a thousand years preserved order in western Europe. Not that it was a very orderly place, as we look back on it. We may think it a mess, even with the church; but it would have been a most unholy mess without it.

Under the shelter of the mighty church, too, it was possible for our western culture to arise. The great universities of Europe, and some in the New World, were founded under the auspices of the Roman Catholic Church. The Dark Ages were really dark; but that they were followed by centuries of increasing light, we owe to the Roman Church and its institutions, especially some of the monasteries. There the light of learning was sheltered and cherished even when great darkness lay upon the world.

Then Why the Reformation?

If the Roman Catholic Church was doing all this, why did any Christian of good sense leave it? The answer to that is in the famed two words of the historian Lord Acton (himself a Catholic): "Power corrupts." The story can be read in the histories of the church and of Europe, how the church which in the thirteenth century seemed to be all-powerful in two centuries shrank, not in temporal but in spiritual power, so that thousands upon thousands of Christians were ripe and ready to leave "Mother Church." A contemporary Roman Catholic Church historian and theologian, Karl Adam, has summed it up:

It was night indeed in a great part of Christendom. Such is the conclusion of our survey of the end of the fifteenth century: amongst the common people, a fearful decline of true piety into religious materialism and morbid hysteria; amongst the clergy, both lower and higher, widespread worldliness and neglect of duty; and amongst the very Shepherds of the Church, demonic ambition and sacrilegious perversion of holy things. Both clergy and people must cry *mea culpa, mea maxima culpa!* [6]

This is not a place to discuss the Protestant Reformation. One word

[6] From *One and Holy,* by Karl Adam, copyright 1951, Sheed & Ward, Inc., New York, p. 25.

of caution is in place at this point, however. It is always a mistake to talk about the Roman Catholic Church as if it were the same church the early Reformers painted in such dark colors. (Not unjustly, as Adam's book shows.) A great deal of water has flowed under the bridge since then. The Reformation sparked a Counterreformation in the Roman Catholic Church which stopped the Reformation from going any farther than it did. The anti-Catholic who goes to a Catholic Church expecting to see indulgences put up for sale à la Tetzel, or who searches for scandal in the Vatican to match the times of the Borgian Popes, will have to invent his own material. There are sufficiently sound reasons for the existence of the Protestant churches today, without dragging up sins which sincere Roman Catholics have long repented.

The Reformation is today viewed, of course, quite differently by Roman Catholics and by Protestants. Leaving out the more violent beliefs about it, such as (on the one side) that it was conceived in sin and born in the iniquity of a monk who was false to his vows, a wolf in sheep's clothing, and (on the other side) that the Reformation gave the deathblow to a mass of organized superstition calling itself a church, or even that it was the first incomplete step toward throwing off the tyranny of *all* religion—a calm and serious Roman Catholic view is that Luther, who had it in him to be "the greatest saint of our [German] people," "let the warring spirits . . . drive him to commit what St. Augustine calls the greatest sin with which a Christian can burden himself: he set up altar against altar and tore in pieces the one Body of Christ." [7] A calm and serious Protestant view of the Reformation, on the contrary, is that it involves a "deeper plunge into the gospel";[8] that it was a return to the creative principles of the New Testament.[9] Protestants have never separated themselves from the Holy Catholic church. They simply deny that the Holy Catholic church and the Roman Catholic are one and the same.

[7] *Ibid.*, p. 26.

[8] See Hugh T. Kerr, Jr., *Positive Protestantism* (Philadelphia: Westminster Press, 1950).

[9] Stanley I. Stuber, *Primer on Roman Catholicism for Protestants* (New York: Association Press, 1953), p. 263.

We Still Have Much in Common

Despite four centuries of separate and generally hostile coexistence, it is remarkable how much Roman Catholicism and Protestantism have in common. Furthermore, our mutual agreements are chiefly in the central areas of Christianity, not in the suburbs. Shall we remind ourselves of some of these?

1. We have a common history down to the sixteenth century.

2. We both recognize the divine authority of the Word of God.

3. For this reason we share the great early creeds of the Church and the doctrines enshrined in them.

4. In matters not spelled out in the early classic creeds, there is much that Protestants and Roman Catholics declare with one voice. Both believe in the destructive power of sin, the necessity for divine grace, the need of repentance and faith. The evangelical Protestant, at least, joins the Roman Catholic in affirming that Christ's suffering was not only vicarious, he himself carrying the burden of man's sin, but also redemptive, setting man free from the power of sin. Both churches agree that the Christian life is a supernatural life, and that the Christian religion is both individual and social.

5. We can all pray to God directly, in the name of the same Christ.

6. Different as life is in the two types of church, there is something in common here also. They both have congregations meeting for worship, led by pastors. They both cherish at least two sacraments, baptism and the Lord's Supper. Paradoxically enough, in the sacraments Protestants and Roman Catholics can sometimes meet at the deepest levels, and yet in the same sacraments they find some of their sharpest differences. But that is another story.

7. Both Roman Catholics and Protestants are aware that Christianity is missionary by its very nature, and support mission enterprises around the world.

Differences We Could Settle

With all this impressive agreement, the fact remains that there are great differences in theory and in practice between the two faiths. Some of these could no doubt be compromised.

1. Protestants might be willing to add the Apocrypha to their Old

162

Testament.[10] In any case it would not hurt Roman doctrine seriously to omit the Apocrypha from the Old Testament, nor would it hurt Protestant doctrine to add them; for no major Christian doctrine receives major support or attack from the Apocrypha.

2. The Roman Church might be willing to hold services in English or other living languages, instead of Latin. As a matter of fact, there is an increasing use of English in the liturgy of many Roman churches.

3. The Roman Church might be willing to give up insisting on an unmarried clergy. They have already done this in taking back into the fold the Maronites, a small Middle Eastern church in which the clergy were not celibate, without holding this group to the Roman rule.

4. While the doctrine of purgatory cannot be called biblical in its Roman Catholic form, the idea that even for the saved there may still be stages of discipline in preparation for final glory, is finding support here and there outside the Roman communion.

5. Conceivably, some compromise on the number of the sacraments might be made by Protestants. Some Protestants already think of marriage, for example, and of ordination, as sacramental. It would be no long step to call them sacraments outright.

6. In some small practices, a Protestant might—indeed some do— adopt Roman examples for his own. The use of incense (surely better than the musty air pervading some Protestant sanctuaries), the practice of making the sign of the cross, the blessing of fields and crops and vehicles, the use of beads in prayers (but not the recitation of the Rosary!): such practices might be abandoned by one or taken up by the other church, without compromising anything essential.

Radical and Irreconcilable Differences

Be all this as it may, it does not affect the main point. There are radical, irreconcilable differences between these two types of Christian-

---

[10] The Apocrypha of the Old Testament, roughly speaking, consists of the books or parts of books which were added when the Old Testament was first translated into Greek, before the time of Christ. Wherever the Bible spread in the Greek-speaking world, the "apocryphal" books were included in it. Nearly all the quotations from the Old Testament, in the New, are from the Greek translation of it. The Christian church, as far as it was Greek-speaking, began its existence with scriptures which contained what we now call the Apocrypha. Hence the Roman Catholic Church cannot be said to have "added" these books. The Protestants gradually eliminated them. There is a New Testament Apocrypha, but none of its books was ever accepted by the Christian church.

ity. On these differences there has never been compromise; there never can be, without one group or the other caving in completely and ceasing to be itself. These differences are in both doctrine and practice.

Protestants have more and more come to regard the thought and practice of the New Testament as normative, setting the standard for all Christians. Keeping the New Testament standards in mind, they see that the Roman Church has in many ways departed from this norm, and so has departed from original and basic Christianity.

First (and, some Protestants would say, worst), the Roman Catholic Church does not take the New Testament as normative, in actuality. Beside it, as an equally authoritative "fount of revelation," is set up the "Tradition." The truth by which the church lives is held to have originated with the actual teaching of Jesus by word of mouth, or by the dictation of the Spirit ("a Spiritu Sancto dictatas"), and preserved by the (Roman) Catholic Church, which accepts and venerates the Scripture and the Tradition with equal reverence and piety.[11] So far so good; the Scripture itself suggests that Jesus said many things not recorded in writing, and many of these sayings would be remembered and repeated through the years. But what makes a Protestant more than suspicious is that the Tradition is often far out of line with the Scripture, and that where there is a difference, the Roman Church goes with the Tradition. If a man writes me a letter I know to be genuine, and I also receive an oral message on the same topics, I judge the genuineness of the unwritten message by its agreement with the letter. If it is clearly in conflict with it, then I have every reason to doubt; and if another man prefers the oral message to the written one, I wonder whether he has even understood the letter in the first place.

Major Deviations from the New Testament

First of all, and involving many another error with it, is the Roman *doctrine of the infallible church.* The New Testament gives no support to the idea that any congregation or aggregation of congregations, any body of Christians then present or in the future, would be in-

---

[11] Council of Trent, Sess. 4. Denzinger and Rahner, *op. cit.*, p. 783. Compare Bishop Gore's statement that the early Church knew of no tradition of doctrine apart from the Scriptures. See W. P. Witcutt, *Return to Reality* (London: Society for Promoting Christian Knowledge, 1954), p. 61.

fallible. But the Roman Church teaches that "the church, by the special assistance of the Holy Ghost, cannot err when it teaches or believes a doctrine of faith or morals." [12] In Roman thought, the church is virtually identified with Christ, who is God and infallible, and who thus makes the church at least semidivine and certainly infallible. This is expressed in categories of authority. Thus Karl Adam: "The whole constitution of the church is completely aristocratic and not democratic, her authority coming from above, from Christ, and not from below, from the community." [13] He goes on to quote Tertullian: "The Church is from the Apostles, the Apostles from Christ, Christ from God." The teaching of the Church, Prof. Adam says, "is, and aims at being, nothing else but a handing on of that message of Christ which was proclaimed by the Apostles." [14] Protestants are not impressed by this, simply because the teaching of the Roman Church, in cold fact, is at many points almost grotesquely at variance with the message of Christ as proclaimed by the apostles whom we meet in the New Testament, and nowhere more so than in the doctrine of the church which, unlike any of its members, is flawlessly right.

From this doctrine, which is essentially an assumption, stem other doctrines which likewise deviate from the New Testament. The best known of these is the supreme authority and infallibility of the Pope. This became a dogma (i.e., to be believed on peril of mortal sin) only in the nineteenth century, but the idea was widespread earlier. We find St. Thomas Aquinas arguing that since it is important that all Christians should believe exactly alike, and since the Pope has authority in all other things, his authority should be first and final in matters of belief.[15] This approaches the dogma of infallibility, if it does not quite reach it. At all events, the Pope is believed to be infallible when he speaks ex cathedra (officially) on matters of faith and morals,[16] not as an individual but as head of the church and "vicar of Christ."

What happens if a priest, for example, does not personally agree with a papal ruling? He must make the *sacrificium intellectus*, the sacrifice

---

[12] *A Catechism of Christian Doctrine*, q. 163.

[13] *The Spirit of Catholicism* (New York: The Macmillan Co., 1948), p. 20. Used by permission of The Macmillan Co.

[14] *Ibid.*, p. 23.

[15] *Summa Theologica*, 22ae, p. 1, Art. 10, 3.

[16] *Catechism of Christian Doctrine*, q. 164.

of his intellect. Recognizing his own fallibility and the church's infallibility, he bows his head and his mind in humble submission. Protestants look on the sacrifice of the intellect as ridiculous at best, vicious at worst, and abjuring of personal convictions, the essence of intellectual dishonesty. Roman Catholics regard this as a high virtue, the surrender of human pride in the presence of the divine. (Again, the divinization of the church.)

From this basic belief about their own church, again, comes the totalitarian arrogance and intolerance toward other churches, wherever this is possible. No other church has a valid ministry, no other church performs valid sacraments, no other church has anything but a distorted version of Christian truth. Every other church is engaged in perverting and confusing people, and concern for the spiritual welfare of mankind leads the loyal and logical Roman Catholic to condemn, oppose, and suppress all other churches so far as this can be done.[17]

The Roman Catholic *doctrine of the priesthood* again departs from the New Testament. The priest is entirely separate from the laity. Ordination being a sacrament, it "imprints a character" on the soul which lasts forever;[18] thus the priest is simply a different kind of being, in his very soul, from the layman. The priest is endowed by ordination with two principal supernatural powers: to change the "substance" of bread and wine into the body and blood of Christ in the Mass, and to forgive sins.[19] Thus the priesthood in the Roman Church has control (as is believed) of the eternal destiny of the laity. The saving grace of God is channeled through the sacraments; the sacraments can be dispensed only by the priesthood. Here lies the force of the interdict, or official censure, in a Catholic parish, forbidding divine services, Christian burial, and the sacraments including penance. Sacraments, it is true, are not refused to the dying; and St. Thomas was kindly enough to believe that infants dying unbaptized might not be lost. Even so, the interdict closes to the living the channels of God's grace. Hence it becomes a powerful weapon to bring the rank and file of church members into line. It has even forced racial integration in regions where all the

[17] See Jacques Delpech, *The Oppression of Protestants in Spain* (Boston: The Beacon Press, 1955), for documented facts about what an unhindered Roman Catholic Church is doing today.
[18] *Catechism of Christian Doctrine,* q. 314.
[19] *Ibid.,* q. 454.

local customs and prejudices and convictions were against it. Another form of priestly power is in the church's alleged relation to purgatory. The church claims the right and the power to shorten the stay of the "poor souls" in purgatory. This is most commonly done by the recital of Masses for the dead. These Masses are seldom free. Hence a wealthy family able to pay for perpetual Masses is in a much better position, purgatory-wise, than a poor one. Again the interdict by refusing permission for Masses to be said clamps down on the laity, not only in this life but also in the next. The priest, again, being the only person duly authorized to receive confession (as the representative of Christ himself), exercises through the confessional a power which no Protestant minister would even attempt, not daring (as the Roman ecclesiastic does) to put himself in the place of God. Needless to say, the Protestant cannot find in the New Testament any justification for this conception of the Christian ministry and its functions.

The conception of *faith* in the Roman Church and in the New Testament are different. In the New Testament, faith is a personal response to God. In the Roman Church, faith characteristically means intellectual assent to doctrine, to propositions as such. Faith indeed is not quite personal, but by proxy; for as the Catholic Baron von Hügel once said, for the Roman Catholic, faith is essentially faith in someone else's faith. The name for this is *fides implicita*, "implicit faith," and it is highly regarded in the Roman communion. A story from Luther will both illustrate this and give the reader a test by which he can tell whether he is a "natural" Roman Catholic or a "natural" Protestant. Luther once asked a charcoal burner what he believed. "What the church teaches," said the worker. "What does the church teach?" Luther asked. "I don't know," said the man. Luther thought that was funny. If the reader does, he too is a natural Protestant. If the charcoal burner's attitude seems sweet, reverent, and right, then the reader belongs in the church where such faith is praised and prized. The New Testament knows nothing of it.

The nature of *sainthood* and of *merit* is another point of deviation. In the New Testament, a saint is a Christian, a living, saved, yet sinning Christian. (*Simul justus et peccator*, as Luther used to say—"at the same time justified and a sinner.") In Roman Catholic thought, a saint is a very special kind of being, always deceased. An officially

167

canonized saint, proved to be such not only by a holy life, but also by at least three miracles performed by him or her before or after death, is believed to have been so much better than God required, that he has literally goodness to give away. "The church . . . supplements the insufficient reparation (for sin) of her weaker members by means of the vicarious superabundance of the merits of Christ and his saints." [20] Again, the Protestant cannot find in his New Testament any saint who was so good he had goodness to spare, who so received merit (even by grace) that he had merit to give away. Still less does the Protestant find in the Bible any power granted the church to transfer merit from dead saint to living sinner.

The cult of the *Virgin Mary* is an area specially dear to the Roman Catholic, specially strange to the Protestant. The Roman theologians make it clear that Mary is a creature, not a goddess. Yet as one observes the Roman Catholic at his devotions, the Protestant is struck by the way in which the Virgin takes the place of the goddesses of pagan religions. To her prayers are said, from her all blessings are expected. She is supposed to have more influence with God, through Christ, than any one else. The whole practice of prayer to saints and to the Virgin, by the way, assumes an omnipresence and omniscience which in the Bible is ascribed only to God. To various saints is ascribed by the church special interest in particular matters: St. Christopher is concerned with transportation, St. Anthony with lost objects, St. Jude with wrecks, and so forth—God's vice-presidents, as it were, in charge of departments. Mary, however, has universal interests and powers. I once had a talk with a Roman Catholic student, who asked: "If you would ask your mother to pray for you, why not ask the Virgin Mary? She prays to Christ and he prays to the Father."

When asked: "But why don't *you* pray to God direct?" the young man said, "I never thought of that." That illustrates the way in which, whatever technical reservations the Roman Catholic theologians lay down,[21] the place the Virgin occupies in the mind of Catholic laity and clergy, tends to push God into the more remote ranges of glory, unreachable by humble prayers, and to leave the Virgin in his place, the

[20] Adam, *The Spirit of Catholicism*, p. 127.
[21] Technically, the saints rate *dulia*, Mary *hyper-dulia*, God alone *latria*. In practice, these grades of veneration merge.

dispenser of grace, the Helper "now and at the hour of our death." (The "Hail Mary.") All this is far removed from the New Testament conception of the Throne of Grace, to which every Christian has access by faith without intermediation by priest, pope, saint, or virgin.

The sacraments are differently regarded in Roman Catholic and Protestant thought. The difference here is to a large extent between a more and a less literal interpretation of New Testament statements. The Roman Catholic reads the passage about being "born of water and the spirit" (John 3:5) literally; most Protestants do not. The Roman Catholic therefore believes in baptismal regeneration, that is, in the power of the act of baptism itself to wash away the guilt of original sin. Without baptism, therefore, the Catholic sees no salvation, and is at great pains to baptize infants. If a Protestant baptizes infants, it is not to save them!

The Mass, the Roman Catholic version of the Lord's Supper, is central in their thought and devotion. The interpretation is again more literal than that of Protestants. "This is my body" is taken literally by the former, who teach that the "substance" (that which underlies all the physical qualities) of the bread and wine is miraculously changed into the substance of Christ's body and blood—a miracle performed by the priest. The Protestant may come very close to the Roman position, as Lutherans do, or may regard the Supper as simply a memorial service; but in any case he never identifies the bread and wine with the literal physical body of Christ. On the contrary, he views the adoration of the host (the consecrated bread) as idolatry, worshiping a *thing* as if it were divine.

Whether the other five Roman sacraments are really such, may be a matter of definition. Protestants practice the equivalent of confirmation, holy orders, and matrimony, but have nothing like penance and extreme unction. Certainly Protestants feel that it is difficult to show that these were *"instituted by Christ* to give grace," [22] which is the Roman Catholic criterion of sacrament.

Sacramentals are "holy things or actions of which the church makes use to obtain for us, from God, through her intercession, spiritual and temporal favors." [23] There is no scriptural authority for these whatever.

[22] *Catechism of Christian Doctrine,* q. 304.
[23] *Ibid.,* q. 469.

They tend to become substitutes for prayer, and collectively are regarded by non-Catholics as examples of superstition and magic. They include, besides blessings given by ecclesiastics, "blessed objects of devotion" such as holy water, candles, images, rosaries, and scapulars. The Roman Church teaches that these should never be made "objects of superstition," but the Protestant observes that that is precisely what they do become. (Inevitably, he would say.) For example, in a pamphlet on holy water, with the imprimatur of the Bishop of St. Joseph,[24] it is said that since this water carries with it the prayers of the infallible church, "one drop of holy water is often more efficacious than a long prayer," for private prayer may be tinged with sin, and the prayers of the church are not. One can see what would happen to the prayer life of a believer who took this seriously. Or again, we may consider the scapular. This is a small object representing the garment of a Roman Catholic order, and it can be worn by any lay Roman Catholic who has the right "intention." Its use was urged upon service men, and no wonder. The wearer of one was supposed to be miraculously protected against many dangers. Of course the wearer even of a scapular must eventually die; but it has been promised (we are told) in a vision seen by St. Simon Stock, that no one who dies clothed in (i.e., wearing) this scapular shall suffer eternal fire. Purgatory? Yes, but not for long. The Virgin Mary has assured Pope John XXII (1322) that she will visit purgatory every Saturday and take out with her every person there who wears this scapular.[25] Obviously it would be to every believer's interest to wear the scapular constantly and to take care to die on a Friday night. The Protestant observer wants to know: If this is not superstition, what is it? But for the loyal Roman Catholic, the church has spoken.

Referring briefly to more secular matters that deserve longer treatment, all the attitudes and practices so annoying or oppressive to Protestants (depending on how powerful the Roman Church is) are rooted in that basic assumption of the one true infallible church. It is sometimes said by critics of Roman Catholic political actions or medical

[24] *Holy Water in the Christian Home* (3d ed.; Clyde, Mo.: Benedictine Convent of Perpetual Adoration, 1928), pp. 6-7.
[25] Pamphlet published by The Scapular Militia, Carmelite National Shrine of Our Lady of the Scapular, 338 E. 29th St., New York City. (Imprimatur: Francis J. Spellman, March 4, 1943.)

ethics or the like, that we have no quarrel with their theology, only with their policies. But the policies are determined by the theology.

For example, in a marriage between Roman Catholic and Protestant, the Roman Church will not recognize the marriage as valid unless the Protestant party sign a document giving up all right to bring up the children in his own religion, or even to persuade husband or wife to become an evangelical Christian; while the Roman Catholic party is bound on the other hand to rear the children in "the" faith, and to do all possible to win over the husband or wife, as the case may be. In other words, the Protestant husband or wife is forced to admit beforehand that his or her religion is false, the other one true.

What is freedom of worship? Where Protestants are in control numerically and politically, it means freedom for all, including the Roman Catholic minority. Where Roman Catholics have preponderant power (as in Spain and Italy), it is quite another story. (See, e.g., Delpech and Blanshard for details.) This apparent inconsistency can be defended only on the supposition that there is but one true religion, the Roman Catholic. The hostility to democratic freedom in general, which is spelled out in the "Syllabus of Errors," [26] also assumes as a basic premise that the Roman Church alone is right, and has a right to power. In that syllabus or collation of "modern errors," are included these for condemnation: that Protestantism is only a different form of the Christian religion, in which it is possible to please God as well as in the Roman Catholic;[27] that public schools should be free from ecclesiastical control;[28] that church and state should be separate;[29] that it is undesirable that the Roman Catholic religion should be the sole religion of a state to the exclusion of all others;[30] that all religions should be allowed equal freedom.[31] Mirbt sums up: "Pius claimed for the church the control of all culture and all science, and of the whole educational

---

[26] Denzinger and Rahner, op. cit., 1700 ff.; also in English in Philip Schaff, The Creeds of Christendom (New York: Harper & Bros., 1919), II, 213-33. References here are to paragraphs in Denzinger. Many Roman Catholics refuse to regard this as in any way definitive (e.g., Auguste Boudinhon, "Syllabus," Encyclopaedia Britannica (Cambridge, England: University Press, 1911), 11th ed., XXVI, 281-82; see as opposed C. T. Mirbt, "Pius IX," op. cit., XXI, 687-90.)

[27] Ibid., p. 1718.

[28] Ibid., p. 1745.

[29] Ibid., p. 1755.

[30] Ibid., p. 1777.

[31] Ibid., p. 1779.

system. He rejected the liberty of faith, conscience and worship enjoyed by other creeds; and bade an easy farewell to the idea of tolerance." [32] Among the most characteristic and cherished features of American life are those condemned most flatly by the utterances of Rome. What the principles of the syllabus will do when long unchallenged may be seen best in a country like Spain.

Conclusions

The Roman Church is willing to consider reunion on her own terms, which essentially demand that the Protestant shall admit that the Roman Church is the only true church, is infallible, and that the Protestant shall give up his right of immediate access to God and shall henceforth depend on the priesthood and the sacraments which the priests alone can administer. Protestants with a genuine experience of communion with God, and who value their freedom in Christ, will not make these admissions and surrenders. Roman Catholicism stands for religious submission, Protestantism for religious freedom.

Protestant leaders should inform their people of their own heritage and show them how Roman Catholicism differs from it. They should make clear what is involved when a Protestant marries a Roman Catholic, and with what dangers Roman Catholicism threatens religious and political freedom as well as the life of the individual. Further, Christians should be well acquainted with and solidly grounded in Scripture teaching, so as to recognize quickly doctrines and practices which distort or deny the clear word of God. Especially, everything should be done to foster a genuine personal experience with God in Christ, through the Holy Spirit, so that Christians who have had these experiences will not be credulous of the Roman Catholic claim to have the keys of the Kingdom in their exclusive possession.

Neither the Roman nor the non-Roman church is without its faults. In cases of unavoidable conflict, nothing is to be gained, and much to be lost, by either shutting one's eyes to deficiencies and sins in Protestantism or by misrepresenting Roman Catholicism. Still less Christian it is to set up one's own church, or Protestantism in general, as a rival sect, with all the narrowness, arrogance, and intolerance which mark

[32] Op. cit., p. 690.

the sectarian spirit wherever found. Roman Catholic and Protestant Christian churches will never be one in this world, unless one or the other changes past recognition. Nevertheless, just because we shall have to remain separate, it is all the more important that we disagree in love and not in contempt or pride; and that we agree, wherever possible, in seeking to do the will of Christ in the world, against our common enemies, in the name of our common Lord. Surely all Christians can say "Amen" to these words of Karl Adam:

The ideal for which Holy Church works . . . is the man of perfect love, the man who has put away from him all self-seeking and who enlarges his little, narrow heart until it becomes a sacred temple of God in which the fire of sacrifice burns, the man who every day fulfils the words of St. Paul: "I will most gladly spend and be spent for your souls" (II Cor. 12:15).[33]

Toward Fuller Understanding

1. Roman Catholicism in Theory. The following brief bibliography will introduce the student to various aspects of Roman Catholicism.

Official Statements and Propaganda

A Catechism of Christian Doctrine (Baltimore Catechism no. 2). Paterson, N. J.: St. Anthony Guild Press, 1941.

Denzinger, Henrici, and Rahner, C. Enchiridion Symbolorum, Definitionum et Declarationum de Rebus Fidei et Morum. Friburgi-Brisg.-Barcinone: Herder, 1953. (Full and accurate—the original Latin texts of official deliverances from earliest times to the present.)

Herbermann, Charles G., et al., eds. The Catholic Encyclopedia. 15 vols.; New York: Robert Appleton Co., 1907-1914.

Jesuit Fathers of St. Mary's College. The Church Teaches—Documents of the Church in Translation. St. Louis: B. Herder, n.d. (Shorter than Denzinger.)

Noll, J. F., and Fallon, L. J. Father Smith Instructs Jackson. Huntington, Ind.: Our Sunday Visitor, 1955. (Used by priests in instructing non-Catholics.)

O'Rafferty, Nicholas. Instruction in Christian Doctrine. 4 vols.; New York: Bruce Publishing Co., 1937.

Sheen, Fulton J. Preface to Religion. New York: P. J. Kenedy & Sons, 1946.

The Sunday Visitor. Huntington, Indiana. ("Popular" weekly.)

Tavard, George H. The Catholic Approach to Protestantism. New York: Harper & Bros., 1955.

[33] The Spirit of Catholicism, pp. 219-20.

More or Less Critical

Blanshard, Paul. *American Freedom and Catholic Power.* Boston: The Beacon Press, 1949.

———. *Communism, Democracy, and Catholic Power.* Boston: The Beacon Press, 1951.

Delpech, Jacques. *The Oppression of Protestants in Spain.* Boston: The Beacon Press, 1955.

Kerr, Hugh T. *Positive Protestantism.* Philadelphia: Westminster Press, 1950.

Kerr, William S. *A Handbook on the Papacy.* New York: Philosophical Library, Inc., 1951.

Manhattan, Avro. *The Vatican in World Politics.* New York: Gaer Associates, 1949.

McLoughlin, Emmett. *People's Padre.* Boston: The Beacon Press, 1954. (Firsthand story of a former priest.)

Nichols, James H. *Democracy and the Churches.* Philadelphia: Westminster Press, 1951.

———. *Primer for Protestants.* New York: Association Press, 1947.

Reynolds, A. G. *What's the Difference in Protestant and Roman Catholic Beliefs?* New York: Abingdon Press, 1954.

Scott, Charles A. A. *Romanism and the Gospel.* Philadelphia: Westminster Press, 1946.

Stuber, Stanley I. *Primer on Roman Catholicism for Protestants.* New York: Association Press, 1953. (Full and objective.)

Witcutt, W. P. *Return to Reality.* London: Society for Promoting Christian Knowledge, 1954. (An Anglican priest who tried Rome and came back.)

Woods, Henry M. *Our Priceless Heritage.* London: Marshall, Morgan, and Scott, Ltd., 1934. (Extended comparison of Romanism and Protestantism.)

2. *Roman Catholicism in Practice.* To enlarge one's personal acquaintance with Roman Catholicism:

a) Visit the nearest Catholic Information Center. Note the kind of information available.

b) Attend a Roman Catholic teaching mission, especially one for non-Catholics.

c) Attend a Roman Catholic service, preferably a Sunday Mass.

d) Visit a monastery, a Roman Catholic school, college, or hospital.

e) Read some of the literature available in hotel lobbies, church vestibules, or other public places.

f) Over a period of time, take note of Roman Catholic publicity and propaganda in your community.

g) Talk with a priest who can give an intelligent firsthand account of Roman Catholicism.

DENOMINATIONALISM AND ECUMENISM

DENOMINATIONALISM AND ECUMENISM ARE NOT MERE ABSTRACTIONS which conveniently end in "ism." They are names of powerful forces in a state of tension. It is like the tension existing in the political world between nationalism and those forces which are constantly thrusting nations toward a fuller realization of the dream of "One World."

It has already been observed that the idea of "isms" as used in this book is flexible. Neither denominationalism nor ecumenism is to be thought of as a sect. Rather they are to be conceived as movements in opposite directions—denominationalism in the direction of fragmentation and separation, and ecumenism in the direction of fellowship and unity. The resulting tension, like an ellipse, has two centers—one within the Church and one outside the Church. But because the Church is in the world and has a mission to the world, the Church is concerned with both centers of tension. Since these terms have been used with such varieties of meanings, it is desirable that their use in this unit be identified.

Ecumenism is derived from a Greek word meaning "economy," or "household." In its broader significance, it is closely akin to the generic idea of catholicism—that which is general or universal. Its meaning in a particular context is determined by the limitations of its frame of reference. Thus, if "seekers after truth" be the frame of reference, then sundry scientists, artists, philosophers, and religionists of all races and nations who consider themselves seekers after truth would be thought of as included in an "ecumenical movement." At the other extreme, if the frame of reference be "the five fundamentals" of fundamentalism identified in Unit III, then fundamentalists of all denominations around the world may be considered members of an ecumenical movement of fundamentalism.

In terms of predominant usage, the ecumenical movement among Christians embraces those trinitarian followers of Christ who are impelled by their faith to reach out in a sharing of that faith with non-Christians throughout the world, and in a sharing of Christian fellowship with other Christians at the level of those beliefs and practices which are common among them and inclusive of the major, historic, Christian convictions. The goal is a wider extension and a fuller realization in the whole world of the experience of oneness in Christ, which the Scriptures set forth as the Christian's heritage.

Thus, in this frame of reference, ecumenism is inevitably concerned with missions and evangelism in extending the experience of Christian unity among peoples of the whole world. In this very effort the movement is thwarted by obstacles to unity both within and among various Christian denominations. But ecumenism takes seriously *both* the world mission of the Church and its catholic, or universal, nature.

In this unit, a denomination is conceived of as any organized communion with a separate and independent existence. Denominationalism is a development within Christendom which has a wide variety of origins and which exercises differing degrees of hindrance to the realization of the catholic nature of the Church. Where ecumenism puts a premium upon those aspects of Christian faith and order which most Christians have in common, denominationalism tends to put a premium upon those aspects of faith and order which distinguish one group of Christians from another. Not all denominations place the same emphasis on their distinctions, to be sure. But by virtue of their very organization, denominations are officially committed to denominationalism—some to the extent of being "sectarian" in the exclusive sense of holding themselves to be the only true church. Others, while inherently committed to denominationalism by virtue of their separate organizations and their exercise of functions which belong to *the* universal Church, vigorously manifest the spirit of ecumenism, deplore the evils of denominationalism, and strive toward an ecumenical goal of world-wide unity in Christ. They recognize other communions as churches also—"branches of the one Church." They seek opportunities for co-operation and union. In them are found strong forces of ecumenism. Indeed, this is the paradox with which this unit is concerned—the tension between the centripetal forces of denominationalism and the centrifugal forces of ecumenism.

It would be superficial to assume the unqualified virtue of all concepts and expressions of ecumenism as identified in this unit, or to regard denominationalism as being uniformly opposed to the world mission and fuller realization of the catholic nature of the Church. Both involve values and weaknesses, virtues and dangers, which need appraisal.

At the level of the reactions of "practical-minded" laymen, the response to denominationalism is often one either of easy acquiescence or of unrestrained disgust. The one says of different denominations, "They are all trying to get to the same place; why be concerned that they travel different highways?" The other says, "Until denominations can get together and quit their mutual denunciations, their deadly and wasteful competition, and their absurd claims to 'infallible' truths which contradict each other, I will have nothing to do with any of them."

Thus, the pastoral minister comes squarely to grip with the tension between denominationalism and ecumenism in his everyday work. He meets it in the financial program of the church when the budget calls for support of some ecumenical agency like the World Council of Churches, the National Council of Churches, or the "Middletown" Council of Churches. He confronts it in the evangelistic program of the church when it involves co-operation with other denominations of the community, or when an evangelistic program of a particular denomination raises the question of proselyting the members of other denominations of Christians. He is faced by it in the missions program of the church at home and abroad. It looms before him in his sermons when he deals with doctrines, rites, ceremonies, or ethical practices which are denominationally distinctive.

For a sympathetic understanding of the tensions between denominationalism and ecumenism, some consideration must be given to their origins and prevalence. And for an intelligent handling of the practical problems growing out of the tensions between them, it is desirable that some appraisal of their respective values and weaknesses be made.

DENOMINATIONALISM

Divisions in the United States

According to the *Year Book of American Churches, 1957,* in 1955 there were 268 religious bodies listed in the United States, of which

258 reported statistics which could be recorded with some degree of accuracy. The total membership reported was 100,162,529 which was 60.9 per cent of the population—the highest yet reported, and somewhat higher in rate than was the increase in population. Analyzed into major groups, they were as follows:

Buddhist	63,000
Old Catholic & Polish National Catholic	367,370
Eastern Orthodox	2,386,945
Jewish	5,500,000
Roman Catholic	33,396,647
Protestant [1]	58,448,567
Total	100,162,529

When the "Protestant" group is further analyzed into "families" of autonomous denominations, a more vivid picture of fragmentized Christianity is presented:

27 Baptist denominations with	18,793,097	members
22 Methodist denominations with	11,784,060	members
19 Lutheran denominations with	7,059,593	members
11 Presbyterian denominations with	3,860,686	members
1 Episcopal denomination with	2,757,944	members
1 Disciples denomination with	1,897,736	members
1 Churches of Christ denomination with	1,600,000	members
6 Latter-day Saints denominations with	1,372,640	members
1 Congregational-Christian denomination with	1,342,045	members
Total	50,467,801	members[2]

Such an analysis provides a statistical basis for Clarence T. Craig's

[1] This total would be more accurately designated as "Protestant and all other reporting bodies," since it includes many groups not properly classified as Protestants. Cf. *op. cit.*, p. 251.

[2] Omitted in this analysis: (1) Christ Unity Science Church—1,581,286 members, (2) Church of Christ, Scientist—no statistics furnished, and (3) numerous smaller Protestant bodies with memberships of less than 1,000,000 and not classifiable in "families" having more than that number. For details, see *op. cit.*, pp. 251-56.

stabbing observation that "if all of the families of churches could be brought together under their respective roofs, 95 per cent of the Protestants would be in less than ten groupings." [3] Furthermore, a glance at this table reveals that only five of these nine "families" are divided into two or more autonomous denominations. When viewed statistically, the task of reducing the number of divisions among Protestants by uniting the most closely related denominations into homogeneous groups seems deceptively easy. The mathematics of such family unification is much easier than either the psychology or the theology of such an effort.

Origins of Denominationalism

Denominationalism has the distinction of being among the few things which Russia has not claimed to have discovered or invented prior to its appearance in the United States of America. But while this country, in which anybody who can get a few followers may start a new denomination, has been the spawning ground of a few new denominations and the battleground of many splits in old denominations, it is an error to infer that denominationalism is a distinctive American product.

Some of the basic psychological roots may be found in the New Testament Church. The New Testament knows only "one body" as *the* Church, having localized expression in congregations at Ephesus, Corinth, Rome, and other places. But in the Jewish-Gentile controversy (Acts 15), and in the party cries at Corinth (I Cor. 1:10-17), one can see the kind of conscientious scruples, loyalty to leaders, magnifying the importance of traditional practices into "fundamentals of the faith," the clash of cultural, linguistic, or other differences, which are among the roots of denominationalism.

But practically every major American denomination traces its ancestry to Europe and to the period following the Protestant Reformation. This fact does not imply that the Reformation movement and its leaders were inherently sectarian and schismatic. Charles Clayton Morrison[4] has pin-pointed some significant observations which challenge this popular inference. The Reformation emerged almost at the same

[3] *The One Church* (Nashville: Abingdon Press, 1951), p. 15.
[4] Cf. *The Unfinished Reformation* (New York: Harper & Bros., 1953), pp. 16 ff.

time in Germany, Switzerland, and England under conditions of geographical, political, and communicative separateness which seriously obstructed efforts for unity on the part of leaders like Luther, Melanchthon, Zwingli, Bullinger, Calvin, Bucer, Archbishop Cranmer, and others. It is chiefly the multiplied divisions of imported denominations which characterize the American Protestant scene as an "ecclesiastical zoo."

The more significant factors giving rise to new denominations, or serving as occasions for the division of old denominations, may be summarized in two categories. First, certain *theological factors* are at least important as affording the rationale and the verbal rallying points of divisions. The doctrine of the Trinity, especially with respect to the persons and work of the Son and of the Holy Spirit; the doctrine of salvation, particularly in relation to the atonement and election; the doctrine of sanctification, notably in terms of perfectionism; the doctrine of eschatology, especially as to adventism; the doctrine of the sacraments, primarily as to the administration and significance of baptism and the Lord's Supper; and various questions of order, relating to forms of government and the status of the ministry—these are illustrative of the theological factors.

Undoubtedly these and other theological doctrines have been in the forefront of the controversies which have produced the state of chaotic competition associated with denominationalism. This is clearly indicated by the number of denominations bearing names which give prominence to some doctrinal distinction or emphasis. But in more recent years, scholars have probed beneath these theological factors and have identified and described a number of *nontheological factors* in denominationalism, some of which are judged to be equal, or even superior, to the importance of the theological factors that have loomed so large in classical studies of church history.

Dean W. L. Sperry, for example, lists eleven such factors—(1) the state, especially where relations between church and state tended to make the faith of the prince the religion of the people, (2) nationalism, i.e., realms of cultural unity which may not conform to state boundaries, (3) race, (4) language, (5) class, either economic or social, (6) varieties of ethical judgment, including manners, mores, and morals, (7) the small communion, with its cherished intimacies of fellowship, (8) the sectarian mind, (9) vested interests, both in property and prestige, (10) differences of educational method and philosophy, and (11) the universality of the sciences and the arts.[5]

In his book *The Social Sources of Denominationalism* H. Richard Niebuhr organizes the nontheological factors differently and lays primary emphasis upon the significance of economic and social classes in producing and maintaining denominational separateness. For example, he observes that denominationalism "represents the accommodation of Christianity to the caste system of human society." [6] And he contends that "the divisions of the church have been occasioned more frequently by the direct and indirect operations of economic factors than by the influence of any other major interest of man." [7]

Granting some place of significance for most of these factors, both theological and nontheological, and a determinative place for some of them in relation to particular denominations, one is impressed with the recurrence of a general pattern in the history of denominational origins.

1. There emerges in an individual or a group a vivid, life-changing religious experience which is capable of reproduction or dissemination under the influence of a dynamic leadership.

2. Tension, mounting to conflict, develops between this pattern of religious experience (or the leaders who seek to propagate it—or both) and the previously established patterns of faith and order (or the acknowledged leaders who personify these patterns of "orthodoxy"—or both).

3. Verbal, theological distinctions are drawn in terms of "heresy," and the nonconformists either withdraw voluntarily or they are forcibly excluded, and they form a new denomination.

In some cases, factor (1) is missing, or it is present in a position of secondary importance. In other cases, factor (2) has its basic origin as a conflict in the political, economic, or social context in which the church operates, and this conflict of the larger context invades the church. One such example is to be found in the North-South divisions produced by the issue of slavery and the sectional strife of the Civil War.

[5] *Non-Theological Factors in the Making and Unmaking of Church Union* (New York: Harper & Bros., 1937), pp. 12-29.
[6] New York: Henry Holt & Co., 1929, p. 6.
[7] *Ibid.*, p. 26.

To the extent that such a recurring pattern is valid in history, it poses the basic problem: How can institutionalized faith remain flexible and inclusive enough to absorb diversities of Christian insight and experience without the impairment of the organic and genuinely spiritual unity of the Church? This problem, among others, ecumenism seeks to answer.

But before considering the unifying movement which is in tension with the separateness of denominationalism, it is desirable to summarize some values and weaknesses of denominationalism.

Some Values of Denominationalism

1. It has often had the effect of reforming and rejuvenating the Church.

2. Both the characteristic vital experience of a new denomination and the tension between it and its environment tend to stimulate new zeal in propagation (evangelism) and a vivid and satisfying sense of unity within the group.

3. Such distinctive and exclusive groups tend to give more sacrificially of both time and money. When such giving is combined with zeal for propagation, the satisfaction of growth and achievement usually follows.

4. Denominationalism provides one means of effective ministry to somewhat different psychological-social groups of people.

Some Weaknesses of Denominationalism

No more valid or incisive critique of denominationalism have I seen than that of Charles C. Morrison, in his *Unfinished Reformation*, which he summarizes as follows:

(1) Denominationalism is exceedingly and scandalously wasteful of the resources of Protestantism.

(2) It is a shameful embarrassment to the missionary expansion of Christianity.

(3) It frustrates the efforts of Protestantism to discharge the responsibility which the social gospel lays upon the Christian Church.

(4) It robs Protestantism of its inherent strength in its inescapable competition with a formidable and aggressive Roman Catholicism.

(5) It provincializes Protestant mentality by erecting barriers against the free flow of Christian thought.

(6) It breeds a subtle and corrosive moral insincerity among Protestant Christians.

(7) It denies to the local church the Christian status, the breadth of outlook, the spiritual inspiration, and the richness of fellowship which is its birthright as a part of the ecumenical church.

(8) It condemns the parish minister to adopt methods and appeals which appreciably stultify his ministerial self-respect as well as the Christian dignity of his high vocation.

(9) Glorying in its false freedom, denominationalism denies the freedom that is in Christ.[8]

ECUMENISM

Ecumenism is no recent development in the Church. Through most of the years since unity was threatened at Jerusalem by the gentile controversy, and at Corinth by personality-party cries, efforts have been made by churchmen to realize more fully the Christian heritage of unity in Christ. It is quite generally agreed, however, that the modern form of ecumenism may be dated from 1910.

Edinburgh to Evanston

From 1910 to 1947, four major ecumenical movements may be identified in relation to conferences with representatives from major denominations of the world.

1. The World Missionary Conference, Edinburgh, 1910. This conference had its roots in such interdenominational organizations as the Y.M.C.A., the Christian Endeavor Society, the Student Volunteers, and others. One of its major fruits was the International Missionary Council, which sponsored further ecumenical conferences at Jerusalem, 1928, and at Madras, 1938.

2. The Life and Work Conferences at Stockholm, 1925, and at Oxford, 1937.

3. The Faith and Order Conferences at Lausanne, 1927, and at Edinburgh, 1937, which, in terms of emphases, were the counterparts of the Stockholm and Oxford conferences.

4. Christian Youth Conferences at Amsterdam, 1939, and at Oslo, 1947.

These ecumenical movements of the modern period were as four

[8] Pp. 28-29. Used by permission of Harper & Bros.

streams which flowed together to form The World Council of Churches at Amsterdam, 1948, which subsequently met at Evanston, 1954, in an Assembly composed of representatives of 163 churches having an aggregate membership of nearly 170,000,000. In the formation of this Council at Amsterdam and in its consolidation and strengthening at Evanston, the ecumenical movement has acquired the status and significance of a "new Reformation."

The justification of the inclusion in this book of ecumenism within the flexible concept of "isms" is twofold. First, its conflict with denominationalism is a focal point of one of the major tensions in the Church. Second, despite the repeated avowals of the World Council that it is only an ecumenical movement, there are those who believe it to be the marks of a superdenomination in the process of being formed.

Grass Roots of Ecumenism

Whatever may be the end result of ecumenism in terms of organic union, it seems evident that the movement is too spontaneous and strong in too many quarters to be interpreted as a "supersectarian bill of goods" which has been sold by a handful of globe-trotters and conference-promoters. Rather it is a movement which has arisen from the grass roots of practical problems encountered in the world mission of the gospel, and from the disturbed consciences of Christian laymen and ministers who have considered earnestly the nature of the Church and the deeper meanings of that "unity in Christ" which the New Testament sets forth as a major heritage of Christians.

Whether regarded as products of the ecumenical movement or as expressions of the same spirit and convictions which have given rise to the ecumenical movement, certainly there has been an impressive number of church unions, reunions, federations, and negotiations looking toward union during the decades since the World Missionary Conference of 1910.

Unions and Federations

For example, in ten countries there have been nineteen organic unions involving forty-seven denominations during the period from 1910 to

1952. These are classified as "introconfessional" unions—unions within theological families of churches.[9]

During the same period, and in addition to these, in ten countries there have been fifteen organic unions involving fifty-three denominations which are classified as "trans-confessional"—unions across confessional or theological lines. The impressive total is thirty-four organic unions, involving one hundred denominations, in eighteen countries, during a little more than four decades.

Even this picture is incomplete. During this period full intercommunion was achieved by two denominations in Europe and two in India. Limited intercommunion was achieved by four denominations in Europe, two in India, and two in the Philippines. Federal unions, involving less than full organic union, have been formed by eighty-four denominations in five countries. As of 1952, seventeen negotiations with a view to organic union, involving sixty-one denominations, were still in progress in nine countries.[10]

Some Weaknesses and Dangers of Ecumenism

While it is my conviction that the ecumenical movement is basically an expression of the New Testament concept of the Church, and that it embodies a needed corrective of the fragmentation of the body of Christ, there are some weaknesses and dangers in such a movement which deserve the scrutiny and evaluation of thoughtful laymen and ministers. Among them, the following may be identified in a summary manner.

One is that in the commendable passion for Christian unity the Church may become uncritically lax in its inclusiveness; and essential distinctions between the Church and the world, or between the Christian faith and other faiths, may be blurred or wiped out. A statement of this danger at once raises the question of the identity of "fundamentals" or "essentials" in the realm of faith and order, as well as of life. This question, in turn, is often the source of as much misunderstanding, tension, and heresy-hunting within a given denomination as it is between denominations. While exaggerated expressions of the

[9] Ruth Rouse and Stephen C. Neill, *A History of the Ecumenical Movement—1517-1948* (Philadelphia: Westminster Press, 1954), pp. 496-502.
[10] *Ibid.*

danger of "inclusiveness" in the concept of the Church may be deplored, the reality of the danger may be ignored only at the jeopardy of that which is important to the vitality of the Christian movement.

Another danger is that, in the zeal for *doing* things together, Christian life, by subtle stages, may be divorced from Christian *faith*. Such a statement assumes the reality and significance of a reciprocal relation betweeen belief and action without implying either that faith is wholly a matter of belief or that theologically correct belief is a guarantee of right conduct. But the mere process of doing things together may have the diverse effects either of strengthening Christian faith or of weakening it by seeming to put faith in one compartment, and life in the form of action in another compartment.

A third danger is that in its concentration upon common doctrines, practices, and ethical objectives the riches of diversity now found in various denominations may be lost in ecumenism. In his *Unfinished Reformation*, Charles Clayton Morrison argues convincingly that the loss of such riches is not inevitable. There is a perverse tendency, however, for an institution, whether it be a church, a school, or a club, to evolve toward a degree of uniformity which may become authoritatively intolerant of diversity. In ecumenism the loss of the riches of diversity is certainly not inevitable, and identically the same danger besets a particular denomination, but the danger is still there to be guarded against in relation to any concept of Christian unity.

A fourth danger is so closely parallel that it may seem to be identical with the one immediately above. It is the danger that unity may be confused with uniformity, and the revolutionary creativeness of Christianity may be squelched by the passion for regularity and conformity. Possibly the chief distinction is that the one points toward the past in terms of heritage, while the other points toward the future in terms of achievement. The root of the danger is undoubtedly the same—the innate tendency of institutionalism toward regularity and uniformity. The concern here, however, is not so much to conserve and perpetuate diversities of the past into the future, but to guard against the danger of stifling the creativeness which might produce valid and desirable riches of diversity in the future.

A fifth danger which is usually given priority by the most theologically conservative critics of ecumenism, is that in the zeal to attain ecclesiastical unity, theological doctrines will be compromised and the distinctive Christian witness of the resulting Church will be seriously impaired. This kind of danger is easily magnified to produce very potent fears, especially in the minds of those who are inclined to identify faith with belief as expressed in propositional form. It is doubtful, however, whether the magnitude of this danger could be documented from actual church unions. Moreover, considerable reassurance may be derived from a look at the very large "denomination" of Southern Baptists in its maintenance of theological conservatism without the benefit of an official confession or of the disciplinary authority of a constitution above the level of the local congregation.

Still another danger is that in the bigness contemplated as the result of unions inspired by ecumenism, the worth of the individual will be ignored. This is a very plausible fear which doubtless grows out of the well-nigh universal experience of feeling "lost in a crowd." Any group which is to be worthy of the name of Christian must diligently seek to guard the rights and maintain the dignity and worth of the individual. But the size of a group is a much less significant factor than the pattern of government and the prevailing mores in the group.

Values in Ecumenism

Increasing numbers of Christians throughout the world see in "the churchism of denominations" a sinful fragmentation of the body of Christ. Each denomination or sect which calls itself *a* Christian church, or takes upon itself autonomously—and with at least implied exclusiveness—the functions and prerogatives which belong to *the* Christian church, thereby denies the Apostles' Creed in its avowal: "I believe . . . in the holy catholic (universal) Church." [11] Thus, on the one hand, ecumenism is an alluring goal to be achieved in the indeterminate future. On the other hand, it is a progressive movement to reduce the evils of

[11] Many consciences are apparently satisfied by the dualism between the "visible Church" and the "invisible Church," which may be regarded as the body referred to in the venerable creed. The invisible Church is real, and a distinction between it and the visible Church is valid, but such dualism hardly solves the basic problems of (1) realizing the unity in Christ of the whole Church—whether visible or invisible, and (2) effectively witnessing to the world as *the* body of Christ.

separateness and schisms in the body of Christ and to reinforce the world mission of the Church.

Viewed in this light, as both goal and process, certain values of ecumenism may be emphasized. One value is that by its co-operative spirit and programs, things may be accomplished together which could hardly be accomplished separately. For instance, in the American context of freedom and of separation of church and state, representatives of a single denomination are likely to find doors closed to their witness in tax-supported universities or public schools. But often those doors are readily opened to a campus mission sponsored by an ecumenical organization like the National Council of Churches of Christ in America.

A second value is that, by its progressive integration of Christian work and worship, the ecumenical movement reduces the wastefulness of time, money, and energy through the elimination of needless overlapping and duplication. Like the consolidated public schools, Community Churches have been formed at various places throughout America to provide centers of work and worship in place of several competing, weaker congregations in the same community. In other areas the Larger Parish plan has been used effectively in grouping rural congregations in unified programs. Closely related denominations have jointly employed officers for similar administrative duties in areas where their work overlapped. The waste which is inherent in overchurching and in the duplication of overhead expenses constitutes one of the most obvious evils of a highly competitive denominational system, and the reduction and ultimate elimination of such wastefulness of resources is a correspondingly obvious value of the ecumenical movement.

Furthermore, through the fellowship of periodic ecumenical conferences, where recognition is given to beliefs and practices which are common to the participating groups, and where differences may be discussed frankly in a context of mutual respect, better understanding is achieved across denominational lines, and distinctions of heritage or practice tend to assume more nearly their proper perspective. Distance does not always lend enchantment; often it borrows prejudices which thrive in separateness and isolation. Quite apart from any resolutions passed, or any co-operative programs initiated, such ecumenical gatherings contribute immeasurably to a kind of understanding and appreciation which is prerequisite to the achievement of other values of ecumenism.

A fourth value is that by the emphasis which ecumenism places upon doctrines, practices, and ethical objectives which are common to various groups of Christians, it helps to keep the current of Christianity in the main channel. The eddies, whirlpools, coves, and tributaries of faith have a strange and perverse fascination for men. We smile, or shudder, at the thought of snake-handling as proof of the reality of one's Christian faith. But one is jerked up with the question, "Lord, is it I?" just by reading the distinguishing titles of some of the denominations listed in the *Year Book of American Churches*. Fortunately, die-hard loyalty to incidentals does not prevent many Christians from participating in those ecumenical gatherings which repeatedly refocus attention upon those doctrines, practices, and ethical objectives which have marked the main channel of the stream of Christian faith down through the centuries.

Moreover, through its persistent emphasis upon those basic doctrines and practices which have marked the main channel of the Christian faith, and which have successfully transmitted Christianity across political, cultural, racial, and linguistic barriers, ecumenism extends the scope of realized unity in Christ. Even such a feeble gesture as the designation of one Sunday in the year as World-wide Communion Sunday has brought a profound sense of unity in Christ as members of congregations throughout the world have gathered around the Lord's Table in obedience to his commission: "This do in remembrance of me." The New Testament concepts of unity in Christ and of Christian fellowship (*koinonia*) are not to be diluted into mere human congeniality. They are not to be associated exclusively with detailed uniformity of rite or ceremony in which people participate. Nor are they to be restricted to that natural gratification which is felt when two or more Christians find themselves in agreement as to the form of words in which they express their faith rationally. Unity in Christ transcends mere human congeniality (or lack of it) and identity of verbal confession (or lack of it). It is given of God, is rooted in faith as trust-belief, and is expressed in love (*agape*) when lives are oriented to God in Christ. Through evangelism, missions, teaching, worship, sacrament, and service, the ecumenical movement seeks to extend the scope of realized unity in Christ.

Thus ecumenism moves, even though at what may seem a crawling pace, toward the goal of "the holy catholic Church." Uniformity of rite, ceremony, government, and creedal forms may not be essential in such a church. To the contrary, considerable diversity and flexibility may be practically necessary and highly desirable. The deadly uniformity of an ecclesiastical Frankenstein is no more the dream of ecumenists than it is the desire of the most individualistic sectarian. But if the body of Christ is to be "the holy catholic Church," members of the Church anywhere must be members of *the* Church everywhere. To the extent that the sin of pride is more catholic than the grace of love, "the holy catholic Church" may remain invisible. But the messages of Amsterdam and Evanston, as well as the frustrations of futile denominational competition in thousands of small villages and rural communities, give hope and courage to ecumenical spirits who cherish the vision of "the holy catholic Church."

Topics for Discussion

The following topics have been suggested by Paul Minear as bases of fruitful ecumenical conversations.[12]

> The Theme (The Nature of the Unity We Seek).
> The Church's Unity in Christ.
> Co-operation and Unity.
> Pressures for United Action.
> Obstacles to Greater Unity.
> The Unity We Seek in Each Congregation.
> The Unity We Seek in Each Locality.
> Consensus in Faith.
> One Baptism, One Altar.
> Oneness in Mission.
> Listening Together to God's Word.
> The Manifestation of Unity in Church Organization.
> Worship in One Spirit.
> Unity in the Beginning and at the End.

[12] "Ecumenical Conversations in Your Church," *The Presbyterian Outlook* (July 30, 1956), p. 5.

Selected Bibliography

Bosley, Harold A. *What Did the World Council Say to You?* Nashville: Abingdon Press, 1955.

Craig, Clarence T. *The One Church.* Nashville: Abingdon Press, 1951.

Douglass, Truman B. *Preaching and the New Reformation.* New York: Harper & Bros., 1956.

Dun, Angus. *Studies in Church Unity.* New York: Joint Executive Committee, World Conference on Faith and Order, 1938.

————. *Prospecting for a United Church.* New York: Harper & Bros., 1948.

Hogg, William R. *Ecumenical Foundations—A History of the Missionary Council and Its Nineteenth Century Background.* New York: Harper & Bros., 1952.

Horton, Walter M. *Toward a Reborn Church.* New York: Harper & Bros., 1949.

————. *Christian Theology: An Ecumenical Approach.* New York: Harper & Bros., 1955.

Latourette, Kenneth S. *Toward a World Christian Fellowship.* Nashville: Abingdon Press, 1938.

Mead, Frank S. *Handbook of Denominations in the United States.* Nashville: Abingdon Press, 1951.

Morrison, Charles C. *The Unfinished Reformation.* New York: Harper & Bros., 1953.

Niebuhr, H. Richard. *The Social Sources of Denominationalism.* New York: Henry Holt & Co., 1929.

Oxnam, G. Bromley. *On This Rock.* New York: Harper & Bros., 1951.

Rosten, Leo. *A Guide to the Religions of America.* New York: Simon & Schuster, Inc., 1955.

Rouse, Ruth, and Neill, Stephen C. *A History of the Ecumenical Movement—1517-1948.* Philadelphia: Westminster Press, 1954.

Scotford, John R. *Church Union; Why Not?* Boston: Pilgrim Press, 1948.

Sperry, Willard L. *The Non-Theological Factors in the Making and Unmaking of Church Union.* New York: Harper & Bros., 1937.

Stuber, Stanley I. *How We Got Our Denominations.* New York: Association Press, 1948.

Van Dusen, Henry P. *World Christianity.* Nashville: Abingdon Press, 1947.

Visser 't Hooft, W. A. *The First Assembly of the World Council of Churches.* New York: Harper & Bros., 1949.

Wedel, Theodore O. *The Coming Great Church.* New York: The MacMillan Co., 1945.

Year Book of American Churches for 1956. New York: National Council of Churches of Christ in the United States of America, 1957.

THE HEALING SECTS

MAN HAS ALWAYS BEEN CONCERNED ABOUT HIS OWN HEALTH. EVERY normal person wants to be healthy, and every "abnormal" person is likely to be unduly and even extravagantly concerned over his body.

The biblical accounts of miraculous healings and Jesus' commission to his disciples to heal raise the question: Should the Church today attempt a healing ministry? The rise of modern healing sects came in the middle of the materialistic nineteenth century. Christian Science and Unity are the best known of the healing sects. They tend to appeal to the middle classes. Those sects which have found their richest recruiting ground among the underprivileged often have healing as a secondary emphasis. By 1956 such main-line churches as the Church of England, the Church of Scotland, and the Presbyterian Church in the United States, had begun to come to grips with the healing question.

Religion and Healing Have Always Been Related

From the time when he first emerged into history, Homo sapiens has had, apparently, some concept of a Higher Being. The priest, the shaman, ministered to body as well as to soul. In all parts of the world religion shows some concern for the physical needs of men. Islam has its healing charms, and the repetition of a verse from the Koran is a good antidote for the toothache. Even today the African medicine man or witch doctor has a strange capacity to heal.

The Bible reveals that God has some relationship to sickness and health. Pain and suffering are often regarded in the Old Testament as signs of God's displeasure. The Book of Job shows its suffering hero as one who maintained his integrity against the judgments of his "comforters." The vision of God in his majesty humbled Job, but it did not solve the problem of suffering. There are many references to healing in the Old Testament. One especially beloved passage is Ps. 103:2-3:

192

Bless the Lord, O my soul,
    and forget not all his benefits,
Who forgives all your iniquity,
    who heals all your diseases.

Forgiveness and healing are also closely associated in Ps. 32:3-5. Our God is a healing God!

In the New Testament we are given many insights concerning God's relationship to sickness and to health. One of the key Bible words is "salvation." In the Greek New Testament we have *sozein*, "to save," *soteria*, "salvation," and *soter*, "savior." *Soter* may be translated "savior"; it may also be translated "healer." William Barclay tells us:

In the papyri by far the commonest meaning of *soteria* is 'bodily health.' . . . Both noun and verb are used of 'bodily health and safety' in the New Testament. . . . "The verb *sozein* means both to save a man in the eternal sense, and to heal a man in the physical sense. Salvation in the New Testament is 'total salvation.' It saves a man, body and soul." [1]

Alan Richardson in similar vein writes concerning Jesus: "Just as his power over the demons demonstrated his conquest of Satan (Mark 3:27), so his power over sickness demonstrated his conquest of sin." [2] The following passage undoubtedly describes a scene often repeated in the life of our Lord:

That evening, at sundown, they brought to him all who were sick or possessed with demons. And the whole city was gathered together about the door. And he healed many who were sick with various diseases, and cast out many demons; and he would not permit the demons to speak, because they knew him (Mark 1:32-34; cf. Luke 4:40).

Matthew, in his account of the same incident, significantly adds, "This was to fulfill what was spoken by the Prophet Isaiah, 'He took our infirmities and bore our diseases'" (Matt. 8:17). The seriousness with which Jesus himself took his healing ministry is memorably clear in his

[1] *A New Testament Wordbook* (London: Student Christian Movement, 1956), pp. 114, 116, 119.
[2] "Heal, Healing, Health," *A Theological Word Book of the Bible*, ed. Alan Richardson (New York: The Macmillan Co., 1951), p. 103b.

reply to the query of the disciples of John the Baptist, "Are you he who is to come . . . ?" (Luke 7:20-33). Jesus healed the sick and cast out demons. He healed those physically and mentally or spiritually ill. Some of the cures undoubtedly were of hysterical patients. We cannot, however, rightly limit Christ's power to heal to the technique of suggestion. God is not the prisoner of his own "laws." God is in control of his creation, including all the "laws of nature," in such a way that he uses his own laws—including higher laws which we do not yet know—to carry out his own purposes in his own creation. Jesus, the Son of God incarnate, was master of far more of the laws of nature and of spirit than we are. He performed his healing miracles out of the compassion of his own great heart and, guardedly, as "signs." Jesus commissioned his disciples to heal (Mark 6:7, 12, 13; Luke 9:1, 2, 6; 10:9; Matt. 10:1, 7, 8).

In the Apostolic Church, the apostles continued to heal. The "many signs and wonders" referred to in such passages as Acts 2:43; 5:12 and 6:8, surely include healing miracles. Specific instances of healing are recorded in Acts 3:2-10; 9:17-18; 9:32-34; 14:8-10; 16:16-18; 28:7-8. In one of the three lists of officers of the Apostolic Church, we read "then healers" (I Cor. 12:28).

Healing apparently did not cease when the apostles had all died. Justyn Martyr (A.D. 100-165), Irenaeus (A.D. 120-202), Origen (A.D. 185-253), Tertullian (A.D. 155-230), all give evidence that in their day the Church continued a ministry of healing. Ambrose (A.D. 340-397) indicates that by his time healing had become very rare; and Chrysostom (A.D. 357-407), though he says miracles had ceased, reports that commonly patients "put away their diseases by anointing themselves with oil of faith." [3] Augustine (A.D. 354-430) stated that miracles of healing were still occurring in his day, but were rare. For some time yet the Church was officially to practice healing. As the Church decayed in the long period of the Dark Ages, however, the healing ministry went into decline. Until very recently the ancient healing art apparently was almost nonexistent in the life of the Church.

The healing methods of Christianity have been three in number and closely related: prayer, anointing with oil, and the laying on of

[3] Quoted in Leslie W. Weatherhead, *Psychology, Religion, and Healing* (Nashville: Abingdon Press, 1951), pp. 77-78.

194

hands. The laying on of hands in healing is not to be confused with the laying on of hands in ordination (II Tim. 1:6; I Tim. 4:14). Jesus touched the eyes of blind men, a leper, and others (Matt. 20:34; Mark 1:41; Luke 8:54; Matt. 8:15). The anointing with oil shows that the healers in the Church were perfectly willing to use "medicine." To this day oil of various kinds serves helpfully in the healing process. But prayer would seem to have been the main feature of spiritual healing on the part of the Church. The classic passage is James 5:14-16.

J. K. S. Reid brilliantly sets forth the thesis that Jesus gave his apostles two commissions, the first immediately after he had called them, the other after his resurrection; and in the second commission the injunction to heal and the admonition to cast out devils are not repeated. He then suggests that with the Great Commission the ministry becomes one of word and sacrament. "It may very well be that the commission to sacramental activity is the continuing form which the earlier command to heal in the first commission now takes. . . ." [4] Reid's thesis would keep us from going off the deep end into an over-emphasis on healing!

Psychology for Centuries Played a Large Part in Healing

Plato knew something of the interrelationship of mind and emotions and body: "For this is the great error of our day in the treatment of the human body that physicians separate the soul from the body." [5] A few centuries later Galen (A.D. 130-200) wrote, "We have proof that many serious illnesses can be cured solely by the shock administered to the mind." [6] And one older than Plato or Galen wrote, "A cheerful heart is a good medicine, but a downcast spirit dries up the bones" (Prov. 17:22).

Man actually did very little with this ancient wisdom, except for the use of suggestion in religious healing. Mesmer towards the close of the eighteenth century and Charcot in the early nineteenth century through hypnotism used psychological forms of healing. Sigmund Freud, who learned much from Charcot, pioneered a new way of thought

[4] J. K. S. Reid, "The Biblical Doctrine of the Ministry," *Scottish Journal of Theology*, Occasional Paper No. 4 (Edinburgh, 1955), p. 13.

[5] Quoted in Weatherhead, *op. cit.*, p. 106.

[6] Quoted in *ibid.*, p. 105.

as the nineteenth century came to a close. Freud made great original contributions to modern knowledge. Today nearly all men know that mind has subconscious or unconscious "depths" and that human beings are moved by dynamic forces, often connected with childhood experiences. Psychiatry has been instrumental in curing the mentally ill. Physicians realize that it is not enough to minister to a broken body and neglect a twisted spirit. Wise doctors have always had some inkling of the truths that underlie current psychosomatic medicine.

Suggestion has always played a major part in the psychological aspects of the healing process. In the miracles of Jesus, for instance, it seems likely that the powers of suggestion often helped greatly in the healings. Where there is an atmosphere of expectation, with witnesses who are hoping, expecting, praying, and where there is a powerful central figure as healer, it is quite possible for healing to take place. This has never been limited to Christians, nor to the Christian religion. The power of fear, or conversely, the power of faith, is great. Look at one of the miracles of Jesus, the man with the withered hand (Mark 3:1-6; Matt. 12:9-14; Luke 6:6-11). "They watched him. . . ." "Come here!" "Stretch out your hand." In Jesus' voice was the authority of certainty and the note of loving concern. The atmosphere was expectant, if hostile. The man really wished to be healed, and he was.

Spiritual Healing Is Being Practiced Today

Spiritual healing in some form is practiced widely today. Below are briefly discussed some of these forms of spiritual healing.

Christian Science. The best known of the healing sects is Christian Science. Around it many verbal battles have been fought. To it many fine people belong. Its pervasive influence extends far beyond the limits of its own church edifices.

Christian Science was founded by Mary Baker Eddy,[7] who was born July 16, 1821, in Bow, New Hampshire. As a child she was of delicate health and highly nervous. Like Samuel and like Joan of Arc, she heard "voices." She was taught at home because she became too excited at school. At twenty she married George Washington Glover. He took her to Charleston, South Carolina, to live; and she became a strong

[7] In this section the writer leans heavily upon the "official" biography by Sibyl Wilbur, *The Life of Mary Baker Eddy* (Boston: The Christian Science Publishing Society, 1907).

opponent of slavery. Mr. Glover soon died of yellow fever. Two months later George Washington II was born. Mrs. Glover was too ill to nurse her son. Later a nurse, much against Mrs. Glover's wishes, took the boy far away to live. Mrs. Glover's health was poor for the next few years. "She was afflicted with a spinal weakness which caused spasmodic seizures, followed by prostration which amounted to a complete nervous collapse. In her moments of utter weakness her father would take her in his arms and soothe her as though she were again his bairn." [8] In 1853, after nine years of widowhood, she married an itinerant dentist, Daniel Patterson. The marriage was unhappy. He refused to keep his promise to bring young George Glover into their home. The spinal weakness and nervousness continued. She became intensely interested in the Bible accounts of healing. She was called "the good sick lady." One day she healed a child almost blind by invoking the power and love of God. Sometime later she met a mesmerist, Phineas P. Quimby, who had gifts of healing. A man without formal education, he had a sincere understanding of the therapeutic powers of suggestion. He hypnotized Mrs. Patterson and immediately she was relieved of her pain.[9] She interpreted Quimby's healing power as divine truth operating through him. They had a number of discussions in the next few weeks. Writers who are critical of Mary Baker Eddy believe that she derived her key ideas from Quimby. Her followers are convinced that, though at first influenced by him, she rose far above him in spiritual understanding, and that her *Science and Health With Key to the Scriptures* was fundamentally her own creation. Mrs. Patterson's mind was tortured with doubt during the years of 1862-1866. On February 1, 1866, she fell on the ice in Lynn, Massachusetts, was unconscious, bruised, and had internal injuries. Three days later, after meditating upon the account of Jesus healing the palsied man, she had a deep spiritual experience during which she heard the Lord say to her, "Daughter, arise." [10] She arose, healed and well. Growing out of that experience, she discovered "the Christian Science or divine laws of Life, Truth, and Love, and named my discovery Christian Science." She began to think

[8] *Ibid.*, p. 54.
[9] *Ibid.*, p. 87.
[10] Mary Baker Eddy, *Science and Health With Key to the Scriptures* (Boston: The Christian Science Publishing Society, 1934), p. 107.

deeply upon the philosophy of religion and the principles of life and health. Her husband, whose amours were already known, ran away with another woman. She divorced him in 1873. In 1877 she married a sewing machine agent named Gilbert Asa Eddy. Seven years later he died of heart trouble. In 1875 she published *Science and Health*. She organized the First Church of Christ, Scientist, in 1879, in Boston. The movement began to spread rapidly. In 1910 Mrs. Eddy died of pneumonia. Christian Science lives on.

Christian Science is a religious sect to which many thousands of people have given their loyalty and in which they have found much help in the form of physical healing, and mental or spiritual peace. The student of philosophy would label it "an idealistic monism."

The basic principles of Christian Science may be derived from a study of *Science and Health*.

The fundamental propositions of divine metaphysics are summarized in the four following, to me, *self-evident* propositions. Even if reversed, these propositions will be found to agree in statement and proof, showing mathematically their exact relation to Truth. De Quincey says mathematics has not a foot to stand upon which is not purely metaphysical.

1. God is All-in-all.
2. God is good. God is Mind.
3. God, Spirit, being all, nothing is matter.
4. Life, God, omnipotent good, deny death, evil, sin, disease.—Disease, sin, evil, death, deny good, omnipotent God, Life.[11]

"God is incorporeal, divine, supreme, infinite Mind, Spirit, Soul, Principle, Life, Truth, Love!" [12] Christ is the true idea of God.

This Christ, or divinity of the man Jesus, was his divine nature, the godliness which animated him. . . . In witness of his divine commission, he presented the proof that Life, Truth, and Love heal the sick and the sinning, and triumph over death through Mind, not matter. This was the highest proof he could have offered of divine Love. . . . Christ is the ideal Truth, that comes to heal sickness and sin through Christian Science, and attributes all power to God. Jesus is the name of the man who, more than all other men, has

[11] *Ibid.*, p. 113.
[12] *Ibid.*, p. 465.

presented Christ, the true idea of God, healing the sick and the sinning and destroying the power of death. Jesus is the human man, and Christ is the divine idea; hence the duality of Jesus the Christ.[13]

Christian Scientists do not ignore that which they consider unreal. Error is defined as "A supposition that pleasure and pain, that intelligence, substance, life, are existent in matter. . . . It is that which seemeth to be and is not." [14] With the help of the law of divine science, Christian Scientists seek to give a demonstration of the true idea of reality as over against error. Some have been known to send for the doctor when they became seriously ill. "If I were a good enough Scientist I would not have a doctor. Error still has a hold on me."

The appeal of Christian Science is great to many people. The belief that God in his goodness wills health, is attractive. To believe, as Christian Scientists do, that pain, sickness, suffering, and death are error and ultimately unreal, aids peace of mind. We long to be healthy, and Christian Science promises to open the way to health. We have a need of serenity, and Christian Science has ministered effectively to this need in thousands of lives. The emphasis of the power of mind over body is sound. This truth was often ignored in the crass materialism of the nineteenth century.

Christian Science has certain weaknesses which evangelical Christians ought to recognize. There are Gnostic elements in its philosophy and in its practice. If one had to choose between the two extremes, "all is mind" and "all is matter," one would choose the former; but that choice is unnecessary, unrealistic, and unbiblical. Both matter and mind are real, and they are in a continuous interrelation, notably in persons. Christian Science declares "the only reality of sin, sickness, or death is the awful fact that unrealities seem real to human, erring belief, until God strips off their disguise. They are not true because they are not of God." [15] The philosophy of absolute idealism, of which Christian Science is a form, simply will not satisfy either the Bible or common sense.

"Spirit is immortal Truth; matter is mortal error. Spirit is the real and eternal; matter is the unreal and temporal. Spirit is God, and man

---

[13] Ibid., pp. 26, 54, 473.
[14] Ibid., p. 472.
[15] Ibid.

is His image and likeness. Therefore man is not material; he is spiritual." [16] The truly Christian understanding of matter, however, is that it is sacramental. Water and bread and wine, the blood of the martyrs and the sweat of the brow, all are matter and all may partake of the sacramental.

The theology of Christian Science is as dubious as is its philosophy. The Bible declares that man is a sinner, in need of redemption; Christian Science calls sin an "error" (though we should remember an error may be operatively real). Jesus Christ is God Incarnate. "The Word became flesh [*sarx*]" (John 1:14), but Christian Science declares matter to be unreal. The view of Christ is Docetic, for his humanity is not *real*. Of the comforter whom Jesus promised to send, Mrs. Eddy says, "This Comforter I understand to be Divine Science." [17]

Mrs. Eddy specifically disavowed pantheism, but there are large elements akin to Neoplatonic pantheism in her philosophy. "There is no life, truth, intelligence, nor substance in matter. All is infinite Mind and its infinite manifestation, for God is All-in-all." [18] Again:

Mind is God. The exterminator of error is the great truth that God, good, is the *only* Mind, and the supposititious opposite of infinite Mind—called *devil* or evil—is not Mind, is not Truth, but error, without intelligence or reality. There can be but one Mind, because there is but one God . . . evil can have no place, where all space is filled with God.[19]

God is impersonal, a Principle, apparently. "To grasp the reality and order of being in its Science, you must begin by reckoning God as the divine Principle of all that really is." [20]

Mrs. Eddy's view of the Atonement does not do justice to the tremendous biblical concepts involved in such a phrase as "He himself bore our sins in his body on the tree . . ." (I Pet. 2:24), or in the words, "For our sake he made him to be sin who knew no sin" (II Cor. 5:21).

At the practical level, the outstanding weakness of Christian Science

[16] *Ibid.*, p. 468.
[17] *Ibid.*, p. 55.
[18] *Ibid.*, p. 468.
[19] *Ibid.*, p. 469.
[20] *Ibid.*, p. 275.

is its failure to realize that some sickness is not psychogenic and cannot be easily dealt with through mind-power spiritually "in tune with the Infinite." Its failure to encourage co-operation with doctors allegedly has led to more than one tragic, unnecessary death. Christian Science is not noted for a ministry to the poor.

Christian Science contains truth, but it is an unbalanced approach to life. To be too concerned about health is to become either neurotic or egocentric. Or both. Such outcomes the founder did not fully avoid. Such outcomes are difficult to avoid. The "cult of reassurance" is appealing, both in its Protestant and in its Christian Science forms, but it is also dangerous.

Unity.[21] The Unity School of Christianity was founded by Myrtle and Charles Fillmore in 1889. "Unity" does not consider itself to be a church. Its followers usually retain their membership in one of the Protestant sects or churches. The influence of Unity is vastly greater than most ministers dream, for thousands read Unity literature, take it very seriously, and perhaps write to Unity headquarters for help. Unity is classified by Elmer T. Clark in *The Small Sects in America* (see Basic Bibliography) as one of the "Egocentric" or "New Thought" bodies. Unity is the only relative of Christian Science that won for itself an important place in the religious life of America. Unity generally takes a more realistic view than Christian Science.

Charles Fillmore was crippled in childhood with a hip disease, while Myrtle Fillmore suffered from tuberculosis. After some time in Colorado the Fillmores moved to Kansas City where Fillmore became wealthy through real estate dealings. Later he lost everything in a depression. One night in the spring of 1886, when Myrtle was seriously ill, they went to a lecture on New Thought given by a Dr. Weeks. Charles was not impressed, but Myrtle received something that sent her out of the lecture hall repeating to herself, "I am a child of God and therefore I do not inherit sickness." [22] It took two years for her to become completely well, but the process was initiated that night. She tells part of the secret in these words:

[21] In this section I have drawn freely upon the approved book, James D. Freeman's *The Household of Faith* (Lee's Summit, Mo.: Unity School of Christianity, 1951).
[22] *Ibid.*, p. 44.

How do we communicate intelligence? By thinking and talking, of course. Then it flashed upon me that I might talk to the life in every part of my body and have it do just what I wanted. I began to teach my body and got marvelous results. I told the life in my liver that it was not torpid or inert, but full of vigor and energy. . . . I told the life in my abdomen that it was no longer infested with ignorant thoughts of disease, put there by myself and by doctors, but that it was all athrill with the sweet, pure, wholesome energy of God.[23]

The Unity publications contain a good many prayers and many biblical quotations. It is no wonder that many Christians, fed on a diet of moralisms from the pulpit, and whose theological education has been weak, accept Unity. The theological errors of Unity are subtle. Jesus Christ is recognized as a person of the Trinity. "Jesus Christ's real name is Jehovah, I AM. The personal man Jesus is merely the veil or mask worn by the spiritual man Christ or Jehovah." [24] Only a theologian would discern the error in such words. And so it is with many another passage. In a chapter entitled "God Presence" Mr. Fillmore wrote:

Being is the consciousness of the one Presence and the one Power, of the one intelligence, and man stands in the Godhead as *I will*. When man perceives his place in the great scheme of creation and recognizes his I AM power, he declares, "I discern that I will be that which I will to be." [25]

In such words there is a kinship to the doctrine of *Imago Dei*, and these words "sound good," but again there are subtle errors. Man does not stand in the Godhead and man is not divine, though man is "a child of God." Two of Unity's teachings are clearly deviant. One is reincarnation; the other, the view that as the believer becomes like Jesus, a spiritual body replaces his physical, so that death should be unnecessary.

In addition to its emphasis on healing, Unity answers requests for prayer for prosperity. "You cannot use God too often. He loves to be used, and the more you use him the more easily you use him and the more pleasant his help becomes. If you want a dress, a car, a house, or if you are thinking of driving a

[23] *Ibid.*, pp. 47-48.
[24] Charles Fillmore, quoted in Freeman, *Ibid.*, p. 274.
[25] *Ibid.*, p. 261.

sharp bargain with your neighbor, . . . or reforming a nation, ask God for guidance in a moment of silent soul desire." [26]

Although Unity groups now meet in a number of cities, Unity's main work is done through its magazines, notably *Unity;* its radio; and its great center at Lee's Summit, Missouri, to which over half a million people annually call for help. The mechanism of autosuggestion is used in healings by adherents to Unity.

Healing in Roman Catholicism.[27] The Roman Catholic Church maintains a number of healing centers, the best known of which is at Lourdes, France. In the one hundred years that have passed since Bernadette Soubirous had a vision and the trickle of water at the grotto began to flow strongly, millions of people have visited the shrine. Pilgrims to Lourdes have been cured of most diseases known to man. At this shrine the Roman Catholic Church has accepted as miraculous fewer than fifty cures in ninety-eight years. The church is even harder to satisfy at this point than the bureau of medical verification. Both faith and prayer are regarded as essential to healing at Lourdes, but not necessarily the faith and prayers of the sick person. Here too healing is from God.

Healing in Churchly Protestantism. Healing missions are conducted in some main-line churches from time to time, usually by representatives of the group who have prompted the "Camps Farthest Out." These services, usually held in the Episcopal Church, are conducted on a high level. A few resident pastors conduct regular public services of healing in their own parishes.

These spiritual healers are fine, consecrated persons of integrity. One suspects they may be rather naïve in accepting some reported cures without adequate scientific check-ups. Their services undoubtedly help some folk. Persons with an inadequate Christian view of suffering may be hurt and disillusioned if they receive no help from such services.[28]

Other Methods of Healing. Those who engage in healing missions in the larger denominations tend to call their work "spiritual healing," or

[26] *Ibid.,* p. 229.
[27] For this section see Weatherhead, *op. cit.,* pp. 142-54, and Ruth Cranston, *The Miracle of Lourdes* (New York: McGraw-Hill Book Co., 1955).
[28] See comment of British Medical Society, quoted on page 204 below; see also W. H. Boggs, Jr., *Faith Healing and the Christian Faith* (Richmond: John Knox Press, 1956).

"divine healing." The "faith healers" are somewhat different. They work in store-front churches, in gospel tents, and among some sects which tend to the bizarre. The faith healers also make much use of the radio. By far the best known radio healer is the Rev. Oral Roberts, who also has a television program. The faith healers in general depend to a great extent on personal magnetism and the power of suggestion.[29]

Toward an Evaluation of Spiritual Healing

Healing is the process by which a person whose functions are disordered is made whole and can function effectively. Healing is a relative term, for disease always leaves some kind of "scar" on body tissue or psychological make-up. Some persons are made relatively whole through spiritual means. In authentic cases of spiritual healing, faith, prayer, and the laying on of hands supplement rather than supplant medical care. There have been relatively few cures purely by spiritual means. The vast majority of spiritual cures have been of disorders that were of psychological origin—psychogenic or psychosomatic, to use the current terms.

A special committee of the Council of the British Medical Association in the summer of 1956 submitted to the Archbishops' Commission on Divine Healing a memorandum on Divine Healing and Co-operation between Doctors and Clergy. Their basic conclusion is:

We can find no evidence that there is any type of illness cured by "spiritual healing" alone which could not have been cured by medical treatment which necessarily includes consideration of environmental factors. We find that, whilst patients suffering from psychogenic disorders may be "cured" by various methods of spiritual healing, just as they are by methods of suggestion and other forms of psychological treatment employed by doctors, we find no evidence that organic diseases are cured solely by such means. The evidence suggests that many such cases claimed to be cured are likely to be either instances of wrong diagnosis, wrong prognosis, remission, or possibly of spontaneous cure. . . . Religious ministration on whatever basis it rests may have an important bearing upon the emotional and spiritual life of the patient and so contribute to recovery.[30]

[29] Boggs, op. cit.; and A. G. Ikin, New Concepts of Healing, Medical, Psychological and Religious (New York: Association Press, 1956), pp. 235-38.
[30] London: British Medical Association, p. 15.

Some General Principles Concerning Spiritual Healing

1. All healing is from God. Whether healing comes through the surgeon's scalpel or the magic of penicillin or the patient, dynamic listening of a psychiatrist or through intercessory prayer, it is God who heals. He has planted in us an inner drive to health, the *vis medicatrix Dei.*

2. Some persons have, apparently, the gift of healing. It was so in the early Church (I Cor. 12:28). It seems to be so today. Cyril Richardson says that we ought to distinguish two types of spiritual healing, the charismatic and the sacramental. The charismatic healer tends to be somewhat visionary and mystical, not of a critical turn of mind. In the other type of healing, "Not the charismatic individual, but the sacramental form is of primary importance." [31] The Sacraments have no magical powers, but they are marvelous channels of divine grace for the healing of the whole person.

3. Spiritual healing is not to be identified with faith healing. In the popular usage, faith healing has more reference to faith in a dynamic healer than it does to the deep spiritual faith Jesus meant when he said, "Your faith thas made you well" (Mark 5:34).

4. Cyril Richardson[32] suggests that sickness is one of the ways in which original sin expresses itself. Job argued vehemently and wisely that sickness does not have a one-to-one equation with sin. Jesus agreed with Job's viewpoint (Luke 13:1-5; John 9:3). When Jesus healed the paralytic borne of four, he said, "My son, your sins are forgiven" (Mark 2:3-12). A study of that incident would suggest a real relationship between some sickness and sin. Sickness is given by original sin a significance which it would not have had in a sinless world. "The connexion between healing and salvation (in the religious sense) is a characteristic feature of the gospel tradition. Miracles of healing are, as it were, symbolic demonstrations of God's forgiveness in action." [33]

5. Healing has eschatological connotations. "Ultimately we all die, and sickness, the consequence of sin, overcomes us all, till in the resur-

---

[31] "Spiritual Healing in the Light of History," *Pastoral Psychology*, V (May, 1954), 18a.
[32] *Ibid.*
[33] Alan Richardson, *The Miracle Stories of the Gospels* (New York: Harper & Bros., 1941), pp. 61-62.

rection we are made one with Christ." [34] Healing is thus a foretaste. "The miracle of healing is but a breaking through of powers to be realized in the future, when death shall be swallowed up in victory." [35]

6. For the Christian the matter of supreme importance is not bodily health but right relations with God. One may be a profound Christian and yet suffer horribly with cancer. On the battlefield bullets strike sinners and saints alike. Being a Christian enables one to triumph over his suffering in dependence upon the all-sufficient grace of God. The inner climate of faith and love often seems to give a kind of charm to some of God's children, so that they manage to cast off sickness to which others succumb. But such is not always the case. Paul did not get rid of his thorn in the flesh! (II Cor. 12).

Some Negative Criticisms of the Healing Sects

In addition to the specific criticisms which were made in connection with Christian Science and the implied criticisms at other points, some fundamental weaknesses of method and philosophy need to be emphasized.

The gospel does not promise that we shall be free from all illness in this world; it promises that we shall be made whole. Through Christ's redeeming work and the power of the Holy Spirit we are "whole" here, but we shall not be perfectly whole this side of death. . . . God's grace is sufficient, however, for our every need.[36]

People who emphasize healing are in danger of placing more emphasis on bodily healing than on the great theme of reconciliation. God is not a tool to be manipulated for human health, either physical or emotional. An overemphasis on health may and often does lead to an overemphasis on self. Ultimately the Christian religion finds a cross at the center of life. The author of Hebrews wrote of Jesus, "Who in the days of his flesh, having offered up prayers and supplications with strong crying and tears . . . though he was a Son, yet learned obedience by the things which he suffered" (Heb. 5:7-9 K.J.V.). Christian Science and Unity do not agree with the biblical realization that sin, sickness, suffering, and

[34] Cyril Richardson, op. cit., p. 19a.
[35] Ibid.,
[36] For an excellent discussion of the fallacy of the faith healers' thesis that all sickness is contrary to the will of God, see Boggs, op. cit., Ch. 7.

death are part of life in this present world. The healing sects overemphasize physical health.

Sometimes in the healing sects there is revealed a gross disregard of medical realities. Few "healers" are competent to make a medical diagnosis. Sometimes persons who desperately need the services of a physician or surgeon have their symptoms removed through spiritual healing— mainly through the technique of suggestion—but their real trouble is untouched and later flares up. Traumatic experiences have occurred to a number of persons supposedly healed under the excitement and mass expectancy of a certain type of faith-healing situation. A collection of crutches does not always mean that the folk who threw away the crutches and hobbled down the aisles of the tabernacle were able to walk the next day.

A quotation from a committee of the British Medical Association is apropos here:

It is undesirable and even dangerous for anyone to apply these methods of treatment without a knowledge of the nature of the disease from which the patient is suffering. To treat certain forms of depression by laying on of hands or resort to the help of spirit media, or by suggestion, when specific treatment is available is to do the patient the gravest disservice.[37]

Those with the gift of healing, may and sometimes do take a self-righteous view of their closeness to God. The less wise among the faith healers are prone to blame failure to heal upon lack of faith in the one who comes for healing. This obviously is distressing to one of real faith who prays for healing and does not receive it.

Positive Undergirding for a Healing Ministry by the Church

The healing sects, despite their obvious weaknesses, remind the Church of its failure to carry out its entire task. Healing continues to be a part of the ministry of the Church. The Church has in Jesus Christ the answer to the deepest needs of modern man, including the need of healing.

1. We speak of the whole gospel for the whole man in his total en-

[37] *Op. cit.*, p. 9.

vironment. Unlike the Greek concept of the immortality of the soul, Christians believe in the resurrection of the body. Salvation is therefore for the whole person, the total man.

2. "Prayer changes things." The Church has always believed in the power of intercessory prayer, following the example of her Lord (John 17; Mark 9:29). Our prayers may not change God; but it is unquestionable that our prayers change us, and the total atmosphere. God uses our prayers to carry out his purposes. Intercessory prayer is a must for the man of faith.

3. "Faith can move mountains" (cf. Matt. 21:21 and parallels). This passage is not to be taken literally, but it has great spiritual significance. Faith in the sense of positive thinking has tremendous power. Faith, in the sense of expectancy, uses the technique of autosuggestion to make possible the seemingly impossible. Faith in the healer is of great value. Phineas P. Quimby, who healed Mary Baker Patterson, claimed that the only cure for disease is the confidence of the patient in the healer. Such faith works, even though occasionally the healer be a hypocrite who is in the game for money. But faith in the biblical sense is a saving, trusting, deeply personal relationship with Jesus Christ. He who has this faith is already a new man in Christ. This is newness of being at the inner core. The Church's healing should be done in an atmosphere of faith in Jesus Christ as savior of one's whole being. For spiritual healing, faith is placed not simply in the healer, but primarily in the power and the love of God in Christ. He is the healer, and we trust ourselves in faith to the great Physician.

4. "Perfect love casts out fear. . . . We love, because he first loved us" (I John 4:18-19). When in saving faith we have found Jesus Christ, when the love of God has been shed abroad in our hearts by the Holy Spirit, fears and anxieties grow less and less potent in our lives. In accepting the love of God, we accept the fact that he has forgiven us, that we are justified by the righteousness of Christ, received by faith alone. Accepting his forgiveness, we can forgive ourselves and begin to feel ourselves again a part of mankind. Grateful for his merciful love, aware of being his child, we want to show his love unto our fellow men. Such is the way to mental health.

5. As has been intimated, the forgiveness of God wipes out our guilt. If we really accept this forgiveness, much of our anxiety and hostility

disappears. We no longer have to hate others because down deep we hate ourselves. No longer are we prey to many bodily disturbances growing out of disturbed emotions.

6. Biblical psychology teaches the unity of the person. The medical profession has rediscovered the ancient wisdom that mind and body interact in amazingly complicated ways so that each affects the other profoundly. Flanders Dunbar, in her popular book, *Mind and Body* (see bibliography), makes it clear that our emotions and our bodily processes are strangely linked. Thus, the child who resents being "smothered" by his mother may develop asthma. The man who harbors resentments may develop high blood pressure and even heart trouble. It is not true, however, that all people with high blood pressure hate, and cherish grudges; and it is not true that all ulcers are due to the worship of the goddess Success. But there are correlations between our emotional states growing out of character states and our physical condition. A prominent Christian psychiatrist writes that research "suggests that spiritual healing fits into the general concept developed by psychosomatic medicine: that bodily diseases express specific psychological conditions of the patient and that they disappear if the underlying condition has disappeared spontaneously or by treatment." [38] This is not to deny the germ theory, nor is it to say that a specific psychological condition always results in a certain physical condition, but it is to say, "there is a meaningful connection between illness and the psychology of the patient." [39]

Perhaps a word of warning needs to be added here. Pastors must not be too quick to attribute all illness to some particular character weakness, either with reference to themselves or to their parishioners. Some ills really are basically physical!

The Church Today Has a Commission to Heal

This is true both in general and specifically.

1. The church hospital has a rich and useful place in every city as well as on the mission field. It bears daily testimony to the belief of the Church in the need of healing, both mental and physical.

[38] Gotthard Booth, "Science and Spiritual Healing," *Pastoral Psychology, op. cit.,* p. 22b.
[39] *Ibid.*

2. The Church should recruit some of its finest young people not only for the ordained ministries of the Church but also for the healing vocations.

3. Institutional churches can carry on health clinics, or even mental health clinics, where needed.

4. Pastors who have excellent training in psychology are using in small church groups—circles and cells—some of the techniques of non-deep-level group therapy. Churches which can call upon psychologists and psychiatrists of deep Christian conviction ought to do more of this.

5. Pastoral counseling has direct relationship to healing. It is a dynamic relationship between two persons, in which the pastor, representing Christ and the Church in the situation, seeks to help the other person to help himself. By the grace of God twisted lives are straightened out, tense emotional attitudes are released, guilty souls receive forgiveness, lives are made better through the counseling process.

The following *specific methods* of healing are used by a goodly number of churches and ministers today.

1. Public prayers for the sick may be deeply vital and a part of the concern of the *koinonia*, "the healing community of concern," to use Wayne Oates's phrase.[40]

2. Many churches have special prayer groups, in which a particular emphasis is laid on intercession for the sick.

3. A few churches have regular public healing services; others have healing missions.

4. Occasionally a minister will carry out a healing ministry to individual patients, with the consent of doctor and family. Such specific healing efforts have to be done without arousing undue expectation, for not all individuals are given healing by God on such occasions. Many ministers who are not ready to test on an individual patient whether or not they have the *charisma* of healing, will present the sick person and his need to God in prayer, at the same time touching in deep empathy the patient's hand or head. Ministers who take communion to the sick know that often spiritual if not physical healing takes place during the celebration of the Lord's Supper.

[40] "Pastoral Psychology and Faith Healing," *Pastoral Psychology, op. cit.,* p. 33a.

Conclusion

The healing sects are a continual reminder to the Church that healing is an integral part of the ministry of the Church of Jesus Christ to a sinful, suffering world. They also remind us of the supreme importance of the spiritual aspects of life.

On both counts the healing sects give an unbalanced emphasis, but we can be grateful to these sects for their reminder to the Church to be about its entire business.

This writer concludes that healing of functional disorders through spiritual means undoubtedly occurs; that possibly healing of organic disorders may occur in rare instances—probably in conjunction with medical means; that those who have the gift of healing should use that gift only in collaboration with doctors; and that healing services of a public nature, with high emotional charge, are so fraught with danger that they ought not to be held. The Church should continue to explore spiritual healing.

Suggestions for Further Study

1. Attend a Christian Science service. Describe, evaluate. What is its appeal? Buttress with the reading of perhaps one hundred pages of *Science and Health*.

2. Attend a meeting of one of the lesser known sects. Describe, evaluate. Read as much literature on the sect as you can secure.

3. If there is a Spiritualist church in your community, attend services, and make a study of the phenomena of Spirit-healing.

4. Investigate the theories concerning Odic-Force. (See volumes in the *Spiritual Seminar* series for 1954-1955.)

5. Work out a paper or sermon on "The Christian Philosophy of Sickness."

Selected Bibliography

Beasley, Norman. "The Cross and the Crown," *The History of Christian Science*. New York: Duell, Sloan & Pearce, Inc., 1952.

Boggs, Wade H., Jr., *Faith Healing and the Christian Faith*. Richmond: John Knox Press, 1956.

Bonnell, John S. "Is Faith Healing Valid Today?" *Religion and Human Behaviour*. Ed. Simon Doniger. New York: Association Press, 1954.

British Medical Association. A special committee of the Council. *Divine Healing and Co-operation Between Doctors and Clergy*. London, 1956.

Cranston, Ruth. *The Miracle of Lourdes*. New York: McGraw-Hill Book Co., 1955.

Dakin, Edwin F. *Mrs. Eddy, the Biography of a Virginal Mind*. New York: Blue Ribbon Books, 1930.

"Deadline for God: Rev. Oral Roberts," *Time*, LXVI (July 11, 1955), 41.

Dunbar, Flanders. *Mind and Body*. New York: Random House, 1947.

Dwyer, W. W. *Spiritual Healing in the United States and Great Britain*. Privately printed. Order from Samuel Weiser, Inc., 117 Fourth Avenue, New York 3, N. Y.; 1956, rev. ed.

Eddy, Mary Baker. *Science and Health, With Key to the Scriptures*. Boston: The Trustees under the will of Mary Baker Eddy, 1875.

Fox, Emmett. *The Sermon on the Mount*. New York: Harper & Bros., 1934.

Freeman, J. D. *The Household of Faith: the Story of Unity*. Lee's Summit, Mo.: Unity School of Christianity, 1951.

Ikin, Alice G. *New Concepts of Healing, Medical, Psychological, and Religious*. New York: Association Press, 1956.

Kew, Clifton E., and Kew Clinton J. *You Can Be Healed*. New York: Prentice-Hall, Inc., 1953.

Mann, Stella T. *Change Your Life Through Love!* New York: Dodd, Mead & Co., 1949.

McCasland, Selby V. *By the Finger of God*. New York: The Macmillan Co., 1951.

McNeill, John T. *A History of the Cure of Souls*. New York: Harper & Bros., 1951.

Oates, Wayne E. "The Cult of Reassurance," *Religion in Life*, XXIV (1955), 72-82.

Presbyterian Church in the United States. The General Assembly. Ad interim Committee on Christianity and Health. "Christianity and Health," *The Presbyterian Outlook*, CXXXVII (April 18, 1955), 5-7.

Pitts, John; Richardson, Cyril; Gross, Don H.; and Johnson, Paul E. "Spiritual Healing," *Religion in Life*, XXV (Spring, 1956), 163-204.

"Psychiatry and Spiritual Healing," *The Atlantic Monthly*, XCCIV (August, 1954), 39-43.

Sanford, Agnes. *The Healing Light*. 13th ed.; St. Paul: Macalester Park Publishing Co., 1951.

Scherzer, Karl. *The Church and Healing*. Philadelphia: Westminster Press, 1950.

Stegall, C. R., Jr., "What About the Faith Healers?" *The Presbyterian Outlook*, CXXXVII (September 18, 1955).

The Spiritual Healing Seminar (series of three reports, 1954, 1955). Rye, New York: Wainwright House.

"The Church and Healing," *Pastoral Psychology*, V (May, 1954) entire issue.

Van Buskirk, James D. *Religion, Healing, and Health*. New York: The Macmillan Co., 1952.

Weatherhead, Leslie D. *Psychology, Religion, and Healing*. New York: Abingdon Press, 1951.

———. Hiltner, Seward, and Outler, Albert C. "Christian Faith and Psychotherapy," *Religion in Life*, XXI (1952), 483-512.

Wilbur, Sibyl. *The Life of Mary Baker Eddy*. Boston: The Christian Publishing Society, 1907.

Wise, Carroll A. *Psychiatry and the Bible*. New York: Harper & Bros., 1956.

———. *Religion in Illness and Health*. New York: Harper & Bros., 1942.

Worcester, Elwood, and McComb, Samuel. *Body, Mind, and Spirit*. New York: Charles Scribner's Sons, 1932.

Zelley, E. S., Jr. "Prayer for the Sick," *The Christian Century*, LXXI (July, 1954), 300-301.

PART FOUR

ISMS PREDOMINANTLY CULTURAL

✚✚✚✚✚✚✚✚✚✚✚✚✚✚✚✚✚

TOTALITARIANISM: FASCISM AND COMMUNISM

IT SHOULD BE CLEAR FROM THE EARLIER UNITS OF THIS BOOK THAT there is no absolute dichotomy between "Biblical Isms" and "Cultural Isms." Complex institutions of culture grow out of biblical interpretation. People may also use biblical or pseudobiblical arguments as bulwarks for their social convictions and prejudices. We have examined some isms in which the principal issue is one of biblical interpretation. We have noted others in which religious belief and particular aspects of social behavior are very clearly interrelated. In this section we are considering isms in which biblical religion is either openly repudiated or else used for purposes which cannot be called religious in the ordinary sense of that word. We shall see, however, that even in the isms described as predominantly secular, men are incapable of complete separation from all religious behavior. Human nature is incurably religious.

Fascism and Marxian Communism, although quite different in theory, are remarkably similar in practice. Both systems are inherently totalitarian, denying basic human rights including religious freedom. Our purpose in this unit is to consider the origin of the movements, their essential characteristics, and the Church's strategy in confronting them.

In the course of this discussion we shall emphasize similarities in the practice of communism and fascism. Real differences between the two systems have been abundantly described by reliable writers; they have been even more frequently exploited through exaggeration or misrepresentation by demagogues of both the extreme right and the extreme left.

Historical Summary

Fascism. The Italian Fascisti organized their program in 1922 to promote conservative ideals of nationalism and to oppose all extraneous political movements, including communism. Fascism became associated with the drive for a revival of nationalism in other parts of Europe as well, notably Germany in 1933 and Spain in 1937. Its chief power lay in the military; hence, in the name of patriotism the military was given more and more authority. "Patriotism" became fanatical nationalism, and conquest in the name of nationalism, the accepted practice. Fascist principles were evident both in communist Russia after 1917 and in noncommunist Japan during the 1930's. In various Latin American countries there has been a succession of dictatorships for many years, but fascism of a more developed variety came to Argentina after 1943.

On the contemporary American scene, fascistic influences are probably more dangerous than communism, because economic and social conditions which nourish the latter in other parts of the world do not obtain here to the same degree. George Younger[1] describes a number of organizations and movements in America as "Old Dealers who judge issues by conditions which allegedly existed in some bygone era." Most of these organizations are isolationist, and all of them are regarded by Younger as insidious and potentially fascistic. The movements described appear to have common sources of financial support and maintain an informal membership. They are dedicated to molding public opinion, and they form channels of propaganda for irresponsible fringe groups "which do not have to be scrupulous about libel laws and which have no status among conservatives."

Communism. Not all communistic experiments have been Marxian or atheistic. A kind of communism is at least as old as Plato, and several communistic religious sects have developed in America. However, in the thinking of most people today, the word "communism" is clearly identified with the political and military expressions of Marx-Lenin-Stalinism.

Karl Marx (1818-1883) and Friedrich Engels (1820-1895) collaborated in writing *The Communist Manifesto* and *Das Kapital*, the infallible scriptures of the communist movement ever since. They inverted the Hegelian philosophy by insisting that "material" rather

[1] "Protestant Piety and the Right Wing," *Social Action*, XVII (May 15, 1951). *Social Action* is a monthly publication of the Council for Social Action of the Congregational Christian Churches and the Commission on Christian Social Action of the Evangelical and Reformed Church.

than "idea" is of the essence; all else was "epiphenomena." In the Marxian dialectic, materialism was further defined as economic determinism; thus all culture is a reflection of and is determined by economic conditions.

Organized communism did not come to power in Germany or England, relatively industrialized nations where Marx and Engels had supposed that it would first gain control. But in 1917 it came to power in Russia, a backward country more than ninety per cent agricultural and largely untouched by the Renaissance. Within a few months after the October Revolution of that year, the Bolsheviks (self-styled majority party of the Soviet Government) gained supremacy over the more moderate Mensheviks. It should be made clear that these Bolsheviks did not overthrow the Czar. Nicholas II, the last of the Romanov dynasty, abdicated well before the October Revolution and his Duma had already dissolved in favor of a Provisional Government which promised the only democratic experiment in Russia before or since that time. It was the Provisional Government which the Communists ruthlessly overthrew without reference to the expressed will of the people.

The Soviet regime is now supported by a powerful military and propaganda organization. The amazing spread of communism throughout other areas, notably in eastern Asia and eastern Europe, has always enjoyed the hearty encouragement and support of the Soviet regime, although it has not usually involved the direct participation of the Red Army, nor has it depended entirely on Russian leadership.

Analysis and Evaluation

William Ebenstein, in his chapter on fascism in *Today's Isms* (1954), describes that form of totalitarianism as ordinarily found in technologically advanced nations, among people who have had some introduction to democracy. A fascistic regime, at least in the initial stages, may have impressive support through popular elections. It is noteworthy that in March, 1933, Hitler received seventeen million votes in Germany, nearly half the total.

Fascism characteristically follows economic depression and utilizes the attending fears and frustrations of depression. It depends upon dictatorial leaders, greedy for power, and upon military force. It builds on foundations of authoritarian tradition and thrives on hostility

217

toward the real or imagined enemies of the nation. This kind of totalitarianism has no universally accepted scripture or doctrinal statement comparable to *The Communist Manifesto*. Yet Hitler's *Mein Kampf* (1925-27) and Mussolini's *The Doctrine of Fascism* (1932) contain widely accepted principles. Unlike communism, which ostensibly champions human equality, fascism affirms inequality as an ideal, justifying both racialism and imperialism on the grounds that superior people have the right and the obligation to dominate the inferior. Like communists, however, fascists govern by a single party, an elite group. They defy international agreements, advocate violence, and exercise totalitarian control over all sorts of human relationships. Fascism, like communism, becomes a way of life, not merely a political order.[2]

Communism does not appeal exclusively to the underprivileged, nor by any means to all of them. Some people of wealth and social prestige have given expression to their idealism through Marxian philosophy. A vivid example of this, and a record of the disillusionment which often follows it, is to be found in the chapter André Gide contributed to *The God That Failed* (see bibliography). In some places, modern India for example, the most vigorous expressions of communistic unrest are in university circles where graduates are frustrated by lack of employment commensurate with their training.

Yet it is unquestionably true, as Warren Austin said, that "we live in a world in which most of our fellowmen eat too little, live too wretchedly and die too young." In countries where many of these wretched folk live, the few abortive attempts at democratic procedure have fallen into the hands of the economically privileged and issued in disillusionment for the masses. Communists regularly and quite deliberately exploit any social injustice for their purposes, turning other revolutionary drives in the direction of Marxianism. Communism offers the masses a plan of action and makes promises which have a winsome sound, even though they are seldom if ever fulfilled. Such slogans as "workers of the world unite, you have nothing to lose but your chains" do not seem absurd to those who have never known anything but chains!

A. Marxian Communism Has the Following Presuppositions:

[2] The ideas incorporated in this paragraph are suggested by and elaborated in William Ebenstein's *Today's Isms* (New York: Prentice Hall, Inc., 1954), *passim*.

1. *The privileged classes will yield only to revolutionary pressure, and only the violent form of revolution can be ultimately effective.* This philosophy forever separates communism from any form of socialism which abhors violence and is characterized by constitutional gradualism. Marx looked disdainfully on the socialistic movements of his day, regarding them as visionary and craven; he would have no higher regard for the modern socialism in England or Scandinavia.

2. *Only the skilled industrial proletariat can be trusted to carry out the revolution.* Marx had little interest in peasants, and he had little confidence in the ability of unskilled industrial workers to lead the movement. But he envisioned a dictatorship of the skilled proletariat as the intermediate stage between capitalism and pure communism (classless society). No Iron Curtain country regards itself as having yet attained pure communism. The most advanced among them claim to have arrived at the dictatorship of the proletariat, but even that misrepresents the fact, because in each case these nations are controlled by an oligarchy whose leadership is chosen without regard to their proletarian status and whose concerns seem to have little reference to expressed proletarian interests.

Capitalists, in Marx's definition of the term, are those who control the means of production while proletarians do all the productive work, receive far less remuneration than is their just due, and are helpless to improve their condition unless they revolt. We should always remember that Marx was familiar with the capitalism of the Industrial Revolution period, and that communists continue to describe capitalism in nineteenth-century terms. The modern development within capitalism of powerful labor unions, favorable working conditions, and the partial ownership of many industries by the workers themselves was unthinkable to Marx, and for his followers to acknowledge its effectiveness would seriously weaken the cause of communism.

3. *Since religion is by nature conservative, it always stands in the way of economic justice.* Thus religion is regarded by communists as the "opiate of the people," lulling them to inertia with promises of a better life in the hereafter. Atheism in Marxian philosophy is of the essence; it is not some later addition intended to protest the more reactionary forms of religious expression. All religion is a superstition

219

to be outgrown, its organized forms merely reflections of an antiquated economic order.

We may rightly admit that the Russian Church was for centuries pretty well identified with the economic *status quo*. But we must insist that Karl Marx was never in Russia, knew little or nothing about the Russian Church, and that he denounced not merely reactionary manifestations of religion, but religion per se.

B. It Is Important to Distinguish Carefully Between Christian and Communist Social Ideals.

There is some truth in the statement that communism is a judgment on the Church for her failures, and it is undoubtedly true that the zeal of communists makes lethargy among Christians even more shameful. But it is utterly naïve to assume that Christianity and communism are "brothers under the skin." Can a Christian be a communist? The following reply was made by Andrew K. Rule of the Louisville Presbyterian Seminary faculty: "No Christian who knows what Christianity is can be a communist if he knows what communism is." There are, to be sure, Christians who have not thought very deeply about the implications of the Christian faith. There are also honest idealists who are intrigued by Marxian philosophy without realizing that the Frankenstein monster of Iron Curtain totalitarianism is a logical outgrowth of the Marxian philosophy. We shall contrast Christian social ideals with the ideals of communism in relation to five important concepts:

1. *The transformation of people.* Marxism proposes to transform the world through economic "liberation," assuming that there can be no transformation except through economic revolution and that nothing else is essentially important. Communists believe that when people are thus liberated other social evils will automatically disappear. Christians believe that apart from the transforming power of God on human character, any freedom may be used for evil purposes as surely as it can be used for good. Communists, therefore, seem unduly optimistic about human nature, even proletarian human nature, in spite of the fact that their history thus far really gives them little basis for such optimism!

2. *The importance of individuals.* In communistic practice, individuals are expendable; only the "social good" is important. Not only

counter revolutionaries but even old-line Bolsheviks who have earlier demonstrated their loyalty, may be liquidated if they are unable to keep pace with frequent changes in the Party line. The Moscow purges of the 1930's give dramatic testimony to this fact.[3] Unconcern for individual human worth is the natural product of a philosophy which denies man's spiritual nature.

Christian theology teaches that man was created in the image of God and that every human being is potentially an heir of eternal life. No individual, therefore, is unimportant even when he fails to contribute to the social good. Thus Christianity and communism find basic disagreement in the doctrine of man. Calvinistic theology, to be sure, is not in the least optimistic about the inner resources of unregenerate human nature. But the supreme manifestation of God's love is that "while we were yet helpless, at the right time Christ died for the ungodly" (Rom. 5:6). So there is a mandatory Christian concern for every human being, whether he be revolutionary or counterrevolutionary, kulak or proletarian, rich or poor, Bolshevik or Menshevik, precisely because each one is so important to God.

Christians, however, have often been so preoccupied with the importance of individual conversions as to give insufficient thought to social problems. We have often been naïve in supposing that converted individuals will invariably solve social problems. Unfortunately they don't—not even among themselves. Yet the fact remains that a regenerate society cannot exist apart from regenerate individuals.

3. *The importance of economic factors to social well-being.* The Bible is not a textbook of economics, and no economic system in the world can properly claim to be distinctively Christian. Yet the Bible has a great deal to say about the right use of material possessions. Note, for example, several of the parables of Jesus: the unmerciful servant (Matt. 18:21-35), the laborers and hours (Matt. 20:1-16), the talents (Matt. 25:14-30), the two debtors (Luke 7:40-49), the rich fool (Luke 12:13-21), the unjust steward (Luke 16:1-9), and the rich man and the beggar (Luke 16:19-31).

[3] The current repudiation of the cult of the leader in Russia lays the blame for the Moscow purges squarely at the feet of Joseph Stalin. But unless the cult of the leader can be superseded by something far better than the cult of a party, comprising a tiny minority of the population, the term "counterrevolutionary" will continue to mean anything standing in the path of party leadership at any given time.

Insofar as I understand biblical teachings on the subject, wealth is to be condemned only if it is wrongfully gained or selfishly administered. The Scriptures do not indiscriminately condemn private wealth, and normal spiritual development is enhanced by a reasonable freedom from want. There is no inherent virtue in being poor, yet virtue is in no way assured among people who are merely free from economic under-privilege. Communists are convinced that classless society, where distribution is "to each according to his need," will be *ipso facto* free from all unrighteousness. This identification of righteousness with freedom from want seems utterly absurd to Christians who know that human sin goes much deeper and is much more inclusive. Yet the Christian doctrine of sin must never be used to justify unconcern about the existence of poverty.

4. *The attitude toward the State.* Communists affirm that since the State exists to protect the selfish interests of privileged classes, it serves no purpose in classless society and is destined to "wither away." They are remarkably vague about what arrangements will be made in classless society to deliver the mail, run the railroads, keep vital statistics, etc., expecting no doubt to cross those particular bridges when they come to them. Quite significantly, however, this withering away of the State seems more remote than ever in the modern practice of communism. Not even the most despotic monarchies remaining in the world control the lives of their people more completely or in greater detail than do the totalitarian governments of the Iron and Bamboo Curtains. The activities of their secret police make all but the worst czars of the Romanov dynasty seem benevolent by comparison.

Christians do not repudiate the concept of the State as such. Even a bad state is better than anarchy. They do not expect the State to wither away in time, and Christian eschatology points to the consummation of the kingdom of God in eternity; a kingdom is fundamentally different from statelessness. Most Christians readily accept the responsibilities of citizenship, ideally including among those responsibilities the obligation to protest when the laws of God are evidently violated by civil authorities. They accept the requirement to render unto Caesar the things that are Caesar's, not expecting Caesar to be perfect because, after all, he is a human being. But the right of totalitarian control over their lives does not belong to Caesar; their supreme loyalty must be to

God. Therefore, they are obliged to reject the principle of totalitarianism, but also to recognize that no existing form of government is distinctively or entirely Christian.

5. *Ethics.* Communist ethics consist in loyalty to the Party. Having no foundation in recognized spiritual values, they are avowedly relative. From the communist point of view, repudiation of local or international agreements is not regarded as inconsistency, nor is the misrepresentation of facts necessarily considered dishonesty. Loyalty means conforming to *today's* Party strategy, and while that may be quite different from yesterday's, the fact that it is the Party's decision justifies it completely.

Ideally, at least, Christian conduct toward all people and at all times depends upon principles which are eternally valid. Christians, to be sure, do not always act consistently with their belief that basic ethical values are rooted in the unchanging will of God; their failures in that regard are frequent and shameful. But for such failures they are rebuked by their Scriptures and occasionally by their consciences and by one another.

C. Both Fascism and Communism Exhibit Interesting Parallels to Religion and Frequently Fill a Religious Vacuum.

In the widest sense of the word, we may regard the totalitarian philosophies as "religions." They have produced their messiahs, holy books, prophets, missionary outreach, organized hierarchy, and even eschatology. And they often guard them as jealously and interpret them as literally as do the most fundamentalist and exclusivist believers of any religious system. It seems plain that dialectical materialism, simply as a philosophy, could not induce men to fight, bleed, and die in its defense. Neither could the merely intellectual concept of racial superiority or national excellence. It is when those ideas penetrate to the emotional and volitional levels and are implemented with slogans, creeds, extravagant promises, and dynamic leaders that full-blown religion emerges from philosophical conjecture. Both communism and fascism demonstrate the terrifying proportions this religious zeal can reach, proportions not even the most fanatical and authoritarian among the religions of the world can match.

All people, communists and fascists no less than others, seem to be incurably religious. People who have repudiated ancient spiritual values almost invariably create substitutes. Those who have joined the Communist Party expecting to escape from religious authority have instead found themselves involved in a philosophy and practice which has developed its own religious symbolism and which is governed by a hierarchy demanding obedience as unquestioning as that demanded in the Jesuit Order.

D. There are Evident Similarities in the Practice of Communism and Fascism Which Show Their Essential Kinship:

1. *In both systems the activity of all opposition parties is eliminated.* Popular elections are frequently held in totalitarian states, but the choice is not between candidates. It is rather the obligation to vote "yes" or "no" in relation to the single issue or candidate proposed. The overwhelming numbers of people who go to the polls indicate the power of these regimes, and the all-but-unanimous approval of the Party's proposal demonstrates the futility of opposition and shows that it is considerably less risky to avoid registering a protest. In the democratic sense, therefore, popular elections do not exist where either communists or fascists are in control. Neither is there the possibility of referendum initiated by the people, and recall is ordinarily accomplished by "liquidation."

2. *In both systems there is absolute economic control from the top level and repudiation of free enterprise.* To some extent during Russia's New Economic Policy Period (1921-1928), and even at present, concessions to a modified form of capitalism have been made. But such concessions are temporary measures to avoid economic catastrophe and are tolerated, much as religion is tolerated, to be outgrown. Communism's long-term goal is clearly the elimination of free enterprise, and even during the transition period there is nothing comparable to the freedom taken for granted in capitalistic society.

Large industries and especially heavy industries have frequently sponsored fascistic regimes in the beginning, ultimately to find themselves pawns of the totalitarian authorities, all their freedom dissipated. Economic controls become as inflexible in fascistic society as under communism, although the theory and practice of the two systems are different in many important respects. Fascists maintain a pretense of free enterprise, denouncing communism, glorifying rank and gradation.

224

They do not even theorize that controls will ultimately "wither away," but openly regard authoritarianism as permanently beneficial.

3. *The glorification of the leader is characteristic of both systems.* There is little essential difference between the apotheosis of Hitler in Germany and of Stalin in Russia. Infallibility and impeccability were attributed to both. There was the same kind of obeisance, similar banners and fanfare, the same aura about their persons. The splendor in which each of them lived was extravagant, Stalin behind a façade of proletarian simplicity, Hitler quite openly.

As has been the case throughout history, even leaders ultimately go the way of all flesh, and there often follows a terrible disillusionment about their alleged impeccability. The lives of both Hitler and Stalin have now been revealed for what they were—lustful, greedy, perverted. In Germany, the fascist regime died with Hitler. Whether it will ever be reborn depends upon many factors. The totalitarian regime in Russia did not die with Stalin. Whether the current denunciation of the cult of the leader in that country is an honest effort to remedy the most despicable aspects of the Party's bloody history, or whether it is intended merely to foster the cult of an oligarchy, is not yet clear.

4. *In both systems freedom of speech, freedom of the press, and freedom of assembly are denied.* We must acknowledge that freedom in the absolute sense is impossible because it would threaten all proper law and order. We must also admit that under wartime conditions a considerable amount of censorship is exercised by the same Western democratic governments which in peacetime relax their controls. But we must insist that the traditions of Hyde Park and of Town Meeting, the freedom of religious assembly and religious education, the freedom to publish and circulate both the *Daily Worker* and the *Chicago Tribune*, could not be tolerated by any totalitarian state.

We are not here suggesting that the practices which emerge in democratic freedom are invariably worthy. Many of them quite evidently are not. Certain conditions, to be sure, might be more speedily ameliorated by the firm control of authoritarian hands. But we could never be sure that such authority would long remain less corrupt than the worst of our social evils. Although the judgment of free people is by no means always trustworthy in what they say or write or meet to accomplish, at least the truth can be as openly declared as falsehood, and we shall have to go on believing that truth will ultimately triumph.

5. *Both systems depend upon secret police and forced labor.* Russia's forced labor camps began with Stalin's efforts to liquidate the kulaks and were created primarily for political prisoners. They are not merely a wartime measure, except as activities in a totalitarian state may be described as continual preparation for war. These camps, located for the most part on the borders of Finland and in the far Asiatic reaches of the Soviet territory, continue to the present time. Their exact location and number are unknown except to Soviet authorities. In addition to providing safekeeping for counterrevolutionaries and prisoners of war, they furnish a regular supply of cheap labor for the enormous industrial development of various Soviet Republics.

The notorious forced-labor and concentration camps of Nazi Germany have been so well publicized that further description is unnecessary. For our purposes it is sufficient to note that such measures are not only typical of totalitarian rule but also seem to be inherently a part of it. They cannot be maintained without an elaborate and comprehensive network of secret police.

6. *In both systems all economic life is subordinated to the military development of the country.* Totalitarianism frankly advocates the use of force, regarding aggression as desirable until the new order is everywhere established. Totalitarian leaders depend on war economy to maintain artificial prosperity and to create the state of excitement necessary for their effective control. They continually emphasize the development of heavy industry at the expense of consumer goods, and the resulting industrial efficiency is often impressive. Railroads run on time, factories spring up everywhere, there is little unemployment. The parade of military power is equally impressive, demonstrating unmistakable preparation for any contingency of internal strife or external attack, all the while publicizing slogans of peace.

Through fear of aggression from totalitarian states, democratic nations of the West have also permitted themselves to be caught in the vicious circle of excessive spending for military preparation. There are at least three real dangers involved: (a) Nations not willingly identified with either democratic or totalitarian spheres of power are led to suspect the Western democracies of aggressive ambitions. (b) The return to peacetime economy becomes increasingly difficult and could be accompanied by serious unrest. (c) Excessive military power is itself a potential invitation to the sort of totalitarian control our democratic philosophy so vigorously repudiates.

7. *Each system makes a scapegoat of some race or class.* It is not uncommon in human society generally to make convenient use of a scapegoat in rationalizing evil, and the practice is always shameful. But when it is implemented by the vicious legislation and purges characteristic of totalitaranism, it is the more reprehensible. "Counterrevolutionaries" are held responsible by communists for all social injustice and are submitted to legal disability and discrimination on account of religion or class. In Nazi Germany, Jews were the scapegoat people. In each case the accusations have been leveled at a minority group whose economic privilege or business acumen is allegedly a threat to the majority.

Communist philosophy affirms racial equality, and in that respect is a rebuke to the segregation and discrimination practiced in both fascist states and Western democracies. Peoples under colonial domination, and minority racial groups condemned to second-class citizenship within autonomous nations, are special objects of communist propaganda.

8. *Both communists and fascists show open disregard for international agreements.* This is to be explained partly by the exclusivism of totalitarian governments and partly by their inherent ethical relativism. We do not mean to suggest that communists and fascists *never* abide by international agreements; some agreements are manifestly to their advantage and even necessary to their livelihood. But totalitarian states cannot permanently collaborate either with the democracies or with each other. An example in point is the nonaggression pact between Hitler and Stalin signed August 23, 1939. That pact was violated by the signatories within a very short time, although it probably helped to make the Second World War inevitable by temporarily protecting Germany on her eastern borders.

In this matter of international relationships, a reasonable humility becomes the Western democracies. We too have sometimes violated agreements. Even more frequently we have felt obligated to temporize, making alliances with strange bedfellows whom we regarded as the lesser of evils. We collaborated with the Soviet Union during the Second World War to oppose fascism, and we have also given open support to

227

fascist states for fear of communism. Confidence in the ultimate efficacy of such alliances would be wishful thinking.

9. *Both totalitarian systems maintain fifth-column activities in other countries wherever possible.* These activities have been so widespread and varied that a comprehensive description would be impossible within the limits of this unit. It is sufficient for our purposes to indicate the essential similarity of the German Bund and the Comintern (later replaced by the Cominform) in various parts of the free world. Those organizations loyally supported the totalitarian doctrines of fascist Germany and communist Russia. They were in regular communication with Berlin and Moscow, from which headquarters they received financial and moral support. They met with varying degrees of success, operating as they did throughout the world either openly or surreptitiously, but always with indefatigable persistence.

"Popular front" is a strategy whereby communists, when they are a minority group, temporarily collaborate with other left-of-center political movements in order to dominate the others through an eventual *coup d'état.* The success of "popular front" is evidence that communists do not need voluntary support from the popular majority in order to dominate. This strategy, comparable in some respects to fifth-column, has met with success in Czechoslovakia and other Russian satellites. Czechoslovakia, a highly industrialized nation, had a fairly well-established democratic tradition for many years. The present regime in that country is a notable exception to William Ebenstein's rule, mentioned earlier in this unit, that fascism and not communism seizes power in post-democratic and post-industrial countries.

The Christian Approach to Totalitarianism

Christians who live behind the Iron Curtain or under fascist governments face a dilemma. Their problem in determining and implementing the proper attitude toward totalitarianism is more trying, though perhaps no more complex or soul-searching than ours. Prof. Joseph Hromodka of Czechoslovakia has succeeded in delineating the problem, even though his evaluations of Western democracy have occasionally seemed more than a little unsympathetic. We should gratefully enjoy our freedom, but not without confessing that the sins which make totalitarianism possible—greed, selfishness, and lust for power—are shared by us all. We too are responsible for seeking the proper Christian approach to whatever human authority attempts to usurp the prerogatives of God. There is no easy solution to this complex problem. We believe, however, that the following suggestions are indicated, at least for us who still enjoy the necessary political freedom to implement them:

A. Insist That All Totalitarianism Is Fundamentally a Denial of Basic Human Rights Including Religious Liberty.

Ecclesiastical as well as civil authorities have violated the principles of liberty. The organized Church has cause for repentance wherever she has been party to the limitations of civil or religious freedom. The political intrigue of the Roman Church in Spain, Italy, parts of Latin America, and elsewhere is well known to Protestants, and we cannot excuse it. Freedom of religion includes both the right to conform and the right to dissent. We must acknowledge, however, that the Roman Church is not alone culpable in the mistreatment of religious minorities. Let us beware of ever engaging in comparable practices. The liberty we expect to enjoy where we are a minority must never be denied others where we are a majority. Neither should we seek privileges for Christians which are not granted to others.

We who can still openly oppose the insidious forces leading to totalitarianism should do so vigorously. To maintain civil and religious liberty where they exist is probably the greatest service we can render those who no longer enjoy them. Ultimately, the most effective enemy of totalitarianism is the existence of freedom in other parts of the world. People who live under the totalitarian heel cannot forever be kept in ignorance and isolation from those whose lot is more favorable, and they are sure to want whatever is manifestly better. A spirit of rebellion from within is still a more formidable danger to any totalitarian regime than the strongest military force from without.

B. Be Alert to the Danger of the Totalitarian Virus, but Not So Preoccupied with Fighting It as to Neglect Positive Christian Witness.

The primary function of Christians is the proclamation of the gospel, joyfully sharing the good news. Although our Christian duties involve both "building up and tearing down," edification is ultimately more important than destruction; proclaiming righteousness is more essential than decrying sin. In a word, it is more important to be pro-Christian than to be anticommunist or antifascist. It is far better to light a candle than to rail against the darkness! Those who allow themselves to become preoccupied with fighting communism or fascism tend to lose their perspective. They not only neglect the more positive witness to their faith, but also frequently become impervious to recognition of their own social evils. Negative preaching so often eventuates in negative living.

The mission of Christianity is a ministry to people in all their needs and relationships. The Church cannot properly remain aloof from the problems of hunger, ignorance, poverty, and disease. The danger that those conditions will be exploited by totalitarianism is real and important, but the primary concern of Christians is with something greater than that. Our first interest must be to show compassion in the name of him who said, "As you did it to one of the least of these my brethren, you did it to me" (Matt. 25:40).

C. Carefully Distinguish Both Communism and Fascism from Everything Falsely So Called.

In some circles there is a regrettable tendency to label any unpopular cause or movement "communistic." This practice is conducive to a hysteria which is as unchristian as it is unrealistic. Surely the Church is obliged to tell people what communism *is* and, as a corollary, what it *is not*. Never be deceived by communism, an enemy of Christianity and of all proper world order, but do not equate it with everything unconventional or disturbing. Christianity itself is both unconventional and revolutionary. Christians were once accused of turning the world upside down; if that charge is never made of us today, can we claim to be truly and vitally Christian?

The modern world is torn by revolution, some of which is very ugly but by no means all of which is communistic. Many parts of Asia and Africa, for example, are presently in a ferment born of an exaggerated spirit of nationalism. Theirs is an understandable reaction against centuries of colonial domination. A third of the world's population has emerged from colonial dependency to autonomous statehood in a single decade since the end of the Second World War; other nations are struggling to be born. These peoples often seem much more suspicious of the Western democracies, who are their former masters, than of Russia, whose oppression they have not known. Permitting Soviet influence in their political affairs is, we believe, exceedingly dangerous.

Let us hope they discover that before they fall prey to the popular-front strategy and are inextricably caught in the web of a new variety of colonialism. But they are not to be regarded as communistic simply because they dislike the West or because they welcome trade agreements with the Soviet Union. We must acknowledge their right to do both.

In the United States, as elsewhere, there are potential fascist inroads through government, military power, business, even organized religion. Yet it is well to remember that Americans do not have and have never had a totalitarian regime. While we shall do well to maintain a watchful eye, it is quite as easy to become needlessly hysterical about the danger of fascism as about the danger of communism. Alarmists are quick to identify with fascism all military organizations, mass media of communication, large corporations, and either "New Deal" or "Old Deal" political thinking. The identification is generally indefensible. Admitting the possibility that those institutions might become tools for fascistic purposes, they do not of themselves lead to totalitarian government. In a democracy we can afford to be less afraid of the sort of fascism which has developed in Germany, Italy, Spain, or Japan, than of slow and insidious encroachment on our democratic processes. Nevertheless, we must not feel smugly secure or relax a reasonable vigilance in the false assurance that "it could never happen here." There are various avenues of psychological preparation for the growth of totalitarianism; a spirit of isolationism is probably the most dangerous among them.

D. Co-operate with Every Worthy Effort to Correct the Social Evils Which Nourish Totalitarianism.

For a hundred and fifty years, Protestant missions have worked heroically, but with limited means and personnel, to alleviate hunger, poverty, and disease. Today the Church has willing allies among secular organizations genuinely interested in better living conditions throughout the world. Agencies of the United Nations, agencies of our government, and private foundations with vast financial resources are everywhere offering their help. A significant factor in their concern is a desire to obliterate communism by draining the swamps in which it most readily breeds. Some of these secular organizations are much more interested in keeping communism out than putting Christianity in; yet they welcome the collaboration of Christian missionaries trained in agriculture, public health, literacy education, etc. The Church has more important business, to be sure, than fighting communism. But since she has neither the financial means nor the technical skills to heal the world's sores alone, she must never look disdainfully on collaboration with other agencies whose purposes are also good.

Conclusion

In this unit we have attempted to show how Marxian communism and fascism, both inherently totalitarian systems, although very different in theory, are remarkably similar in practice. Each denies the principle of religious liberty. Each becomes a way of life, a political and secular faith, eliciting the devotion of millions for whom real religion has become meaningless. In so doing, these systems reveal interesting parallels to religion.

Among those who espouse the social philosophy of communism are visionaries who confuse it with Christian idealism. We have maintained that the differences are fundamental and have indicated that the evils of totalitarian rule are a natural outgrowth of the Marxian philosophy in practice.

We have deplored the tendency of some people to label as "communistic" or "fascistic" almost any thought or practice which they regard unfavorably. We believe it is the business of the Church to help people understand what these totalitarian philosophies really are, and to be more discriminating with respect to movements which are either revolutionary or reactionary, but which are not related to totalitarianism.

Human nature being what it is, the threat of totalitarianism will probably continue to exert itself throughout the world. We have admitted the potential danger of both communistic and fascistic encroachment on democratic society, and we have recommended a reasonable vigilance to prevent such encroachment. But we have also warned against the danger of hysteria with respect to those movements. They are most effectively opposed in the calm assurance and loving concern which belong to the Christian faith.

A final word is of utmost importance: while hating the systems that enslave people, let us never give way to hating the people. Victims of totalitarian rule deserve nothing less than our sympathetic understanding; even their rulers, like all others who succumb to the sins of pride and lust for power, are still potential recipients of God's grace to forgive and power to change. To regard them otherwise would be a denial of Christian faith. To hate them would be capitulation to the very spirit on which totalitarianism itself thrives.

Above all, we must seek to maintain fellowship with Christian communities living under totalitarian governments. It is easy to forget that an Iron Curtain effectively blocks the view from both directions. That explains why they so often regard us, as we regard them, with suspicion. The recent visit of Western churchmen to Russia in the interest of re-establishing lines of communication between churches deserves our wholehearted approval. It is still required of us that we "do good to all men, and especially to those who are of the household of faith" (Gal. 6:10).

Suggestions for Further Study

1. In the available literature, investigate what happens to the Church and religious life generally under fascism.

2. How does fascism affect ethical behavior, economic well-being, such organizations as labor unions?

3. Discuss with a socialist what he regards as the differences between socialism and communism. Find out why socialists are so opposed to communists, and vice versa.

4. Since it is the kind of thing to which ministers and even whole churches are sometimes exposed, it might be worth while to examine such perennial attacks on the National Council of the Churches of Christ in the U. S. A., or The Methodist Church and Bishop Oxnam, or John C. Bennett, or E. Stanley Jones (all of whom are opposed to communism) as are found, for example, in the *Christian Beacon*. Submit them to analysis and determine the basis of the misunderstanding or of the odium.

Selected Bibliography

A. FASCISM

Ebenstein, William. *Today's Isms*. New York: Prentice-Hall, Inc., 1954.

Hallgarten, George W. F. *Why Dictators?* New York: The Macmillan Co., 1954.

Harand, Irene. *His Struggle*. Chicago: Artcraft & Co., 1937.

Hitler, Adolph. *Mein Kampf*. New York: Reynal & Co., 1939.

Krueger, Kurt. *I Was Hitler's Doctor*. New York: Biltmore Publishing Co., 1943.

Roy, Ralph L. *Apostles of Discord*. Boston: The Beacon Press, 1953.

U. S. Library of Congress, Legislative and Reference Service. *Fascism in Action*. Washington: Government Printing Service, 1947.

Van Passen, Pierre. *Earth Could Be Fair*. New York: The Dial Press, 1946.

"The Vatican Lesson," *Christian Century*, LXIX (January 30, 1952), 118-19.

Wagner, Ludwig. *Hitler, Man of Strife*. New York: W. W. Norton & Co., 1942.

B. COMMUNISM

Bennett, John C. *Christianity and Communism*. New York: Association Press, 1948.

Blanchard, Paul. *Communism, Democracy and Catholic Power*. Boston: The Beacon Press, 1951.

Church of Scotland, Commission on Communism. *The Challenge of Communism*. Edinburgh: Church of Scotland Publications, 1951.

————. *The Church Under Communism*. London: Student Christian Movement Press, 1952.

Crossman, Richard H. S., ed. *The God That Failed*. New York: Harper & Bros., 1949.

Ebon, Martin. *World Communism Today*. New York: Whittlesey House, 1948.

Hunt, R. N. C. *Marxism: Past and Present*. New York: The Macmillan Co., 1954.

————. *The Theory and Practice of Communism*. New York: The Macmillan Co., 1951.

Koestler, Arthur. *Darkness at Noon*. New York: The Macmillan Co., 1952.

————. *The Yogi and the Commissar*. New York: The Macmillan Co., 1946.

Marx, Karl, and Engels, Friedrich. *Selected Works*. 2 vols.; London: Lawrence & Wishart, Ltd., 1950.

Miller, Alexander. *The Christian Significance of Karl Marx*. New York: The Macmillan Co., 1947.

Spinka, Matthew. *Christianity Confronts Communism*. London: Religious Book Publishers, 1938.

————. *Nicholas Berdyaev: Captive of Freedom*. Philadelphia: Westminster Press, 1950.

————. *The Church in Soviet Russia*. New York: Oxford University Press, 1956.

Timasheff, N. S. *The Great Retreat*. New York: E. P. Dutton & Co., 1948.

————. *Religion in Soviet Russia, 1917-1942*. New York: Sheed & Ward, 1942.

RACISM

IN THE EFFORT TO SECURE PLAY SPACE FOR THEIR CHILDREN, NEGRO ministers in the city of New Orleans said, "We are not allowed at the parks, although provisions are made for ducks and geese. It is hard for us as ministers to teach our children Christianity under such circumstances." [1]

Racism! It shows up everywhere. It affects our choice of friends and our personal relationships with others. Within the framework of our nation racism has become a crucial problem, dividing us into groups and classes wherein the democratic ideal of the basic rights of every individual is denied to some citizens, and from which groups and classes enmity and strife have exploded. But the problem is not confined to our own nation. It is world wide. There is perhaps not a place on earth where the attitude of racial superiority is not expressed in some form. People throughout the world have been matched against each other because of differences in appearance. The world has been divided into the "white" and "yellow" and "black" areas, with prejudice, hatred, and warfare as the consequence. Racism has made its way into the Christian church. It not only hides within the fellowship of this body, but also in one way or another has been supported and promoted by Christian groups. Thus the message of reconciliation of man to God through Jesus Christ is incongruously proclaimed by people who are not reconciled to one another but isolated by the feelings of racial superiority. Racism is one of the most vicious enemies man ever faces. The Christian church must in these days look at it in all of its terrible reality and examine it in the light of the gospel of deliverance.

What Is Racism?

The fact that people are different in appearance is without question, and racism results from the evaluation given to these differences and

[1] Quoted by William S. Nelson in "Crucial Issues in America's Race Relations Today," *The Christian Way in Race Relations,* ed. William S. Nelson (New York: Harper & Bros., 1948), p. 21.

the attitudes which follow. "Race, then, is not the modern superstition. But Racism is. Racism is the dogma that one ethnic group is condemned by Nature to hereditary inferiority and another group is destined to hereditary superiority." [2] *Webster's New Collegiate Dictionary* defines racism as an "assumption of inherent racial superiority or the purity and superiority of certain races, and consequent discrimination against other races; also, any doctrine or program of racial domination and discrimination based on such an assumption." The definition is not without substantiation. Again and again the distinctions of physical features have been interpreted as marks of superiority or inferiority, and Dr. Alfred Metraux was right when he said,

Racism is one of the most disturbing phenomena of the great revolution of the modern world. At the very time when industrial civilization is penetrating to all points of the globe and is uprooting men of every colour from their age-old traditions, a doctrine, speciously scientific in appearance, is invoked in order to rob these men of their full share in the advantage of the civilization forced upon them.[3]

The Roots of Racism

Attitudes of racial superiority are made possible among other ways, by the fact that human beings differ in physical traits. People have different colors of skin, different kinds of hair, and different facial features. In the past and in the present these distinctions have been used, sometimes ignorantly, sometimes skilfully, as justification for the position that some people by nature are inferior and that this native endowment will always be passed on from generation to generation. As will be discussed in a later section, it is clearly established that this position fails to distinguish between natural and cultural traits. Race is a biological concept from which it is impossible to determine mental capacity. But recognition of these pseudoscientific ideas about physical distinctions has not eliminated the concepts of racial superiorities or resolved the problems of racism. If the Christian church is to understand adequately the problem of racism and is to meet it effectively, we must look further at its roots.

[2] Ruth Benedict as quoted in Edmund D. Soper, *Racism, a World Issue* (Nashville: Abingdon Press, 1947), p. 32.
[3] Quoted in Michel Leiris, *Race and Culture* (Paris: UNESCO, 1951), p. 6.

Racism often develops because of historical precedent and the conditioning atmosphere in which children are reared. In areas where racism prevails, children often grow to be prejudiced because of the position of parents and other adults. It is believed that it is natural and proper for one group to look with disdain upon another. But racial prejudice is not inborn. It is learned. Children who have not been influenced otherwise will live and play side by side with children of other races without question or concern. Attitudes of superiority take root as the child is influenced by the example of others, particularly of parents. This fact is illustrated by the statement of the man who said "I was fourteen years old before I knew I was better than a Negro." The significance of this conditioning atmosphere is vividly illustrated at the present time in widely scattered experiences related to the program of integration in the public schools of the United States. In community after community where school boards have inaugurated a program of integration, white and Negro students have worked and lived harmoniously until interrupted by parents and other adults whose criticisms, accusations, and riotous acts have not only interrupted the program but also influenced school children to take up the banner of superiority.

Promotion of racial prejudice can also be traced to the desire for economic gain. One of the first strong proponents of racism, Count de Gobineau, confessed that his bitter essays were prompted by the desire to defend the threatened interest of the aristocratic caste of Europe. Racial suppressions in the imperial world of the British Empire is clearly identified with vast financial advantages. When other countries were abolishing slavery in the nineteenth century, justification was given to slavery in the southern part of the United States on the basis of the need of this inferior race for its own good to be directed by the superior whites. But behind this attitude was the need for cheap labor so that the production of cotton could maintain the wealthy position the South had achieved. In our own day attitudes toward people of other countries are often regulated by the extent to which their industrial activities threaten the enterprise of our own nation.

One of the most essential starting points for an adequate understanding of the explosive feelings which develop among people is found in the functioning of the personality of individuals who give expression to racism and in the inner condition of groups which hold themselves superior to others. This means that racism is often the expression of a sick personality, the result of unwholesome living.

When an individual fails to face up to himself, he will then often seek compensation by making an attack on someone else. The dishonest man is almost always suspicious of the honesty of others. The liar never believes his neighbor's story. The unfaithful husband or wife usually suspects the fidelity of the other. Man is always tempted to transfer ignorance, trouble, and failure to others; and racial prejudice and discrimination is often the outward expression of frustration, anxiety, insecurity, fear, failure. The racism so prevalent in the rise of the Nazi regime in Germany, was rooted in the frustrations and failures of the German people which under the leadership of Hitler were transferred to the Jews and the aristocrats. The increase in violent attitudes of some white people in the United States toward minority groups can often be seen during periods when there has been anxiety over the economic or political welfare of the nation.

Racism Around the World

Evidences of racism abound everywhere. It is not possible to review here all of the conditions and areas where racism is and has been at work, but some of the more significant situations are now to be noted with particular attention given to racism in the United States.

Nowhere, at least in our own century, has the idea of racial superiority been more explosively, more brutally expressed than in parts of Europe under the domination of Adolph Hitler. His rise to power and temporary control of a large part of Europe was built around one theme—the superiority of the Aryan race. The use of "Aryan race" is incorrect. There is no Aryan race, for the word "Aryan" is a linguistic designation. Hitler did not indicate who the Aryans were or on what bases the claim was made for their superior station in life. He simply started with the thesis and continuously emphasized it. The response is a vivid example of how racism can develop and people be led to believe in their own unique position among mankind. The morale of the German people was low; they were failing in attempts to regain a position of prominence among the nations of the world. Hitler appealed to their vanity and offered a scapegoat.

The position of the Aryan master race was supported by the gospel that all other races were inferior and should be subjugated. *Mein Kampf* abounds with critical, disdainful commentary about other people, especially the Negroes and Jews. At the time of Hitler's rise to prominence there were approximately 600,000 Jews in Germany. The story of what happened to them is well known—the story of confiscation of property, withdrawal of rights, slavery, murder, so that at the close of World War II there were only about 25,000 remaining, and it is estimated that many times this number were murdered in Poland.

The 400,000,000 people of India represent a unique phenomenon in human relations. Significant has been the caste system wherein groups have been separated one from another by such things as occupation, social fellowship, and economic condition, and religious teachings. In the development of the caste system, people have been matched against one another not according to race but according to groupings which have been made within race. Here, then, the assumption of inherent superiority of one group over another, which in racism is expressed by one race against another race, is pointed toward people of the same race.

In South Africa the superior position of the white man has been harshly held. Living quarters have been strictly segregated; taxation of the Africans extremely heavy; pass-laws adopted, limiting freedom of travel; types of employment restricted; and slave wages paid. These expressions of superior attitude have been motivated by a lust for wealth and a fear of the growing desire for recognition on the part of the large native population. Attempts have been made to combat this prejudice, but so deeply rooted is it that some Christian churches have joined the cause of inherent racial superiority.

The most significant expression of racism which has been related to the Far East came out of the position of the Japanese people regarding themselves. For generations the Japanese were taught that they were a superior people. They were ruled by a divine emperor, they themselves were of divine origin, they lived on divine soil. This position, along with economic and sociological motivation, prompted the wars of Japan and China, and together with Hitler's doctrine of Aryan supremacy brought on World War II. The recent renunciation of this divinely destined position on the part of Japan can and should help greatly in resolving the problems of racism within that nation and elsewhere.

In a land which proposed to provide a way of life where recognition is given to the freedom and equality of all men, one out of seven of its citizens belongs to a minority group and suffers discrimination of one kind or another. The people of the United States represent backgrounds from almost every part of the world. While they have had different customs and habits and even physical distinctions, many of them have come from the same racial stock and all have gradually been assimilated. But the story has not been the same for all minority groups. Other groups have dug deep roots here in the United States, but because of racial distinctions have suffered from prejudice and discrimination. Among these are the Chinese, Japanese, Indians, Mexicans, and most of all, the Negroes.

The Negro was brought to America shortly after the white man first set foot on its shore. The superior attitude of the white people has been tragically significant in the events which followed: increase in the slave trade, division of the North and the South, war between the states, and the long, difficult struggle of millions of people who suddenly were made "free." On the one hand, the story of the progress of the Negro in the United States is thrilling, made all the more so by the difficult odds against which growth has been achieved. At the same time there exists the tragic truth that progress has been impeded on every side by the position of so many white people that the Negro is inherently inferior; so that some one hundred years following the war which "emancipated" the Negro, racism remains one of the biggest problems of America. Racial discrimination is practiced in every area of life—in the matter of employment, in the use of public facilities, in social acceptance, in membership within religious bodies—and excitement over progress is always softened by realization of the unfinished task.

This brief review of the rise of racism and the many expressions in various parts of the world of racial superiority indicates how this sin separates man from man. Its false assumption and its tragic path in community, nation, and the world, challenges the Christian church and its mission as an instrument of God in establishing his Kingdom on earth.

Guiding Light on the Problem

The matter of his origin has always been a concern of man. The Bible teaches that man is the crowning expression of the creative activity of God. The scientists themselves say this biblical story of creation foreshadowed the evidence of science that present men derive from a common stock. Although scientists continue to study the origin and development of man, they unhesitantly state there is no pure race, there is no superior race, and there are no absolute and unchangeable race differences.[4]

There are common biological features in all human beings such as the complex nervous system, internal organs, and bone structures. It is now recognized scientifically that human beings have one common ancestor and that inheritance has been passed on by genes which determine the potentials of physical characteristics. It is now determined that the blood of different races is not essentially different. The blood of all people, regardless of race or color, can be divided into four types according to the substances of the red blood cells. It is also recognized that racial groups have formed because of the operation of certain processes, such as mutation, migration, and isolation.

From a common ancestor human beings have multiplied and spread over the earth and formed into groups with different physical characteristics. Scientists recognize that race is not something fixed and unchangeable. Consequently there is no single classification by races to which universal agreement is given. Most racial classifications can be fitted into three major divisions: (1) European or Caucasoid; (2) African or Negroid; and (3) Asiatic or Mongoloid. There is, however, no such thing as a pure race. The very biological processes which are determinative in the formation of racial groups indicate the impossibility of a "pure race." "It is beyond dispute that all the major races are of hybrid origin, and during the millennia which have elapsed since the original fission of the basic human stock, crossings have gone on continuously."[5]

The evidence of science not only provides explanation for the existence of physical differences in the people of the world, but also indicates there are no biological bases for the position of superior and

[4] Diana Tead, *What Is Race?* (Paris: UNESCO, 1952), p. 7.
[5] Juan Comas, *Racial Myths* (Paris: UNESCO, 1953), p. 17.

THE CHURCH FACES THE ISMS

inferior races. The idea that some races are innately inferior in intellectual capacity, in economic and social potentials, is often held; but it cannot be supported by scientific studies. When educational leaders in New York City decided to set up a special school for promising children, it was discovered that the five hundred selected on the basis of intelligence tests given represented a racial distribution corresponding to that of the population of the city.[6] Test after test, study after study, indicates there are superior and inferior people in all races and that the intellectual levels and cultural attainments of groups of people are related to environment and opportunity rather than to biological characteristics. The evidence of science, as it relates to the problem of racism, can best be summed up in one of the concluding statements of a group of physical anthropologists and geneticists who met in 1951 under the auspices of UNESCO to determine, in the light of the latest scientific knowledge available, what could be said with certainty about race:

We have thought it worth while to set out in a formal manner what is at present scientifically established concerning individual and group differences. (a). In matters of race, the only characteristics which anthropologists have so far been able to use effectively as a basis for classification are physical (anatomical and physiological).
(b). Available scientific knowledge provides no basis for believing that the groups of mankind differ in their innate capacity for intellectual and emotional development.
(c). Some biological differences between human beings within a single race may be as great or greater than the same biological differences between the races.[7]

The conduct of man also furnishes guidance in meeting the problem of assuming the inherent racial superiority of groups of people. Racism as known today is of relatively recent origin, although the idea of superior and inferior people can be traced back through history. It was, however, with the westward movement from Europe that racism as we know it today developed with such force. It is clearly to be identified with economic interests. The past three centuries have brought man the greatest civilization in history, and yet the damaging blows

---

[6] Diana Tead, *op. cit.*, p. 57.
[7] *Ibid.*, p. 85.

of racism should serve as sufficient warning for the future. The United States has not yet fully recovered from the war fought between its citizens in the mid-nineteenth century. The past two world wars were directly related to the problem of racism.

The Bible has been used to defend racism. Indeed it has been proclaimed in the name of biblical truth that God created people to belong to races with inferior and superior qualities. Puritans of New England justified their attitude toward the Indians by comparing themselves to the Israelites when they were commanded to destroy the Canaanites living in the Promised Land. Noah's curse upon Canaan and identification of the descendants of Ham with the "Black People" have been used "to prove" that God intended the Negro to be subservient. Paul's injunction "Servant, obey your master," has been applied to the Negro in his relations to the white man; and prior to the War Between the States one minister tried to convince his congregation that "man is made in the image of God, and since God, as everyone knows, is not a Negro, it follows that the Negro is not a man." [8]

A biblical basis for the assumption of racial superiority cannot be established. The Bible does contain examples of racial prejudice, hatred, and acts of discrimination; but these are a part of the biblical reflection of the sin of man. The emphasis made in biblical times on the differences between people was rooted primarily in religious affiliation and not on distinctive biological characteristics. Each nation had its own god, and often people within the nation gave allegiance to different gods. The fortunes and destiny of people were largely measured by the qualities and virtues of the god who was worshiped.

Against this polytheistic background the Bible speaks out with the message that there is but one living and true God, who is God of all nations and all people. He is the creator of all. "In the beginning God created the heavens and the earth" (Gen. 1:1). "And he made from one every nation of men to live on all the face of the earth . . ." (Acts 17:26). This one living and true God rules over that which he has created. "It is he who sits above the circle of the earth, and its inhabitants are like grasshoppers; who stretches out the heavens like a curtain,

---

[8] Quoted by E. R. Embree in "Color and Christianity," *Religion and Racial Tensions,* ed. Willard L. Sperry (Cambridge: Harvard University Press, 1945), p. 43.

and spreads them like a tent to dwell in; who brings princes to nought, and makes the rulers of the earth as nothing" (Isa. 40:22-23).

The Bible speaks to the problem of racism when it declares that all people have a common origin in the creative activity of God. The earth on which man lives has been described as a microscopic dot in the vast expanse of space, on which infinitesimal particles of impure carbon and water stir slightly for an instant of cosmic time and then are dissolved back into the elements from which they were originally compounded. The biblical doctrine of the nature of man does not deny the vast extent of the universe. "When I look at thy heavens, the work of thy fingers, the moon and the stars which thou hast established; what is man that thou art mindful of him . . . ?" (Ps. 8:3-4.) But it does deny that man's appearance is a temporary accident. "So God created man in his own image, in the image of God he created him; male and female he created them." (Gen. 1:27.) The Bible affirms the fact that man is the purposeful expression of God's creation. It is not, however, by tracing the origin of all human beings back to an act of God that the Bible most significantly emphasizes the oneness of all men. The heart of the matter is revealed in the purpose for which man was made. Man was created in the image of God. All men, without distinction as to appearance, are made to have a meaningful relationship with God. All men are given the capacity to love God, to obey God, to serve God. If the Bible is used as the basis of authority, there is no limit placed on the extent to which any person is to love God and serve him. "You shall love the Lord your God with all your heart, and with all your soul, and with all your mind" (Matt. 22:37).

The biblical emphasis on the relationship of man to God reveals not only a common origin but a common need. The will of man is such that he does not pursue God's purpose and cannot by his own desire and power achieve his destiny. Man goes his own way. He rebels. He may ignore his divine origin and destiny, but he cannot escape it. He is made in the image of God and is constantly measured against that which he was intended to be. Man is a sinner and therefore stands under the judgment of God. The biblical revelation of this nature of man begins with the story of the fall of man and continues throughout the Bible. All men are sinners, regardless of wealth, ancestry, position, color, or nationality. The Bible affords example after example of man's transgression and failure, but the biblical picture is that of not only the sins of particular individuals but also the sin of mankind. It is what Surjit Singh [9] calls the solidarity of mankind in sin. When Isaiah so forcibly felt the presence of the Lord in the temple he saw himself not only as one with unclean lips but also as one within a people of unclean lips (Isa. 6:5).

The biblical answer to the common problem of evil, in which all men are caught up, is the Savior Jesus Christ. God's redemptive purpose is forecast in the story of the fall of man. It begins to take form in the call to Abraham and is pursued in the mission given to the chosen people. It is brought to fulfillment in the person of Jesus Christ. "For God so loved the world that he gave his only Son, that whoever believes in him should not perish but have eternal life" (John 3:16). According to the New Testament, Christ is God's answer to the sin, suffering, and death in which all men are involved (Luke 4:16-30), and this gift of God's love is freely expressed to all.

This is good, and it is acceptable in the sight of God our Savior, who desires all men to be saved and to come to the knowledge of truth. For there is one God, and there is one mediator between God and men, the man Christ Jesus, who gave himself as a ransom for all, the testimony to which was borne at the proper time (I Tim. 2:3-6).

The death and resurrection of Jesus Christ are the full expression of the limitless extent of God's love, and here in the mightiest activity of the eternal God in time all men are as one. "The last word about men is that they belong together to that one human race which was created by God and which he desires to save." [10]

The redeeming work of God through his Son reconciles man to God, does for man that which he cannot do for himself, and makes possible growth in fellowship with God. The fellowship of this restored relationship is known as the Church, the body of Christ. Again the biblical emphasis is on the oneness of man. There is one fellowship, one body, one Church. "For just as the body is one and has many members, and all the

[9] "Nation and Race," *Biblical Authority for Today,* ed. Alan Richardson and Wolfgang Schweitzer. (Philadelphia: Westminster Press, 1951), p. 320.

[10] W. A. Visser 't Hooft, *The Ecumenical Movement and the Racial Problem* (Paris: UNESCO, 1954), p. 57.

members of the body, though many, are one body, so it is with Christ. For by one Spirit we were all baptized into one body—Jews or Greeks, slaves or free—and all were made to drink of one Spirit" (I Cor. 12:12-13). In the kingdom of God there is no discrimination, no superior people; but all are sons of men who in his grace have become sons of God. "For in Christ Jesus you are all sons of God, through faith. For as many of you as were baptized into Christ have put on Christ. There is neither Jew nor Greek, there is neither slave nor free, there is neither male nor female; for you are all one in Christ Jesus" (Gal. 3:26-28).

Our Strategy as Christians

Racism is rooted in the sin of man; the answer to racism is in the salvation of man. "When the individual permits his attitudes and actions to be determined by race, he is continuing the Fall in life; he is maintaining cleavage, tension, and disunion; he is rejecting the clear voice of God which calls him to union, communion, and fellowship—to the Kingdom." [11] It is in his relationship to God that the significance of man is revealed. In this relationship there is a basic equality among all people. All men were made for fellowship with God. In Christ all men are brought into fellowship with God. Here the differences between people are resolved in a new relationship in which men, regardless of physical appearance or station in life, share in the same experiences and are united as one with God. This is the destiny of mankind, fulfilled in communion with God. The problem of racism is therefore answered in evangelism. It is resolved as the Christian church spreads throughout the world and becomes truly an instrument through which the whole gospel is proclaimed and the Kingdom comes into the lives of people who are transformed.

By Christian people living in the world as the body of Christ, attention will be given, of course, to the problem of racism. Christ reigns in life, but not from the politician's platform or from the social service worker's desk or from the preacher's pulpit. Rather, Christ reigns from the Cross. "Lifted up there, he draws all men unto him." But the message of the Cross becomes vital and dynamic as it is focused on the places where we live. When the Christian church truly functions as the body

[11] G. D. Kelsey, "The Christian Way in Race Relations," *The Christian Way in Race Relations,* ed. William S. Nelson (New York: Harper & Bros., 1948), p. 36.

of Christ, then by its very nature a stand is taken on all crucial issues of life, which are always measured against him who is life. But there are times when to do this means trouble, and so the Church backs away from the issue, preferring life, even in the name of Christ, where no controversial questions are raised and no dangerous missions are to be fulfilled. The Christian church too often has become simply an ambulance, dragging along behind, picking up the wounded, making bandages and soothing hurt feelings, when it should have been out on the front line, getting hit in the face but leading others and conquering the enemy.

The Christian church, then, in days such as these and in any day must take its stand against racism. There is absolutely no place in the Christian message or in the fellowship of Christian people for the assumption of the inherent racial superiority of any group of people. The message of the Bible and the revelation of Jesus Christ is that God is concerned about people in two ways. He is concerned about them in their alienated state and in their restored relationship made possible by his self-giving love and power. There is no place for hatred and self-righteousness in the fellowship of Christian people. "If anyone says, 'I love God,' and hates his brother, he is a liar. . . . And this commandment we have from him, that he who loves God should love his brother also" (I John 4:20-21). This message must be proclaimed from the pulpit, taught through the programs of the Church and the home, and lived in daily life.

The first place where the message of the right relationship of people made in the image of God is to bear fruit is in the membership and fellowship of the Church. This does not mean that the exclusive concern of the Church is to fill its sanctuary with people from minority races. It does mean that in the membership of the Christian church there is no recognition of race or color or nationality. The doors of the church of Jesus Christ should be open to any and all sinners. For this cause the Lord Jesus came to earth, and only as the Church fulfills this mission is it the body of Christ. The Church does not and cannot answer the problems of racism when it functions on a racially segregated, discriminatory basis. Many ecclesiastical groups have adopted resolutions condemning racial segregation and affirming the brotherhood of the sons of God, but they have only relative value until realized in the experience of the Church at its grass roots.

The Christian church must also provide leadership to combat racism in every area of life—political, economic, social. Here discernment and wisdom will be expressed, but always in the context of constructive, positive approaches. Recognition should be given to special problems in areas where attitudes of racism have cut deep inroads, where emotional reactions are strong, where illiteracy prevails, where minority groups must undergo long-range programs of preparation and training before new and more significant responsibilities can be assumed. Desired changes cannot always be accomplished overnight, but this does not eliminate the change or make inapplicable the Christian gospel. Christians must therefore distinguish between the erection of barriers to protect the *status quo* and long-range programs of a constructive nature. Christians must lead the way in educational approaches which replace misunderstandings and ignorance with facts and truth. Christians must support constructive legislation for community, state, and nation. Christians must give personal testimony in deeds as well as in words.

It has been in the framework of the Christian faith in the nature and destiny of man that the democratic political theory has been applied in the United States and elsewhere with measures of success. Belief in the sacredness of personality, the worth and dignity of the individual, with which democracy is concerned, did not come about in this nation by chance. These concepts of the nature of man are rooted in the Christian faith that all men are created by the one living God, that all men have a recalcitrant nature and stand in need of redeeming grace, that all men are created for the same fundamental purpose to love God and their fellow men. This is God's world. In the doing of his will there is freedom, now and always.

Suggestions for Further Study

1. Discover as many racist groups as possible and find out their origin, distinctive characteristics, means of propaganda, and the success of their efforts.

2. Use the means available to find out what is being done in your denomination to overcome racism in your general locality. What are other religious groups doing in the same locality?

3. Study the attitudes of racism in your own church and plan constructive programs of education.

4. Organize small groups to get acquainted with people of other races. Arrange for discussions and fellowship experiences.

248

Selected Bibliography

American Academy of Political and Social Science. *Civil Rights in America*. In the "Annals"; Philadelphia: American Academy of Political Science, 1951.

Coy, Harold. *The Real Book About George Washington Carver*. Garden City, New York: Garden City Books, 1951.

Davie, Maurice R. *Negroes in American Society*. New York: Whittlesey House, 1949.

Frazier, Edward F. *The Negro in the United States*. New York: The Macmillan Co., 1949.

Loescher, Frank S. *The Protestant Church and the Negro*. New York: Association Press, 1948.

Myrdal, Gunnar. *An American Dilemma*. 2 vols.; New York: Harper & Bros., 1944.

Nelson, William S., ed. *The Christian Way in Race Relations*. New York: Harper & Bros., 1948.

Oldham, Joseph H. *Christianity and the Race Problem*. New York: Association Press, 1924,

Paton, Alan. *Cry, the Beloved Country*. New York: Charles Scribner's Sons, 1948.

"Segregation on Sunday?" *Social Progress*, XLV (January, 1955), in full.

Singh, Surjit. "Nation and Race," *Biblical Authority for Today*. Ed. Alan Richardson and Wolfgang Schweitzer. Philadelphia: Westminster Press, 1951.

Soper, Edmund D. *Racism, a World Issue*. Nashville: Abingdon Press, 1947.

Sperry, Willard L., ed. *Religion and Our Racial Tensions*. Cambridge: Harvard University Press, 1945.

Various articles in *The Student World*, XLIV (1951).

Visser 't Hooft, W. A. *The Ecumenical Movement and the Racial Problem*. Paris: UNESCO, 1954.

Woodward, Comer V. *The Strange Career of Jim Crow*. New York: Oxford University Press, 1955.

Publications on THE RACE QUESTION IN MODERN SCIENCE which may be secured at 25 cents each from the Publications Department, UNESCO, United Nations Building, New York, New York:

Comas, Juan. *Racial Myths*.

Dunn, L. C. *Race and Biology*.

Klineberg, Otto. *Race and Psychology*.

Leiris, Michel. *Race and Culture*.

Levi-Strauss, Claude. *Race and History*.

Morant, Geoffrey. *The Significance of Racial Differences*.

Rose, Arnold. *The Roots of Prejudice*.

Tead, Diana. *What Is Race?* (Price unknown.)

NATURALISM, SCIENTISM, MODERNISM

THERE HAVE BEEN SOME ERAS AND SOME PLACES IN WHICH CHRIStianity has set the patterns for thought and culture. This happened in the Middle Ages in Europe, when laws were made and enforced, kings were crowned and deposed, and society in general was regulated, according to the doctrines of the then established form of the Christian church. It happened in Geneva in the time of John Calvin, in New England during the Puritan theocracy—all of these systems being more or less explicitly based on the ancient Hebrew theocracy, which passed from theory to practice after the days of Ezra and which may be seen to some extent in modern Israel.

This control of society by the Church has not been in effect always, and is not now. Other philosophies, world views, or repudiation of world views, are challenging Christianity directly or threatening to change it past recognition. In contrast to the "Biblical Isms" which are rooted either in Christianity itself or in the Christian Bible, the "Cultural Isms," while they may be historically related to Christianity even if only by way of protest, have their roots actually elsewhere. Some of them start from an entirely different set of presuppositions. Some of them retain some and discard others of the traditional Christian ideas. These cultural isms have only this in common with the biblical isms, that they are part of the contemporary scene and represent (like most isms) the main-stream Church's competition, so to speak. They differ from the biblical isms in that for the most part they are not organized. They are more likely to be part of the general intellectual climate—meaning not necessarily the thought world of intellectuals, but the commonly accepted and perhaps unexamined presuppositions, the mental standpoints occupied even unawares, by people who do any thinking at all. Converts to what in this book are called "Biblical Isms" will very likely leave the established churches and join a rival church, perhaps becoming active proselyters for their new faith. Converts to a cultural ism may not be aware they have been converted. They will perhaps remain in the old-line church, unconscious that its creed and what they actually believe are different; or, conscious of the difference, they will stay on from pure inertia and sentiment; or again they may be aware of a conflict and write off the Christian church as a medieval relic, irrelevant to the modern world. Still another course is to remain in the Christian church, and attempt to alter its creed or its practice, or both, to bring it into line with the newly found point of view. If these alterations are sufficiently radical, conflicts will result; for while Christianity has undergone many changes, it has always in the long run resisted changes which would destroy its essence and transform it into something alien to itself.

The Problem

The three cultural isms which are to be described briefly in this unit give somewhat similar answers to the same problem, yet the answers are different enough so they they can be pretty well distinguished. The problem is this: How far, if at all, can and should Christianity conform to the intellectual and cultural patterns of its time? It has always unconsciously done so, to some degree; can it do so by intention? How far is it possible to restate Christian doctrines in the light of modern knowledge? Or does modern knowledge make it impossible to accept Christianity in any form? At one extreme are non-Christians (so born or so become) who find all attempts at restating, reshaping, or reforming, quite useless; who regard Christianity therefore as quite outmoded, even harmful. At the other extreme are those Christians who would impose, if possible, upon all culture, patterns drawn from their own special understanding of Christianity. Between these extremes are various attempts to arrive at some kind of harmony, or compromise, between Christianity and culture.[1] This unit deals with some isms which are related in various ways to this general problem.

If these isms seem to be loosely defined, so that they tend to melt into one another, this comes from the nature of the case. We are not dealing with organizations and creeds, rather with more or less pervasive points

---

[1] For an excellent analysis of the relation between Christianity and culture during the Christian centuries, see H. Richard Niebuhr, *Christ and Culture* (New York: Harper & Bros., 1951).

of view, or climates of thought, sets of presuppositions, types of *Welt-anschauung*.

Naturalism: What Is It That Is?

Two of these world views, closely related to each other, are naturalism and scientism. Naturalism is a philosophy which affirms that only the universe exists, and interprets this in terms reducible to physical energy and chemical-physical laws. Once called materialism, it is as old as the Greek philosopher Democritus. It is now often called physical realism. In some forms, naturalism frankly discards religion. One distinguished philosopher of this school remarked in a public lecture that he had not been inside a church in forty years. (One wondered how up-to-date his strictures on organized religion could be.) If the universe is all that is, then we have to deny the very first article of the universally accepted Christian creed: "I believe in God . . . Maker of heaven and earth"—or as another creed has it, "of all things visible and invisible." The Christian religion has always offered prayer to this creator. Harmony and union with him have always been the highest aim of the great religions. If there is no creator and there is only the self-existent, self-perpetuating universe, then prayer, the "vital breath of religion," is without meaning. It is of little use to do what some naturalists have done, revise the meaning of "religion" so as to do without any reference to God. For instance, William H. Kilpatrick [2] defines religion as "the spirit with which one holds one's supreme value . . . plus the outworking of this attitude appropriately in life." For the Christian, the supreme value is God. If, on the naturalist hypothesis, there is no God, only the universe, then the Christian's religion, by this definition, would mean the spirit in which one holds—Nothing, an illusion, a vacuum, a mirage. Christianity never has really placed its faith in *faith,* but in *God.* Faith in a mirage will never quench thirst. It is obvious that naturalism and Christian faith are incompatible. This is clearly seen by such logical persons as Lenin and his followers.

In this unit it is of course not possible to attempt a refutation of naturalism. That is the task of Christian philosophy, especially of the branch of theology called apologetics. A short and plain refutation of

[2] *Philosophy of Education* (New York: The Macmillan Co., 1951), p. 157.

252

naturalism may be read in Trueblood's *Logic of Belief* (see bibliography). Here it is possible only to point out that naturalism as a world view is not merely a twist or deviation within Christianity, but a denial of the very central object of Christian faith.

This is true even of those forms of naturalism which attempt to retain "God," redefined in some way. Two or three such attempts may be noted here. One is that of Samuel Alexander, in his Gifford Lectures (1916-1918), *Space, Time and Deity*.[3] In his view, the universe has a kind of direction, a "nisus," or "striving"; it is oriented and not growing at random. If we compare the universe to a great arrow, the target at which it is aimed is Deity; only no one aims the universe. It is more as if Deity were a magnet and the universe a scattering of iron filings. At all events, Deity is the Not-yet of the universe. The universe strives to realize Deity; and does so, for Deity is simply the next step of evolution, the Higher not yet reached—but never the Highest, for just beyond each level is again a Not-yet. In other words, when Deity becomes no longer a God but an achieved pattern, when the universe as it were overtakes and absorbs Deity, then that which was Deity is so no more, and the new Not-yet, the new Goal, is the new Deity toward which the universe yet and forever moves. It is plain enough that this is inconsistent at many points with Christian understanding of reality, not least so in denying personality to this Deity, as well as permanence. The only permanence this Deity has is after it becomes a part of the universe. As an undisclosed Goal it is in constant process of change. Indeed as Deity it has no objective existence. It has whatever reality future time may have in the present, but no more.

Another attempt to have a God and naturalism too is that of A. N. Whitehead.[4] On many pages of his works one finds references to God and to religion which make a reader count him a Christian; and indeed he, like many other naturalists, exhibits a Christian spirit. But when in *Process and Reality* he sets forth in detail his speculative delineations of God, his nature and functions, it is quite evident that this is not the Christian God. His scheme is far too complex to reproduce here. To make a long story short, Whitehead's God is not the Christian God, not be-

---

[3] 2 vols.; New York: The Macmillan, Co., 1920.
[4] See his *Process and Reality* (New York: Social Science Book Store, 1941), and *Science and the Modern World* (Harmondsworth, Middlesex: Penguin Books, 1938).

cause he is given a new name, "The Principle of Concretion," but (among other reasons) because he is non-personal—no "he" at all, at best a complicated dynamic "it"; and because, while he does have creative functions, he has not and cannot have, or have had, any existence apart from the universe. His relation to the universe is correlative; it is as necessary to him—to his very existence—as he to it. Whitehead has made a contribution to Christian thought which many theologians are working out further, namely, that reality ultimately includes and involves process; this against the classic idea that if we could penetrate to ultimate reality we should have left process behind. (The English idealist Bradley put it very neatly: "Nothing real ever moves.") Nevertheless, Whitehead's idea of God is by no means the Christian conception. One may admire it as one admires a Univac; but no one in his senses would pray to it.

Another attempt to fit some kind of God into the naturalist one-story universe is that of H. N. Wieman of Chicago. In much that he writes, one finds the classic Christian expressions; but they have very different meanings. They must; for the central object of faith, God himself, turns out to be nothing more than a quality or tendency of the universe, a characteristic of things-as-a-whole. In general terms, "God" for Wieman is a name for the trend to togetherness in the cosmos. Conflict, hate, war, hostility, tend to be self-destroying. That only endures which is rooted in love. (If we may adopt Wieman's use of a Christian word.) [5] Now it is true that the universe does have this fact about it, that in the long run it encourages co-operation and discourages hostility. But this fact is not at all what the Christians mean by "God." Professor Wieman once engaged in a three-cornered debate with Professors D. C. Macintosh of Yale and M. C. Otto of Wisconsin. Macintosh was a theist and Otto a frank atheist. Wieman prided himself on the fact that contrary to Otto and better than Macintosh, he could actually prove that God exists. The reactions of the atheist and the theist were much the same. In essence, they said to Wieman: "We grant that you prove the existence of what you call God. But this is not God." Both Macintosh and Otto urged Wieman to recognize his atheism and get into the atheist camp. But

[5] His *The Source of Human Good* (Chicago: University of Chicago Press, 1946), offers an elaborate rewrite of Christianity, with all the classic words but none of the classic meanings.

Wieman (along with many of his followers) has remained convinced that one can give the name "God" to something, however real, which is simply an aspect of the universe, and suppose that one has retained a belief in God.[6]

It will be observed that all naturalist reconstructions of the idea of God, while objective, i.e., not an idea but a reality, are realities only of the physical world, describable in terms of the physical world. The naturalist's God is adjectival to the universe, as much as the color white is adjectival to this paper. If there were no white objects there would be no whiteness. Whiteness never comes off things to exist in its own right; still less does it create anything. The naturalist's God cannot be the object of prayer, for he or it is never personal. If the naturalist's God seems to be creative, it is only a way of saying that the universe is self-creative. And a self-creative universe is never like the Christian understanding of it, as owing its very existence to the will and power of a personal God.

Two brief observations may further be made. One is that naturalism often is associated with determinism. The naturalist philosophy, reducing all phenomena finally to chemical and physical laws and elements, has difficulty, even when the attempt is made, to find room for freedom. The "block universe" of the naturalist can hardly accept freedom, for this would introduce something not in the chains of cause and effect, something actually supernatural. Some forms of Christian thought have no room for human freedom either, though for different reasons; but with all varieties of Christianity which leave a place for the freedom of man, naturalism is here in conflict.

The other observation has to do with evolution. There are types of evolutionary theory which are fully compatible with Christian faith. But the type of theory associated with naturalism is reductive, and this again is incompatible with Christian belief. By the reductive type of evolution is meant, in untechnical language, the theory that each successive level of evolution is already present in the lower level, that nothing really *new* emerges, but only a rearrangement of the old. The lower produces the higher, the higher can be explained entirely in terms of the lower. On the human level, this means that man is nothing but a higher animal. There is no new dimension in man that is not already in beast

[6] "A Conversation about God," *Christian Century*, XLIX (1932), *passim*.

and worm. Everything about man—his physical, mental, spiritual life; his hopes, dreams, faith, religion; equally with his digestion and his sweat glands—is to be explained finally in terms of chemical reactions and interrelations of physical elements. This again rules out the essential feature in the Christian belief about man, that he is, in his distinctive essence, of another order from the animals with which, it is true, he has so much in common.

If all this has sounded theoretical and philosophical, as if naturalism were something one would meet only in college classrooms or in books, then perhaps there is need for some reminder that the parish minister runs into this world view, directly or indirectly, in many ways. Since naturalism *is* taught in many a college classroom, and not exclusively by professors of philosophy—quite as often by teachers of the humanities or science professors—taught not always explicitly or even by name, but taken for granted at every turn—college graduates in the community, some of whom may be in the Church itself, may be infected with naturalism. They have taken in the idea that no educated man can think otherwise. For example, a well-known professor of philosophy and popularizer of philosophical ideas, in addressing a philosophy club at another university, started by saying that all educated people now accept the mechanistic theory of man. (He seemed surprised to learn that some distinguished members of his audience did not.) A famous professor in another university, speaking at a meeting of a society for the philosophy of religion, laid it down that everything real is tangible, physical, measurable; and therefore God, if real, must be physical, tangible, measurable. A best seller of a few years ago dealt with the life of a physician, from his childhood on. Whether it was the author's own view, or whether he wished to be realistic about doctors, one cannot say; but in all the long book, ministers almost never appear, not in hospitals, not at deathbeds, not anywhere. And if the doctor in all his life ever went near a church, the reader does not learn of it. The churches in his boyhood home are written off in one scornful sentence: "The priests of Miletta guarded the customs and once a week were vigilant to raise the question of an old fear." [7] Impressionable young people, exposed to

[7] Morton Thompson, *Not As a Stranger* (New York: Charles Scribner's Sons, 1954), p. 30.

naturalism attractively set forth by persons they admire, absorb it with all its implications. A study of high-school education in a region of one southern state recently has indicated that seventy per cent of high-school teachers there are unconnected with any church whatever. This may be a high estimate, and in other regions the percentage is lower, no doubt; but if in the so-called "Bible Belt" one half, or more, of the high school teachers are out of the Church, the reason must lie in their education, not their original home background. Naturalism, in the high school classroom, gets down to the place where the people come from, and counteracts the work of the Church in the most effective way, in the minds of growing boys and girls.

In pastoral work the minister meets with the naturalistic point of view in persons who cannot even spell the word. A man will excuse his sins by shrugging them off as something caused by his instincts, or his glands, or his ancestry. A man regards himself as in chains; he surrenders all claim to freedom. As he is, so he must be, he thinks. All this is precisely the naturalist point of view. An irate mother came into her fourteen-year-old boy's classroom to berate the teacher for having been severe with her boy for failing to do his work as he should and could. All I want, she said, is that he shall be a good animal. The teacher might have told her that that was the trouble: the boy was a very good animal; the school was trying to make something more of him. The mother had never heard any lectures by exponents of naturalism, but she was drawing its obvious inferences. So when the minister is trying to find out why people don't come to church, he will discover that one of the reasons in people's minds is that, from the viewpoint of the pervasive philosophy of naturalism, as it seeps into most American communities, the minister is talking nonsense, or at best "raising the question of an old fear."

Scientism: What Can We Know?

Another pervasive, unorganized, respectable, and spiritually deadly ism closely allied to naturalism but always more sharply cut off from religion than some forms of naturalism profess to be, is scientism. This is an awkward word, but it is being used—never by its exponents, always by its critics, and is a useful way of distinguishing it from *science*, the scientific method or attitude or results. It is a name for a point of view which regards science as "omniscient, omnipotent and the bearer of man's salvation." [8]

It is necessary to keep in mind the difference between science and scientism. Science is a rather omnibus term, referring to a body of specialized knowledge, or to the whole sum of knowledge, which men have accumulated, say in the past three hundred years. Science is more than mere collections of facts. It includes hypotheses and theories built on known facts and leading to further facts. Its method is to start by physical examination of physical objects (which may be quite invisible, and/ or without mass at all), analysis of these facts, putting them together into some kind of systematic connection with one another, and proceeding from these to still others. Physics is a good example, and chemistry is another; biochemistry is an example of a science that rests on other sciences. The scientific method consists not only in observation, but also in control of what is observed and in verification by repeated experiments. If miracles were everyday occurrences, they would still not be subjects for scientific investigation, because by definition, every miracle would be unique, there would be no way of repeating it, it could not be properly observed because no one would be expecting *this* miracle, and it would be completely out of control by any scientific observer.

Whether any but the "natural" sciences can be completely scientific, can be debated; but it would not be to the point here, except to remark that some confusion exists because of using the same word "science" to describe bodies of knowledge and methods of investigation as different from each other, as (e.g.) chemistry and history, or mathematics and psychology. The precise measurement in physical categories, the possibility of control, the verifiability by repetition—characteristic of the natural sciences—are impossible in these more loosely named "sciences." At all events, the social sciences, as far as they pride themselves on being scientific, aim to approximate as closely as possible the precision both of observation and measurement, which characterize the physical sciences.

Now, scientists, being human beings, and often very brilliant human beings, cannot help thinking. And when they think, they often go beyond the limits of their sciences and become, with or without intention,

[8] Derwyn R. G. Owen, *Scientism, Man, and Religion* (Philadelphia: Westminster Press, 1952), p. 20.

philosophers. Philosophy tries to think about everything in the light of everything else, and in the course of its wide-ranging meditations comes to such themes and problems as spirit, values, and freedom. Science properly so called, science in the rigidly controlled sense, has nothing to say about spirit. No microscope can see it, no dial can measure it, no physical instrument can be devised to observe what is not physical. Science, as science, simply can say nothing about spirit. The only strictly scientific attitude is to admit ignorance at this point. If a scientist affirms the reality of spirit, or denies it, in either case he does so as a philosopher or a theologian, not as a scientist. The same holds true of values, of freedom, and of God. There is no scientific proof of these objects, for they are not objects at all in the scientific sense; neither can there be any scientific disproof.

But here scientism steps in, where scientists wisely fear to tread. Unlike the genuine sciences, scientism makes bold to look into such matters as spirit, freedom, and God. Not being able to locate and describe these by any known scientific device, scientism returns the verdict: These things do not exist. More generally, scientism affirms that the scientific method is the only method of arriving at truth. What cannot be verified is not so much false as meaningless. That the moon is made of green cheese is a false statement because we know the meaning of all the words; the proposition can be examined by physical means and shown to be false. But if I say that a whrmpf (sic) is less vital than a glnk (sic), I am not telling a lie; I am talking nonsense. And in the view of scientism, if I say that God is a love, I am talking nonsense also, for "God" and "love" are no more subject to laboratory examination than whrmpfs and glnks.

The alliance of scientism and naturalism can be seen at this point clearly, except that scientism may go further than naturalism. Both affirm there is nothing outside the universe that exists. Both describe the knowable world, ultimately, in terms of pointer-readings and precise mathematical formulae. If naturalism admits the existence of what is not—in the strict sense of the word—physical, it still affirms that it can be explained as a function of what is physical; all is reducible to physical terms. Naturalism may speak of qualities, but scientism can speak only of quantity. Science operates on a quantitative principle, necessarily and usefully; but scientism affirms that the quantitative principle is the only one by which valid knowledge can be ascertained and tested. Science operates also on the mechanical principle; scientism declares that the sole, all-explaining, all-inclusive principle is mechanism. And since machines, no matter how complex, are always fixed, determined in advance, scientism turns the mechanical principle into the dogma of determinism. Professor Owen[9] has shown all this in some detail.

The whole thing comes out to this: science alone gives truth, and this truth is absolute and final. Scientism thus low-rates, if it does not actively oppose, all human efforts which are not in the scientific camp. And it has no use or room for religion. The world of scientism is a world without values, without spirit, without freedom, without God. It is a material, physical, mechanical, determined world. Natural laws "work with iron necessity towards inevitable results." [10] If the exponents of scientism (one wishes for a word like "scientismists"!) seem at times to have a sort of utopian optimism, placing hope in future millenniums such as the classless state, even this is a fixed and necessary future. As Engels wrote: "History proceeds in the manner of a natural process and is also essentially subject to the same laws of movement." [11] And since from the viewpoint of scientism death ends all, the death of the entire human race is absolutely certain; and as Bertrand Russell put it in a famous passage, all the dreams, hopes, and achievements of man are destined to be destroyed in the vast death of the solar system. "Only on the firm foundation of unyielding despair can the soul's habitation henceforth be built." As James Thomson put it:

> I find no hint throughout the Universe
> Of good or ill, of blessing or of curse;
> I find alone Necessity Supreme;
> With infinite Mystery, abysmal, dark,
> Unlighted even by the faintest spark.
> For us, the flitting shadows of a dream.[12]

[9] *Ibid., passim.*

[10] Karl Marx, *Preface to Capital*, Vol. I, p. 13, as quoted by Leopold Schwarzchild, *The Red Prussian* (New York: Charles Scribner's Sons, 1947), p. 127.

[11] Friedrich Engels as quoted in *ibid.*, p. 128.

[12] L. E. Elliott, *The Development of English Theology in the Later Nineteenth Century* (London: Longmans, Green & Co., 1952), p. 7.

The problem scientism raises is not the adjustment of religious beliefs to some findings of science as such, e.g., the date of creation or the historical value of the book of Esther. Such adjustments have been made more than once. The real problem for many persons is this: Has science killed religion by making it impossible to believe in spirit (except as a by-product of matter), in freedom, in final causes, or purpose outside man (or for that matter, even in man!)? Again, this is not the place to debate the matter. But it should be clear that scientism and religion of any kind, to say nothing of Christianity, are incompatible.

A word may be added here about logical positivism, which is often if not always associated with scientism. This is very widely taught in philosophy departments in America and Great Britain, and (like naturalism) seeps down before long to the high-school level. Semantics, in some hands, works out to the same conclusions. Nothing is real that cannot be pointed to. Nothing is real except concrete physical individual things. A popularizer of this general point of view once printed by way of illustration a page on which every abstract noun (such as beauty) was replaced by *blah-blah*; the result of course was sheer nonsense. Only scientific discourse makes sense, on this view.

Meeting Scientism and Naturalism

How can the minister meet this point of view, and that of naturalism? 1. If he has not already, in college or seminary, studied courses (such as apologetics) which are of direct help here, he can read such books as those by Trueblood, De Nouy, and Owen (see bibliography) for discussions pointing out the weaknesses of naturalism and kindred viewpoints, or those by Long and Mather and Eddington to see that not all scientists are atheists by any means.

2. Christianity is not well defended by bad arguments. Scientism is not science, to be sure; but it is never to be refuted by wild statements posing as science. A recent example of bad argument with a religious motive was *Worlds in Collision*,[13] an attempt to demonstrate the scientific reliability of the Old Testament by a potpourri of legends, ideas ranging from fanciful to wild, all under the name of "science." The real truth of religion never can be demonstrated even by good science, much

[13] Immanuel Velikovsky (New York: The Macmillan Co., 1950).

261

less by bad. Many well-meant efforts to "prove" the truths of the Bible are ill conceived. Some years ago a popular clergyman-lecturer thought he had demonstrated the truth of the Exodus story by the "fact" that the mummy of the Pharaoh of the Exodus had been found, and there was *salt in the mummy wrappings*. Now in the first place, nobody knows for certain who the Pharaoh of the Exodus was. In the second place, all Egyptian mummies contain salt in the wrappings. Thirdly, the Book of Exodus nowhere says that Pharaoh was drowned. Such arguments, so far from convincing those who have been carried away by scientism, only confirm their opinion that religion can be taken seriously only by the feeble-minded.

3. Careful distinction should always be drawn between science and scientism. For science every religious person should have respect; to science, in many fields, we are all indebted. (Without its aid most of us would not be living.) Scientism is a philosophy, owing its prestige to the services of science. But it is a poor philosophy and can be met on its own grounds.

4. There is just no use defending the indefensible. To defend religion, it is by no means necessary to defend all the tenets of the First Anointed Church of Myopia. In the course of time the gospel ship has picked up a good many barnacles. One does the ship no good by insisting that every barnacle must remain. To speak without a parable, whenever an article of faith, as held by the Church, can be shown to be false, then it is the duty of the Church to lay that article of faith quietly but definitely aside. Faith goes beyond reason, faith dares to believe beyond possibility of "proof." But faith cannot contradict fact without becoming a form of falsehood.

5. There should be no compromise on the essentials. There has been endless discussion of what *is* essential, and this is not the place to settle the question. Surely we ought not to retain as essential anything that is demonstrably false. This was the mistake of those who battled Galileo and Darwin. The essentials of the Christian faith are set forth in the New Testament. The object of faith is always God in Christ. Sin, grace, and salvation can be redescribed and restated over and over; various sciences may help us to understand our behavior and our experiences better; but science never touches, one way or another, the heart of the matter, man's need of the creating and saving God.

6. If science disproved Christianity, there would be no Christian men of science. One of the best refutations of the position of scientism is the number of scientists who are unashamed Christians. (Again, a word of caution, against identifying Christianity with one's own particular segment of it.)

7. Christianity is a religion that reaches the humblest of men. This is part of its glory. But it does not follow that our religion is good only for dim-wits and ignoramuses. Young people especially who have come under the influence of some brilliant unbeliever, may be helped by being introduced to some of the able minds who today find Christianity by no means too simple for them. To say nothing of the great Christian minds of the past, such writers as the Niebuhrs (Reinhold and Richard), T. S. Eliot, Dorothy Sayers, John A. Mackay, the Baillies (John and Donald), C. S. Lewis, Nels F. S. Ferré, Jacques Maritain—to name but a few— may serve to convince a young man or woman that whatever may be said for Christianity, it cannot fairly be said that no first-class minds take it seriously.

8. It should never be forgotten that, as Studdert-Kennedy said, Christianity is not an argument. It is a choice. Many a person who has been honestly troubled by doubts, intellectual and otherwise, has found those doubts fading in the light of a personal experience with Jesus Christ. Argument cannot produce faith; it can at best make room for faith. But faith may make argument unnecessary. So the best defense against negative philosophies, or against watered-down, halfway, apologetic compromises posing as religion, is to recall and to make real again what Paul was driving at when he wrote "For our gospel came to you not only in word, but also in power and in the Holy Spirit and with full conviction" (I Thess. 1:5). No other argument is as powerful as genuine Christians in whose lives the power of the Spirit is a reality, and who have the full conviction born of experience which they cannot deny.

Modernism

An ism which shares many of the presuppositions of naturalism and scientism, but which is more definitely related to Christianity and indeed is often held to be the only possible form of Christianity for the modern educated man, is loosely called modernism.

The word is a slippery one. It is used to express various general ideas, such as the following:

1. The notion that the likelihood of a proposition's being true varies with its age, and that generally speaking, the newer the truer. This notion hardly exists outside the minds of teen-agers.

2. Fundamentalists use the word "modernism" to describe any deviation from the view of the one who uses the term.

3. Sometimes fundamentalism is equated with literalism, modernism is conceived to be the opposite of literalism. This is misleading, because fundamentalist interpretations of Scripture are seldom literal, but follow approved lines of reinterpretation. The modernist's failure or refusal to be literal merely comes at different points from those taken nonliterally by the fundamentalist.

4. In the Roman Church, modernism has a specific reference to the nineteenth-century movement in which Alfred Loisy and others took leading parts, a movement soon and thoroughly squelched.

5. Still another very general use of the term covers a wide variety of interpretations of Christianity. As defined by Cadoux and Snowden (see below), modernism means a reasoned attempt to harmonize what we know, in all fields, with what we believe as Christians.

With reference to the general problem of "isms," modernism in this sense is both biblical and cultural. It is a biblical ism in that it involves reinterpretation of the Bible; more precisely, it involves departing to some extent from the strictly and prosaically literal interpretation of Scripture, as well as modification of one's understanding of what the Bible is. It is cultural in that it takes culture seriously, accepts it at least partially, and does not leave it out of sight when trying to understand the meaning of Christian faith.

Is Modernism Good or Bad?

As a biblical-cultural ism in this fifth meaning of the word, modernism calls for some comment. There can be no general agreement about it, for while most Christians accept its milder forms, perhaps unawares, and reject its extreme forms, there lies between these an enormous variety of modernisms, sliding into one another, differing in the degree to which contemporary culture is allowed to modify either the doctrine or the practice of Christianity, patterns which were set before modern culture was born. ("Milder forms," above, means those in which modification is very slight and not concerned with basic truths. "Extreme forms" are those closely allied with scientism and naturalism; retaining from Christian thought some of its language, they may actually repudiate all connection with historic Christian tradition.)

Modernism can be bad, most Christians would agree, when it so yields to contemporary culture that essential values of Christian faith are lost. In contemporary culture are included not only all branches of science, but also current philosophies and even the contemporary mental climate.

For instance: Moved either by the "scientific" attitude that so-called moral values are meaningless, or by the optimism of some types of philosophy, or by the general pervasive atmosphere of optimism in the more prosperous layers of our civilization, some modernist versions of Christianity regard man as either essentially quite neutral morally, or essentially good, thus overlooking or even denying the Christian doctrine of sin. Most Christians would call this kind of modernism bad because it denies the actuality of sin, as sin, carrying guilt with it—a doctrine which is not dispensable, but is close to the center of any Christian understanding of man which is based on the Bible and religious experience.

This may seem to affect but one doctrine. But when it is seen how many other Christian beliefs are tied in with the conviction of sin, and what radical differences there are between theories of personal ethics which disregard sin and theories which take sin seriously, it will be plain why Christians so widely oppose this particular kind of modernism.

There are also varieties of modernism which frankly cut themselves off from main-line Christianity. For example, a well-known visiting preacher, in a sermon at the Yale Divinity School about 1935, raised the question: "What does the religion preached in my church [congregation] have in common with Eastern Orthodoxy?" His answer was, "Nothing." Now a reader who belongs to almost any of the main-line churches may be aware that his church differs at many points from Eastern Orthodoxy. But there is so much in common that the World Council of Churches has no qualms about accepting the Orthodox Church into as full membership as the Orthodox leaders themselves will permit. To cut oneself off absolutely from the Orthodox Church is to cut oneself off from the

World Council of Churches and from Christianity as it had hitherto been understood.

Or let the reader consider the following ideas from A. C. McGiffert's *Christianity as History and Faith:* [14]

God needs no propitiation. Our sins against man do not need the divine forgiveness . . . the modernist feels little or no need of forgiveness from God. Much has occurred to make the old evangelical experience unnatural to the modernist. In place of salvation, a negative category, modernists have *substituted a different category altogether* (McGiffert's own expression), namely enrichment of life or devotion to the kingdom of God.

It is quite obvious why the church as a whole rejects modernism as extreme as this.

At the other end of the spectrum are forms of modernism which may not use the name, or may even disown it, but which still are departures from views once held in the Church, through the pressure of culture in one way or another. Three examples will suffice; these are all but universally accepted by the Christian world.

Once upon a time Christians believed that this earth was flat and immovable; the Bible, literally understood, teaches this. Christians also believed that the sum of all the changes which the entire universe underwent, between nothing-at-all and the forms we now see, took not over six 24-hour days. They believed furthermore that if women take any part in the Church it must be a listening part only. They believed all these things because "The Bible says so." The Bible still says so as plainly as it ever did, but the main-line churches of today are modernist on these points. That is, they take it for granted that the earth is a flying globe, that the earth required millions of years to reach its present form, and that women should have free opportunities for leadership in the Church. These ideas were suggested first not by the Bible but by science and the social climate in which we now live. The churches that have not come to this much "modernism" are precisely those that are most cut off from modern culture. The reader will think of many other examples.

Some who have thus modified old beliefs, or have inherited such modi-

[14] New York: Charles Scribner's Sons, 1934, pp. 88, 89, 93, 95.

fications, would deny the label of modernists. Two who accept the label "modernism," while holding to its milder forms, have defined the viewpoint thus: Modernism is

that willingness to modify doctrine, in the light of newly acquired truth, which is fully compatible with a firm adherence to the Christian Gospel and so preserve a real continuity with the essential spirit of the New Testament.[15]

This progressive spirit of theology by which the old faith ever absorbs and assimilates new knowledge and keeps abreast of our growing life is the principle and process of modernism.[16]

Contemporary Debates

The modernist-fundamentalist debates of the 1920's have passed into history and are not now an issue. But there are contemporary debates in which the word may never appear, yet which express modernism's perennial problem, the relation of faith to culture and the harmonizing of knowledge and belief.

1. Rudolph Bultmann, professor at Marburg, Germany, has started an immense discussion with his proposal of "demythologizing" Christianity.[17] There is nothing essentially new about this. It is the old question of reinterpretation. Once upon a time Adam was considered in the Christian church to have been a historical character living about four thousand years before Christ, a man so superb in all respects that Aristotle, one of the greatest men of all time, can be called no better than "the ruins of an Adam." Now we know more about primitive man, and Adam has become for many theologians a symbol and type of all men; "every man's name," as Brunner puts it, rather than one historical man who for a time lived a perfectly sinless life. The Christian church has absorbed the facts that this earth is not the physical center of the universe, that death was at work on this planet before ever there was a man to sin, that heaven is not "up" any more than it is "down," and so forth. But exactly where does reinterpretation stop? Bultmann is

[15] Cecil J. Cadoux, *The Case for Evangelical Modernism* (Chicago: Willett, Clark & Co., 1939), p. x.
[16] James H. Snowden, *Old Faith and New Knowledge* (New York: Harper & Bros., 1928), pp. 53-54.
[17] See H. W. Bartsch, ed., *Kerygma and Myth* (London: Society for Promoting Christian Knowledge, 1953), for an extensive reprinting of articles called forth in the discussion, with Bultmann's original essay.

right (everyone says) in insisting that we Christians must speak to modern man in terms modern man can recognize, in categories he uses. Whether Bultmann himself has demythologized Christianity so that its essential meaning is made at last clear, or is finally destroyed, theologians are still debating.

2. Karl Barth and Oscar Cullmann, among others, are biblical theologians in the sense that they propose to eliminate from Christian theology all elements drawn from nonbiblical, that is non-Hebraic, sources. Since at some crucial points the categories of theology are Hellenic rather than Hebrew (as for example in the doctrine of immortality and the concepts of time and eternity and perfection), what these and similar theologians are doing is to repudiate bygone modernisms. Whatever syntheses or weldings of biblical with (then) contemporary ideas may have been worked out in times past by such giants as Augustine and Thomas Aquinas, are now under attack from many contemporary theologians.

3. An influential form of contemporary philosophy is existentialism. In its classic form it is atheistic, but many theologians believe that it makes a sound analysis of the human situation and therefore propose an "existentialist theology." [18] This debate, unlike the famous one of the twenties in America over evolution, goes on over the ordinary Christian's head. But it can be called a highbrow modernism, set in intellectualist terms.

4. Two distinguished contemporary theologians illustrate another phase of this problem, possibly the most important. One of the most influential interpreters of Christianity, Paul Tillich, has often been charged with Gnosticism. In a review of his book, *The New Being*, Nels F. S. Ferré[19] sharply challenges the whole position, affirming that one must choose between Christianity and Tillich's reinterpretation of it. This particular debate hinges on the problem of the "supernatural": What does the concept mean? Tillich represents the modernist who finds a historic Christian element of belief no longer tolerable for the modern mind; Ferré, those who find that to eliminate this is not to cross out one particular outmoded idea, but to dissolve the very foundation of faith itself.

[18] Cf. John McQuarrie, *An Existential Theology* (New York: The Macmillan Co., 1955).
[19] *Interpretation*, IX (1955), 465-67. See also the debate at length in *Religion in Life*, XXV.

Thus, long before the word "modernism" was invented, and long after it has been discarded, the kind of problem it presents has been and will be before the Church, and the dangers inherent in it will always threaten; and yet the answer can never lie in ignorance nor in endless repetition of old formulas.

Ethical Culture Society:
An Organized Form of Modernism

A form of Modernism which is definitely organized is the Ethical Culture Movement. Numerically small, and confined chiefly to urban centers—seven out of twenty-two listed groups or societies are in the New York area—it not only possesses considerable dignity and influence, but illustrates a conscious and rather radical form of modernism. In addition, some congregations with old-line denominational connections are essentially "ethical culture societies" without the name.[20]

It was founded in 1876 by Felix Adler, son of a New York rabbi, as a "Society imbued with the spirit of religion but without its dogmas." From the beginning it was a family movement, and education has been one of its principal activities. The Workingmen's School was opened in 1878, and there are now four schools in New York City which take children through high school. Free kindergartens, visiting nurse services, and settlement houses have been among the activities of the Society. A keen interest in social legislation, such as affected child labor, housing and labor arbitration, has marked the movement. More recently there has been work with refugees from Europe, operation of a camp for underprivileged children, a project known as Citizenship Encampment for young people, and John L. Elliott Institute for adult education.

Spokesmen of the movement repudiate the idea of its being merely a social agency or reform movement. Not only because of its educational efforts, but also because its leaders are authorized to conduct weekly meetings for meditation and worship of a sort, to conduct christening, marriage, and burial services, and also because it has a

[20] Information in this section is derived from various pamphlets issued by the American Ethical Union, 2 W. 64th, New York, N. Y. For a fuller exposition, see D. S. Muzzey, *Ethics as a Religion* (New York: Simon & Schuster, Inc., 1951).

philosophy which is religious in the naturalist sense, Ethical Culturists regard themselves as religious, and indeed the movement is listed as a religion in the Federal Census of religions.

It is, however, strictly a one-story religion, able to fit in with naturalism easily, though hardly with scientism. The Ethical Societies are "devoted to a faith in man, a belief that it is possible for human beings to raise ever higher our standard of living together." "We regard nothing more important to people than people." In several of the meeting places of the Society is inscribed the quotation from Felix Adler: "The Place Where Men Meet to Seek the Highest is Holy Ground." Instead of a one-story religion it might be called a one-commandment religion: "Thou shalt love thy neighbor as thyself." Even more emphatically than the Unitarian Church, Ethical Culturists repudiate any creed whatever, outside of their "faith in man" and in man's ability to solve his own problems and to answer his own needs. They neither insist on a belief in God, nor would they exclude a believer. With respect to theological and metaphysical questions, the Ethical Movement is neutral. "Whether one does or does not believe in God, prayer, and immortality, is one's own affair."

The nearest thing to a creedal affirmation to be found in this movement is a belief in "human dignity and potentiality." "Bring out the best in others and thereby bring out the best in yourself," is one of its slogans. God is not denied; but belief in him is optional, and officially he has no standing. At the Ethical Culture Christening or Naming Service one form begins: "You have brought your child today in the face of this congregation, that the sacred occasion of the bestowing of his name may be hallowed by the benediction of religion." A Marriage Service begins: "We are assembled here in the name of all we reverence as highest and holiest to join together this man and this woman in the sacred bond of matrimony." A benediction called characteristic is quoted: "May the blessing of all who are just and merciful, your own honor and chivalry and the Eternal Order of things, be your strength and peace unto the end."

Whether Ethical Culture is a religion or not, seems to be uncertain among its adherents. Lester Mondale, leader of the Philadelphia Society, says the leaders do not preach ethics as a religion; but this is in contrast to the title of Prof. Muzzey's *Ethics as a Religion*. At all events, ethics for this movement constitutes the standard by which all else is judged. Religious values are, in the last analysis, tested by the degree to which they affect the conduct of men.[21]

By way of brief comment, it may be noted:

1. This movement is a child of religion. Its ethical ideals are those of the Judaeo-Christian tradition rather than (for instance) Buddhist. Its characteristic emphases would have been different in a different milieu.

2. Just as truly as Christian Science, Jehovah's Witnesses, or any other ism, this movement represents a reaction against a lack or an overemphasis in the Christian (and perhaps Jewish?) organized religion. Against an overstress on theological problems and ideas, against churchly indifference to social problems and to submarginal people, this movement has borne its needed witness. Without its initiative, such movements as the Child Study Movement of America, the Legal Aid Societies, and the Visiting Nurses' Association (all projects of the movement in their beginnings) might not have been born.

3. Its very slow growth, however, may indicate a weakness, in that it attempts to grow the fruits of religion without its roots. As between faith in God and faith in man, experience has shown that there can hardly be comparison. Felix Adler himself progressed to the point where shortly before his death he wrote: *"I bless the universe. And to be able to bless the universe in one's last moments is the supreme prize which man can wrest from life's struggles, life's experience."* [22] This goes beyond naturalism, to be sure. But one is reminded of Thomas Carlyle's comment on Margaret Fuller's "I accept the universe"; "Gad—she'd better!" A more consistent naturalist might have reminded Adler of his own words uttered at an earlier time: "In hours of great sorrow we question the sleepless stars; they are cold and distant; the winds blow, the rivers run their course, the seasons change; they are careless of man." [23] Blessing such a universe will not waken it to love, and it is a poor exchange for knowing the Creator who is Love.

---

[21] See David S. Muzzey, *op. cit.*, p. 77.
[22] *An Ethical Philosophy of Life* (New York: D. Appleton & Co., 1925), p. 360.
[23] Felix Adler, *Creed and Deed* (New York: G. P. Putnam's Sons, 1877), p. 132.

Suggestions for Further Exploration

To fill in the outlines of this necessarily sketchy unit, the interested student is invited to explore for himself. A few suggestions follow.

Naturalism and Scientism: Look around you; consider to what extent naturalism and/or scientism have invaded and pervaded contemporary life and thought. Significant areas for investigation would include curricula of schools and colleges; vocational guidance in the public schools; current literature, including the "quality" magazines; philosophies of education.

Modernism: Get acquainted with the local Unitarian Church. Study its service, sermons, hymnal, literature. Why does it have no creed? What is its outreach, locally or world wide? Study the Sunday school literature promoted by your own denomination. Does it show evidences of modernism in any of the senses noted in this unit?

Ethical Culture: Write for the literature of the movement; attend some of its meetings if accessible. Consider your own church. Is there a possibility that its teaching (as in sermons, Sunday school literature, and the like) is so theological and other-worldly as to make the Ethical Culture movement a natural reaction? On the other hand, does the current teaching of your church interpret religion in terms largely of ethics—in other words, is your church an Ethical Culture Society without the name?

Selected Bibliography

Bartsch, Hans W., ed. *Kerygma and Myth, A Theological Debate.* Translated by R. H. Fuller. London: Society for Promoting Christian Knowledge, 1953.

Broad, Charlie D. *Religion, Philosophy, and Psychical Research.* New York: Harcourt, Brace & Co., 1953.

Cadoux, Cecil J. *The Case for Evangelical Modernism.* Chicago: Willett, Clark & Co., 1939. (More radical than Snowden.)

De Nouy, le Comte. *Human Destiny.* New York: Longmans, Green & Co., 1947.

Eddington, Arthur S. *Science and the Unseen World.* New York: The Macmillan Co., 1929.

Herrick, Charles J. *The Thinking Machine.* Chicago: University of Chicago Press, 1929. (Sheer naturalism.)

Kilpatrick, William H. *Philosophy of Education.* New York: The Macmillan Co., 1951.

Lewis, C. S. *Miracles.* New York: The Macmillan Co., 1947. (Defense of their possibility.)

Long, E. LeRoy. *Religious Beliefs of American Scientists.* Philadelphia: Westminster Press, 1952.

———. *Science and Christian Faith.* New York: Association Press, 1950.

Mason, Frances, ed. *The Great Design.* New York: The Macmillan Co., 1934.

Mather, Kirtley F. *Science in Search of God.* New York: Henry Holt & Co., 1928.

Muzzey, David S. *Ethics as a Religion.* New York: Simon & Schuster, Inc., 1951.

Myers, Alexander J. W. *Religion for Today.* New York: Association Press, 1941. (An example of modernism which has little that is distinctively Christian.)

Owen, Derwyn R. G. *Scientism, Man, and Religion*. Philadelphia: Westminster Press, 1952. (Deals broadly with social and sociological angles.)

Raven, Charles E. *Christianity and Science*. New York: Association Press, 1955. (The author is both theologian and scientist, professional in both fields.)

Sellars, Roy W. *Philosophy of Physical Realism*. New York: The Macmillan Co., 1932.

———— et al., eds. *Philosophy for the Future*. New York: The Macmillan Co., 1949.

Snowden, James H. *Old Faith and New Knowledge*. New York: Harper & Bros., 1928.

Temple, William. *Nature, Man, and God*. New York: The Macmillan Co., 1949.

Trueblood, D. Elton. *The Logic of Belief*. New York: Harper & Bros., 1928.

White, Andrew D. *History of the Warfare of Science with Theology in Christendom*. New York: George Braziller, Inc., 1955.

Whitehead, Alfred N. *Process and Reality*. New York: Social Science Book Store, 1941.

————. *Science and the Modern World*. Harmondsworth, Middlesex: Penguin Books, 1938.

Wieman, Henry N. *The Source of Human Good*. Chicago: University of Chicago Press, 1946.

———— Macintosh, Douglas C.; and Otto, Max C. "A Conversation about God," *Christian Century*, XLIX (1932), *passim*.

Wilson, Edmund. *The Scrolls from the Dead Sea*. New York: Oxford University Press, 1955. (A sample of sophisticated unbelief.)

SECULARISM

AT THE JERUSALEM CONFERENCE IN 1928 THE GREAT QUAKER, RUFUS M. Jones, presented a forty-three-page document in which he maintained that the real rival of Christianity in the world is not Buddhism, or Islam, or any other of the great historic religions, but secularism. This he defines as "a way of life and an interpretation of life that include only the natural order of things and that do not find God, or a realm of spiritual reality, essential for life or thought." [1] This discussion occupied the attention of almost half of the delegates to the Jerusalem Conference, and since that time much has been said and written of the threat of secularism.

Definition

Secularism is difficult to define because the word has come to mean different things to different people. This is well illustrated in the definitions quoted below:

1. A system of social ethics based upon a doctrine advanced by G. J. Holyoake (1817-1906) that ethical standards and conduct should be determined exclusively with reference to the present life and social well-being. [2]

2. Any view of life, education, etc., or any policy or program referring to such, based on the premise that religion and religious considerations, as of God and a future life, should be ignored or excluded. [3]

3. Secularism . . . is a world-view limiting itself to life on the human plane . . . . [4]

4. Secularism is the ordering and conducting of life as if God did not exist. [5]

---

[1] "Secular Civilization and the Christian Task," *The Jerusalem Meeting of the International Missionary Council* (New York: International Missionary Council, 1928), I, 230.

[2] *Webster's New International Dictionary* (Springfield: G. & C. Merriam Co., 1952), p. 2263.

[3] *Ibid.*

[4] Theodore O. Wedel, *The Christianity of Main Street* (New York: The Macmillan Co., 1950), p. 31.

[5] Georgia Harkness, *The Modern Rival of Christian Faith* (Nashville: Abingdon Press, 1952), p. 16.

5. Secularism is our failure to let God be God in our lives.[6]

For the purpose of this discussion secularism will be defined as the tendency on the part of people to leave God out of one or many areas of life. Thus there are degrees of secularism. An individual may be devoutly religious in one aspect of life, but at the same time effectively lock God out of other areas. So when it is said that secularism is a view and practice of living which leaves God out—it must be recognized that there are many varieties of the secularist. The most easily recognized are those who might be called practical atheists, who live as if God did not exist. These people turn their backs on the Bible and the Church; they make the Lord's day a holiday instead of a holy day; and they conduct their business, professional, and personal lives without taking God into account. Within this group will be found great variety. It is possible to include among the practical atheists some humanists who are pleasant, gracious people, accepting many of the by-products of the Christian faith, such as honesty, morality, and service to one's fellow man. Many in this group will be relatively good citizens, pleasant neighbors, and loyal friends. On the other hand, many of the practical atheists will be immoral, dishonest, and generally lawless people. It will often be true that respectable secularists will accept the by-products of the Christian religion apart from a personal Christian faith. Some of them will even join the Church.

This is what T. O. Wedel calls "The Christianity of Main Street," which he defines as

A Christianity without doctrinal foundations .... The very word "Theology" ... has become suspect. The Christianity of Main Street has, in fact, become a kind of Christianity *without* theology, one which does not repudiate the name of God, but which has basically little to do with Him. Man and not God has become the chief actor in the drama of moral progress.[7]

T. O. Wedel goes on to say that this Christianity which is a Christianity of ideals resembles a "civilization which turns its energies to per-

[6] Leroy E. Loemaker, "The Nature of Secularism," *The Christian Faith and Secularism,* ed. J. Richard Spann (Nashville: Abingdon Press, 1948), p. 11.

[7] *Op. cit.,* p. 2.

fecting light switches upon walls, but which neglects the generators in its power plants." [8] Others have called it a "cut-flower religion."

Those who hold this "religion of moral ideals" find it practically impossible to pass on to their children these moral ideals, because they have none of the soil of revealed religion in which to root the ideals.

The Secularist Within the Church

Secularists within the Church are of three general types. The first is the church member who too readily accepts the standards and values of the society of which he and his church are a part. Wesley Schrader writes of such a person in his fascinating satire *Dear Charles*. The hero of this book is a successful minister by the name of Charles King, of whom his wife Priscilla says, "Charles entered the ministry with a well defined set of secular values and to his death these values never changed." [9] Priscilla goes on to say of all ministers, "Your weakness has been in permitting a materialistic and success-hungry world to mold the ministry in its own image." [10] The idea of success held by a minister is usually the reflection of the image of success in the minds of the congregation. Far too often, to them success is to be measured in terms of buildings, equipment, budgets, and numbers. Wesley Schrader in an article in *Life*[11] has pointed out that the conflict in the mind of the minister, between the idea and standard of success set forth in the Word of God and the kind of success demanded by congregations, leads the minister to a feeling of frustration and sometimes to a mental breakdown.

The second type of secularist within the Church is the person who restricts his religion to one or more compartments or areas of his life. To him religion is concerned with certain things which he designates as "spiritual" and has little to do with such things as politics, economics, or questions of social ethics. To such a person religion is a purely private matter. This secularist will tell his preacher to stick to the preaching of "religion" and leave politics, economics, and the race question alone. A churchman in the deep South who is a bitter

[8] *Ibid.*, p. 23.
[9] New York: The Macmillan Co., p. 8.
[10] *Ibid.*
[11] "Why Ministers Are Breaking Down," *Life*, XLI (August 20, 1956), 94-104.

foe of the National Council of Churches, when questioned as to the reasons back of his animosity, freely admitted that he feared that representatives of certain departments of the Council would try to tell him how to run his business.

William Muehl in *Politics for Christians* tells of the visit of a group of Christian young people to Washington, D. C. While there they interviewed a senator who had taken a strong stand against the United Nations and all programs of foreign aid. The senator expressed his gratification at seeing Christian young people concerned about affairs of state and reminded them of his own great interest in "religion." When one of the party asked how he related his Christian faith to his stand against the United Nations and all programs of foreign aid, he replied more in admonition than in anger, "Son, I never mix religion and politics. They just don't go together." [12] It was apparent that secular values reigned supreme in all of the compartments of his life except that tiny segment which he labeled "spiritual matters." This type of secularist can be more dangerous than the out-and-out kind which makes no pretense of being concerned about things spiritual. H. Richard Niebuhr in his book *Christ and Culture* well says:

Where the claim is made that Christianity or religion should be kept out of politics and business, or that Christian faith must learn to get along with other religions, what is often meant is that not only the claim of religious groups but the claims of Christ and God should be banished from these spheres where other gods called values reign.[13]

It is distressing to note that it is sometimes the people who shout most loudly and with the most pious tone about the deity of Christ in the sphere of religion that are the ones who deny his lordship and authority in the everyday activities of life. An elder in a church made his wife a Christmas present of a well-known Bible commentary; and each day, year after year, they read a section of this commentary as a part of their daily devotions. They can give the arguments which support the doctrine of the deity of Christ or the Virgin Birth on a moment's notice. But they grow red in the face with anger when de-

[12] New York: Association Press, 1956, p. 182.
[13] New York: Harper & Bros., 1951, p. 9.

segregation, public housing, or the T.V.A. are mentioned in general conversation. It is a revealing fact that this same couple find great difficulty at the point of engaging effectively in a program of personal evangelism.

The third type of secularist frequently found within the Church is associated with that expression of religion which pictures God as a glorified Santa Claus and prayer as a means by which man attains his selfish ends. He is concerned with using God rather than with letting God use him. To such a person religion is the key to gaining peace of mind, security, success, or the power to influence or control the lives of other people. An ultimate end of this emphasis in religion is well illustrated in a portion of a sermon by A. Powell Davies in which he gives an imaginary radio religious commercial satirizing what he called the "huckstering of religion."

Try God, folks, He will clear away your troubles in a twinkling. . . . Works for you all the time. Cures your worries instantly. Nothing for you to do and so inexpensive! Go to your corner church today, folks, and get God! G-O-D, easy to pronounce, easy to remember, easy for you in every way.—This program is brought to you by self interest and Vulgarity, Incorporated, with branches all over America.[14]

The Christian religion calls on man to put self to death, whereas this secularized version of it tends to pamper and glorify the self.

Secularism an Inclusive Term

The great difficulty faced in trying to define or illustrate secularism lies in the fact that secularists are not organized into groups as are Christian Scientists or members of Unity. They rather infiltrate many groups and travel under varied banners. One writer has said that secularism has become "a catch-all for whatsoever things Christian leaders want to criticize in the social order." [15] It may include scientific humanism, dialectical materialism, naturalism, and scientism. A person is on the way to becoming a secularist when he leaves God out of all or any part of his life.

[14] Louis Cassels. United Press Writer. Column in *Louisville Times*, Nov. 1, 1955.
[15] Edwin E. Aubrey, *Secularism a Myth* (New York: Harper & Bros., 1954), p. 26.

Ideas Usually Associated with Secularism

The secular man's basic tendency is to magnify the importance and self-sufficiency of man. Man is inherently good and has within himself the power to achieve good ends. This seems to be the philosophy of most of those who have contributed to the book by Edward R. Murrow, *This I Believe*.[16] One after another these writers testify to their faith in the essential goodness of man, the value of service, and the primacy of honesty and the Golden Rule as values in life. Man, not God, has become the chief actor in the drama of moral progress. The exaltation of man tends to crowd God out of his rightful place in life.

The secularist also tends to believe that whatever gets good results is good. Men's needs can be met through prayer; therefore, pray. Church attendance and participation makes man better; therefore, go to church. Bible reading and study will improve the personality; therefore, join a Bible class. Try tithing, because it is the key to success. Religion brings peace of mind; so turn to religion. Get rid of negative thoughts, think positively, and your troubles will vanish. There are of course elements of truth in all of these ideas, but they are at best only partial truths. The fallacy of this partial-truth approach is made crystal clear in the following "Simeon Stylites" quotation from *Christian Century* entitled "The Power of Negative Thinking":

EDITOR THE CHRISTIAN CENTURY:

Sir: We have heard much in recent days about the Power of Positive Thinking. And we are all for it. It *has* power. We can well call down blessing on each other and intone, "More power to your elbow and to your positive-thinking apparatus."

But we are in danger of much confusion if we are led to believe that "positive" thinking is the only kind of real value. Too many people today regard "positive thinking" as a form of self-assertion, an act of will, which demonstrates what Powerful Boys and Girls they are. That type is pictured in the classic verses:

> There was a young man of Kilpeacon
> Whose nose was as red as a beacon.
> But by saying "It's white!"
> Thirty times, day and night,
> He cured it and died an archdeacon.

[16] "The Living Philosophies of One Hundred Thoughtful Men and Women in All Walks of Life," ed. Edward P. Morgan (New York: Simon & Schuster, Inc., 1952).

When positive thinking is identified with a psychological pep talk to oneself, the best things of life and of true growth of mind and heart are left out. We see that in the title of the French translation of one of the most popular of the pep-talk roads to salvation, Dale Carnegie's *Stop Worrying and Start Living*. It came out this way: *"Triomphez de Vos Soucis. Vivez! Que le Diable!"*— which, being interpreted, means: "Overcome your troubles. Live! What the devil!" Just a bit thin!

So in these positive days we may well turn to some pictures of the Power of Negative thinking, found in an old book that is still read in some quarters— the Bible. The beginning of Christian experience is not in confident self-assertion, but in very negative self-depreciation. The first Beatitude, "Blessed are the poor in spirit, for theirs is the kingdom of heaven," describes the root from which true blessedness grows. The blessed are those who remember their dependence and enter life through the door of humility. That is negative thinking which is the prelude to fruitful living.

We also see the power of very negative thinking about oneself in the words of Peter to Jesus: "Depart from me, for I am a sinful man, O Lord." Again, at the conclusion of the first Christian sermon, men who had been stabbed to the heart by Peter's words asked, "What must we do?" The answer was, in effect, "Do some negative thinking for a change. Repent!"

The power of negative thinking is beautifully and profoundly pictured in the words of the returning Prodigal to his father: "Father, I have sinned against heaven and before you; I am no more worthy to be called your son." That is about as negative as a person can get. And such self-awareness and consciousness of failure is the gateway to power. Humility is the first step in learning.

Such a feeling is very different from the kind of "positive thinking" to which many today are painfully aspiring, the kind that says, "Watch me, boys! I'm going places." That mood may be the beginning of becoming a Big, Booming Success. It is not the door to the life which is Life indeed.[17]

It is striking how this pragmatic approach to life, which is often associated with both religion and humanitarianism, can lead to the adoption of some very strange and questionable efforts to meet human needs. This can be clearly seen in types of effort put forth to raise money for good causes. A group of people dedicated to the cause of

[17] LXXII (January 5, 1955), 9. Copyright 1955 Christian Century Foundation. Reprinted by permission from *The Christian Century*.

providing wholesome recreation for young people can see no harm in operating a game of chance at the fair. It brings in the money. It will support the recreational program. A public-spirited citizen very much interested in raising money for the erection of a building for community recreation, dreams up a game in which people throw nickels at spots on a table in the hope of winning five dollars. Unblushingly, as he rakes in the nickels for the community building, he whispers as an aside, "It is not a game of chance, because you haven't got a chance."

A third concept frequently held by secularists is a very light view of sin. Whereas the Bible pictures sin as being so terrible that only the death of Christ on the cross can atone for it, the secularist will think of it as a matter of no great consequence, a thing to be laughed at or treated with indulgence. He tends to feel that the improvement of education, the eradication of poverty, and better health care will be effective in overcoming sin. After all, man is the product of his environment—just change his environment and all will be well. Little Johnny is rebellious and disobedient because he has bad tonsils, poor hearing, or weak eyesight. The juvenile delinquent is the product of his home environment, and therefore he is not to be held responsible for his violent acts. Again there is an element of truth here, but there is a failure to recognize that by the grace of God men have been enabled to resist temptation and overcome their environment. It is true that a guilt complex induced by certain types of religious teaching can bring about harmful results to the personality—but it is also true that, when sin is dealt with as a thing of no great consequence, even greater damage can be done to the personality.

Often the secularist will hold to a relative ethic as opposed to an absolute moral code. Thus drinking, immorality, or gambling may be accepted as the thing everybody practices in certain circles. If a thing is legal or widely practiced, it is too lightly accepted as right. The last two generations have seen great changes as to what is considered proper and morally right, and a light view of sin has gained wide acceptance. Things which are clearly labeled as evil in the Bible often become quite acceptable in a society which has become secularized. Over against the biblical idea that "Wine is a mocker and strong drink is raging, and they that are deceived thereby are not wise" (Prov. 20:1

281

K.J.V.), the secular world will place a picture of "men of distinction" enjoying strong drink. Where Christian faith challenges men to deny self (Matt. 16:24 K.J.V.), the faith of secularism urges men to pamper self. Among secularists, conduct is to be governed by what is customary, legal, or popular, whereas the true Christian is concerned to know what is eternally right in the sight of God.

The goodness of material abundance looms large in the thinking of the secularist. Better housing, the satisfaction of hunger, the mastery of disease, increased longevity, and the acquisition of education and culture are greatly sought after without fully realizing that when they are coveted as ends in themselves they are often accompanied by an increase in crime. It is hard for the secularist to realize that gold without God can be a curse instead of a blessing. Advertising, in its enthusiasm to sell, tends to bombard the public with the secular idea that all needs can be met with things. Are you unhappy? Then cheer up with a glass of your favorite beer. Are you plagued with undefined hungers? Then light up your favorite cigarette and find satisfaction. Are you unpopular at social functions? Do not bother to go through a searching examination of your character; just get the newest deodorant. Are there lines of selfishness in your face which mar your good looks? Do not bother about the unwholesome inner life; just get the latest thing in the way of lipstick, face lotion, or shampoo. Athletes who have been endowed with strong bodies and unusual skills by their Creator and have developed their native gifts by healthful living and strenuous exercise, give all of the credit to their use of some breakfast food or the smoking of a particular brand of cigarettes. How silly can we get?

Again we are indebted to Simeon Stylites for a very clear statement of this issue:

EDITOR THE CHRISTIAN CENTURY:
Sir: Some people today find it so simple and easy to bow God politely out of the universe that it raises the wonder whether they have ever looked clearly at what life in a spiritual vacuum would be like. There is a notable phrase of Emily Dickinson's, about people bereaved: they "have lost the face that made existence home." But the vivid phrase covers much more than personal loss. People who think of themselves as living in a merely mechanical universe, where the highest hope is in the creation of man's wit, have also "lost the face that made existence home"—the face of God.

A number of efforts have been made to picture life where man depends on the ingenuity of his creations. They are often in the form of parodies of classic expressions of faith and prayer. Here is an affirmation of faith cast in the framework of the Twenty-third Psalm—a devout meditation on gadgets of every sort. It was written by the Rev. Edward K. Ziegler of Roanoke, Virginia.

THE 23RD PSALM
(Materialist's Version)

Science is my Shepherd,
  I shall not want;
He maketh me to lie down on foam-rubber mattresses;
He leadeth me beside six-lane highways.
He rejuvenateth my thyroid glands;
He leadeth me in the paths of psychoanalysis for peace
  of mind's sake.
Yea, though I walk through the valley of the shadow of
  the iron curtain, I will fear no communist; for thou
  art with me; thy radar screen and thy hydrogen bomb,
  they comfort me.
Thou preparest a banquet before me in the presence of the
  world's billion hungry people.
Thou anointest my head with home permanents.
My beer-glass foameth over.
Surely prosperity and pleasure shall follow me all the
  days of my life; and I will dwell in Shangri-la forever.

Here is another, an attempt to examine how the general confession would fit into a world of mechanics, where men reserve their worship for the things they manufacture:

Almighty and everlasting machine, we have erred and strayed from thy ways like lost screws. We have put in those bolts which we ought not to have put in, and left out those bolts that we ought to have put in, and there is no cogginess in us.

That sounds like blasphemy. More than that, it *is* blasphemy. But it is well to realize that it is the only prayer that can be made in a spiritual vacuum.

Yours,

SIMEON STYLITES.[18]

[18] "In a Spiritual Vacuum," *The Christian Century*, LXXIII (March 7, 1956), 300. Copyright 1956 Christian Century Foundation. Reprinted by permission from *The Christian Century*.

The Roots of Secularism

In the vegetable kingdom it is a well-known fact that the plant seen growing above the ground is determined in large part by the roots below the ground. It is equally true that secularism has roots which determine both its character and its fruit. The first root of secularism is man's preoccupation with what he conceives to be objectively real. Nothing can be believed unless it can be seen, handled, measured, or tested by so-called scientific analysis. Years ago there was a movie in which a minister became involved in a discussion with a secularist at a drugstore counter. The secularist insisted that he could not believe in God because he could not hear, see, or touch him. Later in the conversation the secularist referred to the fact that he had a toothache and must go to the dentist. The preacher assured him that the toothache could not possibly be real, because he certainly could not hear, see, or touch it. Faith, hope, and love cannot be measured or analyzed in a chemist's test tube; but if they are experienced in the test tube of life, their reality and value will become apparent.

A second root of secularism is the tendency on the part of some people to be concerned only with the otherworldly aspects of religion. The goal of their religion is to go to heaven when they die. In the future life all of the evils of this present world will be left behind. For the present they endure evil but do nothing to overcome it. As far as possible they withdraw from the world and live a life apart. Sometimes this is coupled with the idea that the more rapidly evils multiply the sooner their Lord will return to make up his jewels. Those who hold to this otherworldly concept of religion, must, of course, live in this present world, but they do little to bring the light of the gospel to bear upon those aspects of life which they consider to be secular. This sometimes leads to strange extremes.

A third root of secularism goes to the opposite extreme. There is the tendency to concentrate on the fruits of religion. Years ago when church courts met for a whole week with three long doctrinal sermons a day, on one such occasion the first sermon was delivered by an eloquent preacher on the theme, "The Fruits of Religion." That afternoon an equally eminent minister spoke forcefully on the subject, "The Roots of Religion," setting forth the idea that ought to be self-evident, that without roots there can be no fruit. This is the whole gospel. Jesus says, "Ye have not chosen me, but I have chosen you, and ordained you, that ye should go and bring forth fruit" (John 15:16 K.J.V.). The first part of this verse has to do with God's side of religion, his electing grace; and the last part has to do with man's side of religion, the bearing of fruit to the glory of God.

A fourth root of secularism is to be found in the denominational divisions of Christendom, which make it difficult for the Church to make an effective approach to many problems. Pitman B. Potter of the American University of Washington, D. C., in commenting on secularism in diplomacy says,

> Is it not true that the splitting up of the church into many sects intensified the danger of secularism in the conduct of public affairs? It was obviously impossible to split up the public interest and government in this same manner, and the only remedy was to transfer this section to a secular plane.[19]

Unquestionably a case can be made for the proposition that secularism has been hastened in American life by denominationalism and by the tendency of some people to make religion a segment of life concerned largely with life after death.

In a sense it can be said that the development of a secular view of life has been hastened by a misapplication of the doctrine of the separation of Church and State. One illustration will suffice to make this clear. In the beginning of America the matter of education was pretty much in the hands of the Church and its leadership. The old blue-back speller, the primers, and the reading books took much of their material directly from the Bible. In the early period of the nation's history the content of the Bible was widely taught. As ecclesiastical divisions became more pronounced, and as society assumed a greater responsibility for education, it became increasingly difficult to retain the biblical content in the schoolbooks. As denominational controversy increased in intensity, practically all "religious material" was dropped from the public school curriculum. At this point a great concern was shown to get the Bible and religion back into the school curriculum, but the effort has been

[19] "Secularism in Diplomacy," *The Christian Faith and Secularism*, ed. J. Richard Spann (Nashville: Abingdon Press, 1948), p. 106.

beset by opposition from certain groups who want to know what view or interpretation of the Bible is to be taught. The movement to restore the teaching of religion to the school curriculum has also been handicapped by the fact that the churches have been unwilling to underwrite the expense of teaching the Bible in the public schools unless they can dictate just what is to be taught. It is true that opposition has also arisen from nonecclesiastical sources, but the Church will have to accept its part of the responsibility for the lack of religious instruction in the public schools.

The inability of the Church to present a united front in bringing the implications of religious life to bear upon all facets of everyday life, has allowed many areas of life to become more or less secularized. This is notably true in the fields of recreation and entertainment. The Church and the nation need to heed the warning voice by George Washington in his Farewell Address:

Of all the dispositions and habits which lead to political prosperity, religion and morality are indispensable supports. In vain would that man claim the tribute of patriotism, who should labor to subvert these great pillars of human happiness, these firmest props of the duties of men and citizens. . . . let it simply be asked, where is the security for property, for reputation, for life, if the sense of religious obligation desert the oaths which are the instruments of investigation in courts of justice? And let us with caution indulge the supposition that morality can be maintained without religion. Whatever may be conceded to the influence of refined education on minds of peculiar structure, reason and experience both forbid us to expect that national morality can prevail in exclusion of religious principle.[20]

A Christian Approach to Secularism

To a greater or a lesser degree, every minister and every church is confronted with the challenge of secularism. It may be a formidable rival to true Christian faith or it may be an enervating influence which waters down effective Christian witness. But to whatever degree it may be present in the lives of the people, it must be understood and dealt with by church leaders.

First of all, there must be a recognition of the honest concern for

[20] *The Academy Classics* (New York: Allyn & Bacon, Inc., 1923), p. 16.

human need on the part of some secularists. This idea is well supported by Aubrey in his book, *Secularism a Myth,* where he says:

I am deeply distressed by the tendency of the Church to attack, when it might be learning, and to treat with contempt forces which might be allies in the struggle for righteousness. Secular movements which are maligned in so much contemporary Christian writing have produced spiritual values.[22]

To illustrate the truth of these two statements, a long list of values which have been produced by secular organizations could be cited. Government has taken many forward steps to improve housing, health, and education. The Red Cross has been the neighborly arm of the people in times of disaster and has conceived and executed the truly great blood bank program. The National Polio Foundation has master-minded the battle against that dread disease. Luncheon clubs and lodges have inaugurated magnificent programs of service for all kinds of human need. The Parent-Teacher Associations organized in practically every community in the land have strengthened school and home. Boy Scout and Girl Scout organizations have made tremendous contributions toward enriching the lives of American youth. The Agricultural Extension Service with its clubs for women and its Four-H Clubs and Older Rural Youth organizations has brought a new way of life to rural America. Any reader could add to this list the names of many organizations with which he is personally acquainted, that have made significant contributions to the betterment of the American way of life.

How well I remember a lesson learned at the meeting of the American Country Life Association which met in East Lansing, Michigan, in June, 1946. The program had been set up on the basis of four seminars. One of these groups was to discuss "Religious and Moral Values in Rural Life." It was expected that this group would be small and largely made up of the clergy in attendance at the meeting. Imagine the surprise of the leaders of the conference when more than half of the registered delegates enrolled for this seminar. And even more surprising was the fact that those who crowded into this seminar were representatives of schools, Scouts, the American Library Association, Agricultural Ex-

[21] *Op. cit.,* pp. 105, 134.

tension Services, and farm organizations. They came to say that they were vitally interested in spiritual and moral values for rural life. At one point in the meeting, when the problem of the delinquent child was under discussion and much was being said about what the Church could and should do, a representative of the Parent-Teacher Association made an excellent case for the claim that the P.T.A. could do a better job than the Church in this area, because the Church would go as a representative of a particular denomination—while the P.T.A. could go to the home as representative of the whole commuity. Many of these so-called secular organizations can be a tremendous asset to the program of the Church if church people will work in and through them to effect its program for a better way of life.

Along with this recognition of the good that sometimes accompanies a secular point of view, there must be a concern on the part of the Church to bring the leaders of the so-called secular organizations and causes to know the love of Christ and to accept Christian motivation for their good works. A good deed done in the name of Jesus and for the glory of God, has a greater power for good than does the same sort of good deed performed from a purely secular motivation. It would be of great interest and value to the Church to have a survey made to determine the proportion of Christians to non-Christians among social workers and other staff people in the various "do-good" efforts being put forth in the United States. It might show this group to be the greatest evangelistic opportunity of this generation. The Church is obligated to present the gospel of Christ in a forceful and appealing way to the personnel of these great service arms of society.

The Christian minister must be aware of the great inroads secularism has made in the life of the minister. Let repentance begin with the minister himself, as he carefully evaluates his own life to see just how secular he has become. What are his standards of personal success? Do they vary significantly from the standards of the world about him? How concerned is he to have all of the comforts and conveniences of life for himself and his family? Does he preach with more enthusiasm to the well-to-do than he does to the poor? How much of his zeal is for the glory of God? When the preacher in the pulpit is willing to confess to and repent of the inroads which secularism has made in his own life, he will see more clearly how to help his people at this point (Matt. 7:1-5).

The Church, too, must do some soul searching and face up to the charge which is being made in some quarters, that in many respects the Church herself is a secular organization. Far too often decisions of policy in church courts are made on the basis of what is practical and expedient, rather than on the basis of what is the will of God. Property and social position all too frequently outweigh faith and love as values when leadership is being chosen. God is no respecter of persons (Acts 10:34 K.J.V.), but often churches are (James 2:1-9 K.J.V.). Is your church a social club of like-minded people, or a fellowship of those who love the Lord? Let the Church get the beam out of her own eye and then she shall see clearly how to remove the mote from the eye of the secularist (Matt. 7:1-5 K.J.V.). It ill behooves a church honey-combed with secularism to attack secularism and secularists outside the Church. Especially is this true of the judgments of the Church upon those organizations which are dedicated to the meeting of human need outside the framework of the Church. The so-called secular organizations for the meeting of human need are outside the Church because the Church is too disunited to do the job effectively. Let the Church make an honest confession of her own secularist tendencies and seek divine help in overcoming them.

The most effective approach the Church can make to the secularist is that of a vital witness to a personal experience of God in Christ. It is impossible to say just how this is to be done, because witnessing is in a very real sense letting Christ Jesus show himself through the personality of the individual. In fact, when it becomes stereotyped, it ceases to be a witness. This witness may be a testimony of sins forgiven; of victory over temptation; of light received on a dark path; of a new insight into truth; of peace of mind given; of grace sufficient in a time of suffering; of a richer, fuller understanding of the greatness and goodness of God; or of strength received in a time of weakness. A witness cannot be faked, but must grow out of an experience. When the witness is real, it carries its own credentials. The witness may be given in word, deed, or attitude. It is most effective when all three are present and agree. The effectiveness of a personal witness is measured by the degree to which the self is crucified and Jesus Christ is glorified.

When the person who has tended to leave God out of his life, hears or sees evidence that God is real to another, it makes a tremendous impression.

Finally, the threat of secularism, this modern rival to Christian faith, is overcome most completely when the Church teaches and practices the full doctrine of Christian vocation. This means bringing to bear upon every area of life the good news that man can by the grace of God become a new creation. There was a time when the Church called upon a select group to become "full-time" servants of God as ministers or missionaries. It is heartening to know that now the emphasis is on the idea that every Christian ought to be in full-time Christian service. That is, he ought in every area of his life to be seeking to do the will of God.

This emphasis has expressed itself in many ways. When Shirley Greene, now with the Farmer's Union, was in the Social Action Department of the Congregational Christian Church, he encouraged the formation of groups of Christian farmers who gathered week after week to discuss what it means to be a Christian farmer. In recent years the Christian Faculty Movement has gained great momentum and holds real promise for a revival of vital religions on the campuses of the schools of higher education in the nation. The concern of these Christian teachers is to discover new ways in which they can make a Christian impact upon the lives of their students. It has been a thrilling thing to learn that a number of congressmen and senators in Washington meet in early-morning prayer meetings to seek the guidance of God in their daily lives. Louis Evans, minister at large of the Presbyterian Church in the United States of America, is in great demand as a speaker at conventions of businessmen, educators, and labor leaders. Recently he has been asked to give the religious emphasis message at gatherings of military men in the Pentagon. There have also been invitations to give religious messages before state educational associations and even to the great crowds gathered at state fairs. All of this is encouraging evidence that increasing numbers of Christians are thinking in terms of using their vocations as pulpits from which to give their witness for Christ.

When we are told that Jesus "increased in wisdom and stature and in favor with God and man" (Luke 2:52 K.J.V.), it means that he grew in every area of his being. The mature Christian of today is the

Christian who allows his Christian faith to influence and control every area of thought and action. He is not only Christian on Sunday, but also on every other day of the week. He acts from Christian motivation not only in so-called spiritual areas of life, but also in the everyday affairs of life. As the number of mature Christians increases, secularism will cease to be either a rival or a threat to the Christian religion.

Areas to Be Explored

1. Analyze and evaluate as to evidence of secular tendencies: *a*) the testimonials in *This I Believe* by Edward R. Murrow; *b*) the writings of Norman Vincent Peale; *c*) the advertising of the "Religion in American Life" campaign; *d*) the concept of God and religion in popular musical numbers such as: "Crying in the Chapel," "Talking to the Man Upstairs," "Faith, Hope, and Charity," and "This Ole House."

2. Just how far should the Church go in becoming a part of society and to what extent should it stand over against society in judgment? For example, should the Church receive people on a simple profession of faith, or should they be required to give evidence of a mature faith before being admitted to the Church?

3. Examine current standards of success held by church people, in the light of Christian values.

4. Make a study of the Christian doctrine of work or vocation. Does the Roman Catholic doctrine of vocation have any relation to secularism?

5. Make a study of the effect of denominational divisions in the Church upon the participation of the Church in efforts to meet human needs, such as health, welfare, education, and the use of mass media in the spread of the gospel.

Selected Bibliography

Aubrey, Edwin E. *Secularism a Myth; an Examination of the Current Attack on Secularism.* New York: Harper & Bros., 1954.

Dakin, Arthur H. *Man the Measure.* Princeton: Princeton University Press, 1939.

Dewey, John. *A Common Faith.* New Haven: Yale University Press, 1944.

Harkness, Georgia E. *The Modern Rival of Christian Faith.* Nashville: Abingdon Press, 1952.

Hartshorne, Charles. *Beyond Humanism.* Chicago: Willett, Clark & Co., 1937.

Lippman, Walter. *A Preface to Morals.* New York: The Macmillan Co., 1929.

Loew, Cornelius. *Modern Rivals to Christian Faith,* "Layman's Theological Library." Philadelphia: Westminster Press, 1956.

Muehl, William. *Politics for Christians.* New York: Association Press, 1956.

Murrow, Edward R., comp. *This I Believe: the Living Philosophies of One Hundred Thoughtful Men and Women in All Walks of Life.* New York: Simon & Schuster, Inc., 1952.

Niebuhr, H. Richard. *Christ and Culture*. New York: Harper & Bros., 1951.

Schrader, Wesley. *Dear Charles*. New York: The Macmillan Co., 1954.

Spann, J. Richard, ed. *The Christian Faith and Secularism*. Nashville: Abingdon Press, 1948.

Wedel, Theodore O. *The Christianity of Main Street*. New York: The Macmillan Co., 1950.

INDEX

INDEX

Freedom
naturalism and, 257
of religion, 171-72, 229
of speech, press, and assembly, 225
Freeman, James D., 201n.
Freeman, James D., quoted, 202
Freud, Sigmund, 195-96
Fundamentalism, 36-37
approach to, 63-67
ecumenical movement in, 175
evaluation of, 61-67
five points of, 47, 52, 63-65
history of, 45-61
interdenominational efforts of, 58-61
literalism and, 264
militant, 62-63
modernism and, 267-69
perfectionism and, 122
pietistic, 61-62
rationalistic, 62
Fundamentals, The, 48
Furniss, Norman F., 55
Furniss, Norman F., quoted, 59

Galatians, 18, 22, 102, 104, 107, 146, 153, 233, 246
Galen, 195
Gemara, 135
Genea, 105
Genesis, 12, 13, 96, 243, 244
Gentiles, salvation of, 99, 100, 101
Germany
concentration camps in, 226
Nazism in, 138, 144, 150, 226, 227, 238
racism in, 238, 239
See also Hitler
Gide, André, 218
Girl Scouts, 287
Glover, George Washington, 196, 197
Gobineau, Count de, 237
God
all healing from, 205
in Christ, personal experience of, 289-90
fatherhood of, in Judaism, 142
as a God of action, 19
Jesus as expression of love of, 245
kingdom of, 99-100, 222, 246
mind as, 200
naturalist reconstructions of, 253-55
redemptive purpose of, 17-18, 245
relationship of man and, 244-45, 246
as supreme value, 252
God That Failed (Gide), 218
Gradualism, 219

Graham, Billy, 54
Great Awakening, 45, 115
Great Commission, 195
Great I Am, 30
Greene, Shirley, 290
Griesbach, 106
Group therapy, 210
Guide of the Perplexed, 136
Guilt, 112-13, 115, 208, 281

Habakkuk Commentary, 12
Halakoth, 135
Hanasi, Judah, 135
Hanukkah, 141
Harris, Richard, 84
Harrison, G. T., 88, 92
Harrison, G. T., quoted, 90
Hayes, Carlton J. H., 152
Healing
Christian Science and, 192, 196-201
evaluation of, 204
Jesus' ministry of, 193-94, 196, 205
as part of church ministry, 207-10
principles of, 205-6
in Protestantism, 203
psychology and, 195-96
relation of religion and, 192-95
in Roman Catholicism, 203
spiritual, 196-206
Unity and, 192, 201-3
Healing sects, 33, 34, 192, 196-204, 206-7, 211
Heaven, kingdom of, 99-100
Hebrew University, 139
Hebrews, 23, 81, 96, 99, 108, 127, 206
Henschel, Milton G., quoted, 84
Heresy, 181
Herzel, Theodor, 139
Highest Critics vs. the Higher Critics (Munhall), 55
Hinckley, Gordon B., quoted, 92
Hinduism, 28
Hirsch, Samuel R., 138
Historical interpretation of Bible, 15-16
Historicism, 23-24
History of the Brethren (Noel), 106
Hitler, 139, 150, 217, 218, 225, 227, 238, 239
Holdheim, Samuel, 138
Holiness sects, 55, 117, 118, 121
"Holy Rollers," 30
Holy Spirit, 20, 180
Holyoake, G. J., 274
Hosea, 13

Reformation, 28, 40, 81, 82, 159, 160-61, 179-80
  biblical study in, 14
  role of Jews in, 137, 144
Reid, J. K. S., quoted, 195
Reincarnation, 202
Religion
  communism and fascism as, 223-24
  in eyes of communists, 219-20
Renaissance, 40, 137, 144
Repentance
  in Judaism, 143
  salvation of Jews by, 99
Republican Party, 28
Research Science Bureau, 60
Reuchlin, 144
Revelation, 22, 70, 98
Revivalism, 45, 76, 115-16, 118
Revolution, world, 230
Rice, John A., 51, 56
Richardson, Alan, quoted, 193
Richardson, Cyril, 205
Riley, William Bell, 49-50, 58, 60
Rimmer, Harry, 60
Ritschl, 46
Roberts, Oral, 204
Rockefeller, John D., 50, 51
Rocky Mountain Bible conferences, 47
Roman Catholicism, 12, 36, 39
  claims and counterclaims of, 157-59
  contributions of, 159-60
  deviations of, from New Testament, 164-72
  healing in, 203
  modernism in, 264
  perfectionism in, 114
  Protestantism and, 33, 161, 162-64, 172-73
  Reformation and, 160-61
  as a sect, 29-30, 157, 158-59
Romans, 18, 23, 97, 100, 102, 113, 127, 151, 153, 221
Rome, early church in, 179
Roosevelt, Theodore, 28
Rosh Hashana (New Year), 141
Rowley, H. H., quoted, 147-48
Rule, Andrew K., 220
Russell, Bertrand, 260
Russell, Charles Taze, 71, 82, 83, 84
Russia
  communism in, 217
  forced labor in, 226
  Jewish refugees to, 139
  New Economic Policy in, 224

Russia—cont'd
  repudiation of cult of leader in, 221n., 225
Rutherford, Judge, 82, 83, 84, 86

Sabbath
  Jewish observance of, 141
  Saturday observance of, 77-79
Sacrament(s)
  Catholic and Protestant, 162, 163, 166, 169, 172
  as channels for healing, 205
  doctrine of, 180
  healing as, 195
Sacramentals, 169-70
Sainthood, 167-68
Salvation
  doctrine of, 180
  healing and, 193, 205
  for the total man, 208
Salvation Army, 87
Samuel, 12
Sanctification, 117-18, 124, 126, 180
Saturday observance of Sabbath, 77-79
Sayers, Dorothy, 263
Scapegoats, 227, 238, 239
Scapular, 170
Schleiermacher, 46, 63
Scholasticism, 28
Schrader, Wesley, 276
Science
  and race, 241-42
  and scientism, 258-60, 261, 262, 263
Science and Health (Eddy), 197, 198
Scientism, 39, 257-61
Scientism, Christian approach to, 261-63
Scofield Reference Bible, Notes of, 95, 98, 100, 101, 102, 103, 104, 105, 106, 108, 109
"Scotch-Irish," 29
"Second blessing," 113, 117-18
Secret police, 226
Sects and isms
  in America, 29-31
  contemporary, 28-29
  defined, 26
  denominations and, 26-27
  formation of, 27-28, 31-37, 123
  in Judaism, 137
  progressive and conservative interaction through, 38-39
  unwholesome, 34-37
  wholesome, 32-34, 38
  See also various sects